In-Law Relationships

IN-LAW RELATIONSHIPS

Mothers, Daughters, Fathers, and Sons

Geoffrey L. Greif and Michael E. Woolley

OXFORD
UNIVERSITY PRESS

OXFORD
UNIVERSITY PRESS

Oxford University Press is a department of the University of Oxford. It furthers the University's objective of excellence in research, scholarship, and education by publishing worldwide. Oxford is a registered trade mark of Oxford University Press in the UK and certain other countries.

Published in the United States of America by Oxford University Press
198 Madison Avenue, New York, NY 10016, United States of America.

Library of Congress Cataloging-in-Publication Data
Names: Greif, Geoffrey L., author. | Woolley, Michael E., author.
Title: In-law relationships : mothers, daughters, fathers, and sons /
Geoffrey L. Greif and Michael E. Woolley.
Description: New York : Oxford University Press, 2021. |
Includes bibliographical references and index.
Identifiers: LCCN 2020021974 (print) | LCCN 2020021975 (ebook) |
ISBN 9780190928131 (hardback) | ISBN 9780190928155 (epub)
Subjects: LCSH: Parents-in-law—Family relationships. | Communication in
families. | Interpersonal communication.
Classification: LCC HQ759.8 .G74 2020 (print) | LCC HQ759.8 (ebook) |
DDC 306.85—dc23
LC record available at https://lccn.loc.gov/2020021974
LC ebook record available at https://lccn.loc.gov/2020021975

9 8 7 6 5 4 3 2 1

Printed by Sheridan Books, Inc., United States of America

CONTENTS

PREFACE

One of our ancient Webster's dictionaries defines "in-law" as "a relative by marriage." The definition falls on the same page and one inch up from "inmate," which is defined as "1. A person living with others in the same building and 2. A person lodged with others, and often confined, in an institution, asylum, etc." An appropriate juxtaposition of definitions? The reader can decide and take comfort in this being the only in-law joke in these pages.

The information for this book on this kaleidoscopic family relationship was gathered from two primary sources: a national, non-representative survey sample and a mixed-methods survey and interview study, both inquiring about daughters-in-law, mothers-in-law, sons-in-law, and fathers-in-law and their relations with their same-gender in-law (e.g., daughters-in-law and their relationship with their mothers-in-law). The first source is a survey of over 1,100 participants that was carried out with the assistance of Qualtrics, a national survey firm. Qualtrics was engaged to seek responses from 250 of each of the four in-law groups. They collected more responses than we asked for, resulting in 267 mothers-in-law, 351 daughters-in-law, 294 fathers-in-law, and 263 sons-in-law, totaling 1,175 surveys. These were people who self-identified as being in one of these in-law roles. We acknowledge that we have limited the research to people who identify as male or female and that we may have missed people who are non-binary or who do not wish to define themselves by gender. Participants answered 115 survey questions and were given the option of describing briefly, in their own words, what the in-law relationship was like. One year later, the original survey respondents were contacted to complete a second survey that included some of the previous questions as well as new questions so that we could explore any changes that occurred over that time period and could get answers to questions we wished we had asked the first time. For this longitudinal portion of the research, an additional 551 surveys across all four in-laws were completed, allowing us to study what might change in these dynamic relationships.

The second source for information about in-law relationships was collected by Master of Social Work (MSW) students. The students were enrolled in an advanced research class that was held every year from 2015 to 2019. Students surveyed and conducted in-depth interviews with people with a living in-law of the same gender. We included respondents or their in-laws who were in same-sex and opposite-sex marriages. No two members of the same family were interviewed. The students could interview people they knew, people whose name they acquired through acquaintances, and people they met in public places. Before beginning the interviews, the students completed required Institutional Review Board coursework and were trained how to administer a consent to participate in research form, the survey, and a qualitative interview. Survey items were initially informed by our reading of the literature. Open-ended questions were used during the qualitative interviews to guide the discussion and, informed by grounded theory, interviewers could pursue topics as they arose during the interviews. Over the course of five years, qualitative questions were refined as we became increasingly sensitized to the topic and new areas of exploration arose. In addition, the authors interviewed people using the same survey and interview guide. In total, 182 children-in-law and 164 parents-in-law were surveyed and interviewed.[1] Please see the Appendix for more information on our methods, the limitations inherent in them, and areas of future research.

In total, over 1,500 people have participated from a variety of sources. This multi-methods data-collection strategy allowed us to get a large enough sample of survey respondents to do rigorous statistical analyses and to consider, with the follow-up survey, what may change over time. The large number of qualitative interviews allowed us an important level of insight into the lives of in-laws. For statistical analyses, we draw on the Qualtrics data. The qualitative interviews illustrate, through examples, the findings and bring the voices of in-laws to the fore. Sometimes lengthy case studies are provided with demographic information; other times brief quotes are used. We have changed names and highly identifiable descriptors. We have edited the quotes for ease of reading while taking great care not to change the meaning of what the in-laws told us.

Following an opening chapter that describes the position of in-laws in society and sets the context for what follows, we offer, in Chapter 2, a brief review of others' research. In Chapters 3 through 6, we look extensively at each of the in-law groups and answer a series of questions about our research findings relevant to their relationship with their same gender in-law. We take a similar approach in each of the chapters, so the context offered for understanding the findings may seem repetitive to some readers. This, however, provides consistent and complete portrayals of the data. Chapter 7 focuses on the in-law experiences of gay and lesbian married couples as well as on the experiences of parents-in-law of married gays and lesbians. We have published articles in peer-reviewed journals on each of the four in-law groups and on gay and lesbian in-law relationships. These form part of the content for Chapters 3 through 7, to which we have added significant additional qualitative and quantitative information. The articles are on the reference list.[2]

Chapter 8 looks at the differences we found across gender and across generations. These differences help place mothers-in-law, fathers-in-law, daughters-in-law, and sons-in-law into a broader social context. The final chapter, Chapter 9, discusses clinical implications of our findings and suggests ways that family members, as well as clinicians working with family issues, can improve their in-law relationships.

Together we, the authors, have collective experiences as sons-in-laws, as a father-in-law, and as spouses. We both have children; one of us has grandchildren; we both have large extended family networks that include divorce, interracial, and interfaith marriages. Together we have more than 70 years' experience as clinicians, researchers, and teachers of clinical practice. While interviews and surveys formed the backbone of this book, these personal and professional narratives drove our conceptual approach to the design of the research and to how we interpreted what we learned. We cannot separate ourselves from what we wrote just as the reader cannot separate him, her, or their self from an interpretation of what we have written.

The topic of in-law relationships is not a simple one. As we discuss, it is multigenerational, multilayered, and, like a kaleidoscope, a shifting amalgam of emotional colors. Beauty, as Margaret Wolfe Hungerford wrote, is in the eye of the beholder, and no two beholders are the same.[3] Underpinning this marital merger are these considerations: How do families open themselves to a new person? How do parents accept that their child is an adult and can make a choice that forever changes the family? Furthermore, how does one enter, even create, a new family while maintaining a sense of self-identity and a loyalty to one's own family of origin?

When times are tough, family members need each other. Whether it is due to global health concerns, social change, political division, or personal struggles, we do better if we love and support each other. We hope this book will help anyone with an in-law relationship to better understand its complexities and to make it more successful. For researchers and clinicians, we hope we have provided roadmaps for increased understanding.

CHAPTER 1

Perspectives on In-Laws

Parents and Children

FROM PARENTS-IN-LAW

My relationship with this daughter-in-law is extremely important. It was something I really hoped for and wanted. I am the mother of two sons so I welcomed the idea of having a daughter-in-law and I just assumed since my son had picked her that she would be wonderful. I was totally ready to love her as she is and include her in our family and it was just shocking to me that she wasn't interested and that she didn't feel the same way and, for a long time, I thought that I must be doing something wrong and then I realized, nope, she just isn't interested. It didn't matter who I was. So I had to accept it. She loves my son; my son loves her. I'm happy that my son has someone who loves him and who he's happy with. I would never interfere with that. The beauty now is that I have my other daughter-in-law in my life and I know that it can be what I hoped it to be.

Alice, a 67-year-old White mother-in-law

My relationship with my son-in-law is very important in the sense that he's married to my daughter and is the father of my granddaughter. They mean the world to me, and I want them to be happy. Having a good relationship with my son-in-law is important because it makes them happy.

Carter, a 65-year-old African American father-in-law

He (son-in-law) is an integral part of the whole family. So if I'm doing something and I want the whole family to attend, I want him to attend. There was an occasion when he was angry and he pulled himself away from it. This was at a wedding of one of my other children and he decided he didn't want to be part of it. He refused to be part of the pictures. It made a hole in the wedding service. In that kind of situation, it's hurtful if he's not part of the family. On the other hand, he has his own family and his family is his family. His loyalties are his loyalties. He has several sisters and brothers and he owes them a lot of loyalty. If there's a conflict, I would expect him to be with them.

Abram, a 64-year-old White father-in-law

FROM CHILDREN-IN-LAW

My relationship with my mother-in-law is very important. Because she's my husband's mother, I feel like I need to put a little bit of extra effort into it. I want to make sure that I have a respectful relationship with her because my husband is a big part of my life. My relationship with her is good. He takes care of her rent, so I always try to encourage him to make sure that everything is okay with her financially. I maybe talk to her once every three months on the phone, but when I go visit, which is twice a year, I spend a lot of time with her. I try to do things with her because even though I sometimes get caught up with things with my school, with work, with internship whatever it is, I don't always have the time to call her.

Lina, a 27-year-old Latina daughter-in-law

The relationship that I have with my father-in-law is very, very important. From Day One of being in a relationship with my now wife, from when we were boyfriend and girlfriend, he has taken the step and really gotten involved. Never to the point of being overbearing or where it was too much. But I could always tell that he cared a lot about Jami and our relationship and where it was heading. He's always had a good sense of guidance and he has always cared about us.

Nemo, a 21-year-old Latino son-in-law

I would say my relationship with my father-in-law is very important to me because it directly affects my wife. In order to keep the peace at home, it's easier for me to get along. Tabatha and her parents are close and if I am not getting along with them, it breeds tension in our marriage and their family relationships.

Monty, a 27-year-old African-American son-in-law

In-law relationships, as exemplified by these brief quotes from a mother-in-law and two fathers-in-law and from a daughter-in-law and two sons-in-law from different cultural backgrounds, are exceptionally important and, often, extremely complicated. They can be joyous and comforting and they can be disappointing and tension-filled. They can serve as a model for how to stay connected across generations and as a bellwether for what to avoid. In-law relationships can also be a totem to the distance between families and a cauldron for receiving support and love without it being overbearing.

Jokes aside, in-law relationships are serious business. They are often of survival importance to marriages and families given the potential caretaking needs of children and grandchildren as well as aging and dying parents. And, if as journalist Mignon McClaughlin opined, "A successful marriage requires falling in love many times, always with the same person," a successful marriage also requires figuring out how to love, at many different times across the lifespan, the family members connected to one's spouse. This requirement gets tested every day: according to the U.S. Census Bureau, over 2 million couples marry every year, joining the ranks of nearly 60 million already married couples.

At the conclusion of the wedding ceremony, three new families are formed—each newlywed's family of origin has added a son-in-law or daughter-in-law, thereby forming two new families, and the couple forms a new, third family. Parents of the newlyweds become parents-in-law for the first time (unless they have other married children) and newlyweds become a son- or daughter-in-law for the first time (unless they have been previously married). The six people referenced here (there will be more if stepparents are involved and sisters- and brothers-in-law are included) may all be learning what it is like to be an in-law at the same time and, perhaps, with little prior thought or discussion about what their new roles entail. And even if the parents have other married children, they have never been parents-in-law to this *particular* son- or daughter-in-law with his or her personality and family background married to this *particular* son or daughter.

Today, in most communities in the United States, parents have little influence over who their children marry (highly religious communities and some immigrant populations are exceptions). Yes, covert and overt pressures can be, and often are, applied by parents or siblings to end a relationship if the potential in-law appears to be inappropriate, but the marriage will still go forward if the determination to marry is strong enough or the objections are poorly received. Thus, parents who have helped raise a child to marital age may find themselves involuntarily "married" to a highly welcome or, in a worst-case scenario, to a highly unwelcome new person, forever changing the family structure and, potentially, the parents' relationship with their child. Note the disappointment for Alice, the mother-in-law quoted at the beginning of this chapter, as she recalled having high expectations dashed in not getting initially the daughter-in-law she always dreamed of having. She had such hopes based on how favorably she viewed her son and was frankly shocked at how the relationship turned out with his wife. She is lucky in that she found that dreamed-of relationship with her second daughter-in-law. However, many parents are not so lucky. They may only have one chance at it.

PURPOSE OF THIS BOOK

In this book, we describe the difficulties that people encounter with their in-law relationships from the perspectives of both generations and suggest ways to work through these difficulties. In-laws cannot only strain a marriage, they can be one of the causes for a divorce, as they were credited with doing in one Minnesota study where 18% of the sample identified in-law problems as a reason for the breakup.[1] While the majority of the more than 1,500 in-laws we researched describe being close with their child-in-law or parent-in-law, many feel under stress to maintain a relationship that can, at times, be quite difficult. Even underneath some of the descriptions of the positive relationships, we see ambivalence, ambiguity, and tension that accompany the genuine affection that in-laws feel toward each other. In a study by University of North Carolina researchers of a population of Midwest families, ambivalence, the holding of conflicting feelings toward someone, characterized adult children's relationship with their parents and in-laws in over one-quarter of the sample.[2] In another study, ambiguity characterized the parents-in-law's interactions with their children-in-law due to uncertainty in how to fulfill family roles and establish norms around the relationship.[3] When people are unsure how to act with each other, they struggle with the relationship.

Such struggles are related to boundary ambiguity, a construct used to further describe when family members are unsure how to interact with each other. The concept deals specifically with *how* family members participate in the family. It also has implications for *who* is considered to be in or out of the family.[4] For example, a mother-in-law might wonder what part she will play when her daughter-in-law gives birth to a grandchild. She may hope to be included in caring for and raising the child but also be wary about intruding and about the role of the mother of the daughter-in-law. When families are functioning well, the mother-in-law may be included with little or no boundary ambiguity.

In the next chapters, we describe these in-law relationships from each of the four perspectives: mothers-in-law, daughters-in-law, fathers-in-law, and sons-in-law. We have chosen to focus on the same gender intergenerational relationships. We ask fathers-in-law about sons-in-law, sons-in-law about fathers-in-law, mothers-in-law about daughters-in-laws, and daughters-in-law about mothers-in-law. We include cross-gender descriptions but our interest is centered on how men interact with men and how women interact with women in their in-law relationships, as well as the differences and similarities between these dyads. We believe learning about how women and men fulfill these roles will help us understand their ever-changing dynamics and provide potential roadmaps for improvement. We acknowledge that there may be great gender fluidity in any of these roles, that notions of gender are not fixed, and that traditional gender roles in families have been changing. We also acknowledge that people may have identified as one gender to participate in the research and may live as another gender or as no gender.

With these survey and interview data, we also look at the relationships across multiple phases of the typical lifespans of families. Three key phases are (1) the relationships between in-laws prior to and at the beginning of the children's marriage; (2) the relationships between in-laws when the children have children/grandchildren; and (3) the relationships when children and children-in-law take care of aging parents/parents-in-law. Each of these phases places unique opportunities as well as demands on intergenerational relationships. By understanding these phases better and placing them in the context of gender, families will be better equipped to anticipate and adapt to these naturally occurring life phases.

While the number of people living together without being married is on the rise, we focus on families where children are married. Same-sex marriages are included in our research, though they make up a small percentage of those we studied. In understanding how in-law relationships work and in suggesting ways to improve them, we apply major family therapy theories: Murray Bowen's family processes, where family history is emphasized; Virginia Satir's communications theory, where clear communication between family members is applied; Salvador Minuchin's structural family therapy theory, where boundaries between and within generations are the focus; and narrative therapy, developed by Michael White and David Epston and where families weave stories that become part of their history. We also use a framework of intergenerational ambivalence to help explain that mixed emotions may typify relationships between parents and adult children[5] and that those mixed feelings may be conferred on a child-in-law or parent-in-law. When family members understand the complexities of in-law relationships and begin to set realistic expectations for each other, there is less ambiguity. With clear role definitions for both generations, their interactions can become more satisfying, which can strengthen the marriage of the younger generation, help parents-in-law as they age, and provide greater nurturing for grandchildren while leaving a legacy of healthy family connections.

Across cultures and for millennia, marriage has been the axis around which families revolve and continue through raising the next generation. Marriage creates more than babies; it also creates in-laws. The selection of an appropriate partner is the stuff with which family dynasties, royalty, businesses, religions, castes, and communities both rich and poor are concerned as a marriage defines who is included and who is excluded, the most basic of human concerns. According to sociologist Stephanie Coontz, "Marriage usually determines rights and obligations related to sexuality, gender roles, relationships with in-laws, and the legitimacy of children . . . It usually defines the mutual duties of husband and wife and often the duties of their respective families towards each other . . . It also allows the property and status of the couple or the household head to be passed down to the next generation."[6] Marriage is such a seminal institution worldwide, she notes, that only one society, the Na of China, does not use marriage as a central way of organizing social and personal life. For the Na, brothers and sisters live together; there are no in-laws. In ancient Egypt, pharaohs married sisters and half-sisters, a practice that also occurred between commoners but less frequently. Such marriages helped families maintain property.[7] Coontz explained that the rules governing who can marry whom vary greatly from one society to the next, with first-cousin marriage and polygamy being discouraged in some societies and encouraged in others.[8] Polyandry, wherein women have more than one husband, has been in vogue in some countries, though never in North America.[9] From the view of researchers studying in-law relationships, consider how polygamy and polyandry would complicate matters!

Sometimes the role of child-in-law and parent-in-law gets flipped on its head. Consider Bill Wyman, the former bass player of the Rolling Stones. Wyman was, at one point, married to a woman 34 years his junior. He became, at that point, a son-in-law to his young wife's mother, a woman named Patty Smith. A few years later, Patty Smith married Wyman's son (16 years her junior) from a previous marriage. As a result, Wyman had the unique experience of being both a son-in-law and a father-in-law to the same woman. Turnabout is fair play, we suspect: Neither marriage lasted.

As anthropologist Janice Stockard wrote, marriage is not just a private, intimate affair. It is ineluctably tied to social, political, and economic life. It is gendered in that marriage has meaning for women and meaning for men and for the roles they are expected to fulfill in the family. It also has meaning for the roles men and women play in relation to the other men and women in the family.[10] One way this has played out over time is in the treatment of females. Historian Elizabeth Abbott documents the early ages at which girls were married off in China over a thousand years ago, sometimes as young as babies, with the thinking that young brides are less likely to run off than older ones. This young bride practice has not been confined to China. Even today, we find child brides. In West and Central Africa, for example, of women between the ages of 20 and 24, 14% were married before the age of 15, presumably in arranged marriages.[11] Worldwide, about 250 million women were married before the age of 15.[12]

Because daughters were not valued as highly as sons, a dowry was also a central component of marriage contracts and the burgeoning in-law relationship. Whether the dowry contained money, property, or something else of value, without it most women would stay single. The dowry could safeguard a woman from mistreatment by her husband or his family (her in-laws) if it was paid out over time as future payments could be curtailed. The amounts involved in dowries could be significant. Abbott explained that dowries were given regardless of class and, in one area of Italy in the 15th century, equaled what a worker might earn in 10 years. "The size of dowries depended on several factors. After searching out a suitable candidate for their daughter, parents offered a dowry based on the work she would do in the house and, sometimes, the field, and how many children she would bear and raise . . . A younger daughter, with more years of work and child-bearing to offer, could be married off with a smaller dowry."[13]

While daughters were seen as more of a drain on family resources than sons, the context in the community could change their relative value as a marriage partner. In North America in the 17th century, women were at a premium, being outnumbered five to one by men. Dowries, while they still existed then, were not as integral a part of the marriage arrangement. As to parents' role in the mate selection during the Colonial period, Historian Maren Wood writes that marriages were not arranged (i.e., parents did not pick a partner for their child), but marriage to an unsuitable person would be blocked as marriage tied families together socially and financially. Common-law marriage was quite frequent given the expense of a marriage license. Slaves could not marry legally and often used the African tradition of "jumping the broom" to announce to the community their commitment to each other.[14]

While arranged marriages were disappearing in the Americas, among the royal families of Europe they were central to consolidating power. Spanning the Colonial and Revolutionary Eras in America, Catherine the Great of Russia came to power, ruling from 1762 to 1796. Hailing from Prussia and having royal blood, she was matched with Peter III, heir to the Russian throne, in order to weaken Austria's influence and consolidate the two countries' alliance. Catherine fully embraced her role in the arranged marriage once she arrived in Russia, learning the language and converting to Eastern Orthodoxy. When she became a mother-in-law, she was initially pleased with the selection of a German princess for her son, similar to her own background. Over time, Catherine clearly changed her opinion. She is quoted as saying, "Everything is done to excess with this lady . . . in short, the middle way is unknown here . . . There is neither grace nor prudence, nor wisdom in any of this and God knows what will become of her . . . Just think that after a year and a half she does not speak a word of the language."[15] Catherine did not contend with this daughter-in-law for too long; she died in childbirth. Catherine was much happier with her son's second wife.

Customs around marriage in 19th-century Europe were characterized more by variation—differences between countries, regions, and economic classes within a country—than by similarity. Mate selection was usually left up to the partners, especially among the lower class. People rarely married outside of their class because they often only socialized with people from their same social class.[16] Young adults' contacts among the wealthier classes were at galas, family events, and concerts. These staged events meant that, to a large extent, marriages were "arranged" within the community. Attraction to another then would be shaped, in part, by what was considered typical of one's social group.[17] Fathers held more sway within the Eastern European countries than the Western European countries. In the Balkans, for example, a daughter refusing a father's (and family's) request to marry someone was unheard of, although, at the same time, a "kind" father or brother would not force the issue.[18]

As for in-law contact, newlyweds usually lived with one set of parents before they established themselves on their own. In one English town in the 1850s, at least half of newlywed couples lived with family or as lodgers in the homes of non-kin. When they had children and set up their own home, they were often in buildings shared by kin.[19] When peasant families thought about marriage, it was likely to be with an eye to what specific farming skills each partner could perform for the well-being of the family into which they were marrying. A young couple was not expected to be independent but to be integrated into an existing farm.[20]

Therefore, the careful and evolutionary selection of a mate for an adult child has been a primary consideration for thousands of years. While capital, power, and social class help drive the selection among the wealthy, other considerations appear in less industrialized societies. Menelaos Apostolou has explored marriage cross-culturally. Drawing on anthropological data from 67 pre-industrial societies preferences differ for what parents are looking for in a son-in-law and a daughter-in-law. For example, youth is more valued in a daughter-in-law due to her potential fertility; a man's fertility is not as limited by age. Chastity is valued more in a daughter-in-law than a son-in-law.[21] Good family background, good character, and industriousness are highly valued in both daughters- and sons-in-law, and wealth is more highly valued in a son-in-law.[22]

TODAY IN THE UNITED STATES

In the United States today, the parents' role in selecting mates for their children has diminished (though arranged marriages still exist in some cultural and religious communities in the United States). Almost half of those in our research indicated they did not know their in-law well before the marriage. For some families, this can result in a steep learning curve in adapting to a new family member.

Adults marry for their own reasons, and those reasons vary. According to the Pew Research Center, in a survey of Americans, love is the most important reason to get married (88% endorsed this), followed by making a lifelong commitment (81%), companionship (76%), and having children (49%).[23] According to the same Pew survey, women are more likely to be looking for a spouse with a steady job (78% of women endorsed) while men are most interested in a wife who shares his parenting philosophy (62% of men endorsed this). Nowhere is "to please one's family" mentioned as what a person is looking for in a spouse.

This does not mean, as Apostolou notes, that parents refrain from wielding some influence on their child's mate selection. Parents would naturally prefer a child-in-law who will adhere to the parents' and the community's values.[24] Children may be more attracted to someone who fits their parents' values. In the complex courtship phase, what attracts one partner to another is a myriad of factors that may include finding a partner that one's parents and brothers and sisters like. Attraction to a mate may also be driven by the welcoming nature of the future mate's family, as in the case of Nemo, who found his wife's father very warm. Family therapist Judith Silverstein writes that people often seek a relationship with someone who will make up for perceived deficits in their own family of origin.[25] For example, someone who comes from a small family may be attracted to a partner from a large family. Someone who comes from a large family and finds there is a lack of privacy and too much intrusion from family members may be attracted to someone from a smaller family. Someone from a family that does not show affection may be drawn to the family of a potential spouse who are all huggers.

It could also be that someone falls in love with or is strongly sexually attracted to his or her soul mate and does not give much thought to the family attached to that soul mate or to how well that soul mate will fit into his or her family. He or she may naively (or correctly) believe that love conquers all.

Of course, sometimes a spouse may be attractive because he or she will *not* be accepted and will help the child gain distance from a dysfunctional family of origin. If a child is searching for ways to separate from her or his family, what better way than to marry someone of whom they would not approve? Among our sample, close to 10% of the daughters-in-law and sons-in-law believed at least one of their parents-in-law did not approve of their marrying into the family and another 10% believed their in-laws were neutral when asked if their parent-in-law approved of the marriage. Of the mothers-in-law and fathers-in-law, 7% replied they did not approve of their child's marriage and 5% said they were neutral about the child-in-law. It is not clear to what extent disapproval was voiced to the marrying children, yet the marriages went forward. As we discuss, and as might be expected, relationships between parents-in-law and children-in-law who were not approved were more problematic.

With marriage as the derivation of in-law relationships, we see how often today's families are formed with little control over who is included. We also see how gender has played a key role for women (dowries paid; child brides handed off; daughters seen as drains on family resources; women valued for their youth and fertility) and how gender has played a key role for men (work prospects and wealth highly valued). In the chapters that follow, the differing roles of men and women in the family are discussed, but it is important to preface this by stating the obvious—women and men typically fulfill different, although increasingly overlapping roles in the family. Those roles often drive in-law relationships, and mothers-in-law and daughters-in-law are frequently central characters in family narratives.[26]

IN-LAWS IN POP CULTURE AND IN FAMILY CULTURE

We do not know when the first mother-in-law joke was told, but given the history of patriarchy across cultures (and that most comedians have traditionally been men), she may have been a safer target than the father-in-law. Clearly societal tropes, expressed in TV, film, and music, affect how we view ourselves and others. Not surprisingly, Wikipedia has a page describing mother-in-law jokes, while the page "father-in-law jokes" does not exist and there are no entries for daughter-in-law or son-in-law jokes. Wikipedia lists various television shows and movies from years back in which mothers-in-law are portrayed: Eve (Eve Arden) and Kaye (Kaye Ballard) starred in the sitcom *The Mothers-in-Law*; Viola Fields (Jane Fonda) in the film *Monster-in-Law*, Marie Barone (Doris Roberts) in the sitcom *Everybody Loves Raymond*, Adele Delfino (Celia Weston) on the television series *Desperate Housewives*, Endora (Agnes Moorehead) in the sitcom *Bewitched*, Olivia Jefferson (Zara Cully) in the sitcom *The Jeffersons*, and Mrs. Gibson (Ethel Owen) in various episodes of the TV show *The Honeymooners*. For a more recent and harrowing portrayal of a mother-in-law, view Meryl Streep as Mary Louise Wright in *Big Little Lies*.

We can add fathers-in-law found in TV and movies, too, all of them meant to be comical. Carroll O'Connor, who played Archie Bunker as the politically conservative father-in-law from hell (from the perspective of his liberal son-in-law, played by Rob Reiner) in the 1970s television show *All in the Family*, could have populated his own page. Don't forget Robert DeNiro opposite Ben Stiller in *Meet the Fockers* and Bryan Cranston opposite potential son-in-law James Franco in the 2016 movie, *Why Him?*

One notable exception to the comedic side of fathers-in-law appears in the 1967 Oscar-winning film, *Guess Who's Coming to Dinner*. Spencer Tracy, a White man, is asked to accept his daughter marrying Sidney Poitier, an African American man. Poitier tells Tracy, "I love your daughter and there is nothing I wouldn't do to keep her as happy as she was the day I met her. But it seems to me, without your approval, it would make no sense at all. That is why I am asking for the clearest possible statement of what your attitude is going to be." Tracy evolves by the end of the movie and says that, if they love each other, his approval is not needed and that love will prevail. Most in-laws do not face such a potential barrier when they join a family as being a different race was more than 50 years ago but marriage still often requires accommodation on both families' parts.

Websites devoted to "mothers-in-law from hell" are active as of this writing and a comparable one on daughters-in-law is also active. Fathers- and sons-in-law do not draw the same attention online today, a situation similar to what sociologist Deborah Merrill found in her survey of websites more than a decade ago as she studied the place of in-laws in popular culture.[27] Fathers-in-law did rate a line in the song by Snoop Dogg and Lil Dicky, Professional Rapper, "I'm taking over and they mad like father-in-law." But that's about it.

Mothers-in-law in songs are most memorably represented by Allen Toussaint's *Mother-in-Law*, sung by Ernie K-Doe and released in 1961. The British group Herman's Hermits covered the song a few years later. The lyrics? The song begins with "The worst person I know, mother-in-law, mother-in-law. She worries me so, mother-in-law, mother-in-law." The song goes on, refers to her as interfering, and suggests that she "don't come back no more." While attacking the role unfairly, the song captures much of the advice commonly given to parents-in-law—don't interfere and keep quiet!

This was K-Doe's only hit and he rode it to the bank, according to Chris Gray of the *Houston Press*. K-Doe opened a bar called (what else?) the Mother-in-Law Lounge.

K-Doe's song is sung by a man, typifying a son-in-law's issues with his mother-in-law—but a son-in-law is not the only one with conflicts with a mother-in-law. In the 1950s, Evelyn Duvall, a sociology professor at the University of Chicago, spearheaded research based, in part, on a CBS radio contest asking people to write in, "Why I think mothers-in-law are wonderful people." Despite the obvious attempt to reframe mothers-in-law by seeking the positives, the research findings did not save the day. From the 3,683 responses (and 1,337 subjects interviewed in focus groups), mothers-in-law were consistently ranked the most difficult of in-laws by all family members, with sisters-in-law a distant second and brothers-in-law and fathers-in-law alternating between the third and fourth most frequently mentioned. Daughters-in-law and sons-in-law were cited much less frequently, with daughters-in-law cited as troublesome more often than sons-in-law. Other research has also found that female in-law relationships are more strained than male in-law relationships.[28] But unlike the stereotype generated in K-Doe's song, it is not the son-in-law who pulls his hair out, according to Duvall; rather, "it is the woman who feels the mother-in-law problem more often."[29]

Duvall asked for in-law jokes in her research and only received them about mothers-in-law. She notes, and this was more than 60 years ago, that, "Mother-in-law jokes . . . quite possibly support some older value system that may or may not have meaning for modern families."[30] She analyzed the content of mother-in-law jokes and found them to center on the mother-in-law talking too much, being a know-it-all, being a meddlesome troublemaker, acting in an ego-deflating manner, and being mean.[31]

Why are these pillars in families (mothers-in-law are also mothers, grandmothers, sisters, and wives) derided so? A list of well-known exemplary mothers-in-law (starting recently with Barack Obama's mother-in-law, Michelle Obama's mother, who played a stabilizing role to the Obama girls, and Barbara Bush, who reportedly had wonderful relationships with her daughters-in-law, married to George and Jeb) would be endless. Add to the well-known mothers-in-law those who are not famous and are loving and supportive of their children and their spouses of both sexes; add to those names the grandmothers who help raise grandchildren when parents are at work or are absent. Consider that the term "mother-in-law" conjures up trepidation for some, while the word "grandmother" conjures up worth to all.[32]

We believe part of the reason for the assault on mothers-in-law is that mothers are central in most families and do not necessarily lose that centrality when their children marry. Women are "more involved in kin networks and function as social managers and thus may be more attuned to both supportive and strained interactions."[33] In the United States, since the Industrial Revolution pulled fathers away from the home and agriculture in search of factory work, mothers have largely had responsibility for raising children. Freudian psychology reinforced the crucial role of the mother in childrearing and that has continued in, for example, attachment theory. According to the Pew Research Center, global changes have occurred in relation to greater gender equality in the home and the workplace.[34] Yet women in the United States still do the bulk of the childcare, according to another Pew Research Center report that details the increase in stay-at-home mothers as the cost of day care goes up.[35] Women also are less likely to be in the workforce even as their children age into their teen years and, generally, spend more time in raising their children.[36] They are more likely than men to make the difficult choice between career and time with children. In China today, women's roles as in-law caretakers are a mixed bag, too. Women are required to retire 10 years earlier than men so they can take care of grandchildren and older relatives, a role that further cements their importance as in-laws while diminishing their importance in the workforce.[37]

Yes, today's fathers are involved in family life and play a much more active role in childrearing than their fathers or grandfathers did. And, yes, fathers continue to out-earn their wives (often for similar work) and thus play a highly important role in the financial well-being of the family. But as we see in our research as well as in other research, one-fifth of the way through the 21st century, fathers-in-law (hence fathers) are not as actively engaged with their families if we think of engagement in purely non-monetary terms. Men's contributions to the family have historically been focused on the financial, as well as the emotional. Tropes in society reaffirm that this is what men "should" be doing. Fathers' work, which often enables some mothers to stay home with children as the Pew Research Center reported, pulls husbands away more than some mothers are pulled away by work. As a result, mothers often sit more squarely in the internal workings of family life. And this is just in the two-parent family home. Extending the discussion to include single-parent families, the mother's role becomes even more central as single mothers are more likely to raise children alone than single fathers.

Being a mother is only one of several roles that women fulfill in families. As sisters, as we detailed in a previous book about adult siblings, women play a more central role in communicating and making arrangements between siblings than brothers.[38] While there is some evidence these gender roles are changing, the evidence does not yet support that sisters and brothers approach each other similarly or share equally in the caretaking of their own parents, much less their in-laws.

The roles that mothers fulfill place them in greater communication with their adult children and children-in-law as, our research shows, they typically are more active with childcare of grandchildren. With such activity, there may be a thin line between being an engaged parent who is helping out with childcare and being seen as an interfering mother-in-law by a son- or daughter-in-law. The fathers-in-law in our research do not engender the same feelings of interference.

At the same time, these relationships are two-way streets. Impressions of sons-in-law and daughters-in-law also differ. Daughters-in-law, perhaps because they are usually the gatekeepers to grandchildren, seem to draw more negative attention than sons-in-law. This may again be due to the roles that women, as kinkeepers and switchboards, play in the family. Women are often responsible for the couple's social calendar[39] and may be more interested in maintaining contact with both sets of parents if they carry more of the childrearing role. In-laws often have to coordinate with the daughter-in-law to see the grandchildren. As such, daughters-in-law may draw both more positive and more negative attention depending on the way the communication flows and visits are arranged.

DETERMINANTS OF SUCCESS
Parents-in-Law

What often determines parents' abilities to sustain a successful relationship with their new child-in-law is multifaceted and based on their personality fit with their own child, their child-in-law, and the dynamics of the parents interacting separately and together with the younger couple as a unit and as individuals. Parents remain parents to their now-married son or daughter whom they now must get to know, perhaps anew, as a married person and as a parent. They are also "parents" to a new son or daughter as well as to a new couple. Adding this all up, nine new interactions, at a minimum, are created just from the parents' perspective when the marriage vows are finished. For example, a mother of a daughter is interacting with:

1. her now-married daughter;
2. a new son-in-law (or daughter-in-law if it is a same-sex marriage); and
3. the newlyweds as a unit.

Add to these three solo interactions that the mother has, she and her husband (or wife if she is in a same-sex marriage) *as a couple* are interacting with:

4. their now-married daughter;
5. their new child-in-law; and
6. the newlyweds as a unit.

Add to this the father's interactions with:

7. his now-married daughter;
8. a new son-in-law (or daughter-in-law); and
9. the newlyweds as a unit.

The number of interactions will be many more if the parents are divorced and step-parents are involved and if siblings and siblings-in-law are on the scene. Add to these interactions a similar and simultaneously unfurling scenario with the new child-in-law's family as those connections have a great impact on this focal family! Of course, there are also the interactions between the two sets of parents, the potential capstone relationship. Historically, they would have arranged the marriage and now are most likely involuntary bystanders to their children's decision. And, when children/grandchildren arrive, a whole new set of roles must be navigated.

Relations between in-laws are nested in the dynamics of the parents-in-law's marriage, their history with their own in-laws, and even, potentially, their parents' relationships with their in-laws. In-law relationships are influenced multigenerationally as parents and children stand on the shoulders of past family relationships. If in-law relationships are notoriously strained in previous generations, perceptions about in-laws and new people marrying into the family may affect the current generation. If the family is historically an open system and is comfortable talking about their past history, the new member will feel more included than if there is great concern about what to share.[40]

What is impossible to calculate is how many of these potential interactions and variables have to be satisfying to make the overall in-law relationship work. What can outweigh family history? It is possible that a strong relationship between a mother-in-law and son-in-law can counterbalance an uncomfortable relationship between the father-in-law and son-in-law and make time together for both generations pleasant. It may be that time alone between a mother-in-law and daughter-in-law works for them yet, when all family members are together, feelings emerge that are difficult to address. Relationships are often fluid and involve many players.

Returning to Alice, she may have everything perfectly aligned for her to establish a satisfying relationship with her daughter-in-law. Yet, and here are the wild cards in family relations, the daughter-in-law brings a whole other set of expectations and family history to the table that does not fit well with Alice's experiences. Alice could come from a long line of family togetherness (for example, vacationing together, frequent and intimate conversations, family rituals around holidays and birthdays) and her daughter-in-law could come from a long line of family autonomy and individualism. For example, the daughter-in-law's family may own a small cabin in the woods where major life events are marked by alone time to contemplate. Or her family could be a mixture of both togetherness and separation—even Henry David Thoreau kept in frequent contact with others while living at Walden Pond. Alice and her daughter-in-law could end up happy with the in-law relationship if there is enough closeness for Alice and enough support for separation for her daughter-in-law.

Children-in-Law

As for sons- and daughters-in-law, newlyweds face a different and yet interconnected set of issues. Primarily, they must learn to be marital partners. Their first responsibility is to make the marriage work. With the divorce rate in the United States having tripled in the last 65 years,[41] success as a married couple is far from a given—still, a marriage can more likely last when in-law relations are comfortable. To sustain a marriage, the couple must recognize that, in most cases, their identities include not only being part of a couple but also being a daughter- or son-in-law and a member of a new extended family. If there are nine familial interaction patterns for the parents-in-law, 18 patterns are operating for the couple who have to adapt to *two* sets of parents as individuals and as units as the couple simultaneously is adapting to each other. In making their decisions, the members of the couple also have their own family histories that may be consciously, or unconsciously, driving their behavior. One set of parents may be more emotionally or financially needy than the other, live farther away, or present with a language barrier if the marriage is intercultural. Thus, simply deciding whose family to visit for that first major family holiday can be a test of multiple relationships.

The demands on the new couple do not stop there. They have friends, both as couples and as individuals, who need their time. They may have siblings (and their spouses) who affect family ties. They may have jobs, educational degrees to complete, as well as hobbies, community service, and religious connections to pursue. The couple needs to agree on exercise schedules, housekeeping chores, financial savings philosophies, and when each can have alone time. One study found that figuring out how much time to spend with each family of origin was the most common stressor for newlyweds.[42] Ultimately, it may be impossible and not even desirable to balance time and resources exactly between the families.

How those components of their lives are balanced with loyalty to each other, to their families, and to their social networks is the tricky part. We know that positive interactions between spouses and between parents and children are related to positive mental health outcomes.[43] But where do the newlyweds draw boundaries that are protective of their relationship yet inclusive of parents? For Abram, the father-in-law whose quote begins this chapter, his son-in-law seems to have drawn a boundary that excludes Abram and Abram's family while simultaneously privileging loyalty to his own family, something that Abram reluctantly accepts. For Nemo, this is not an issue: He sees his father-in-law as being lovingly engaged without being interfering. Again, to have a successful in-law relationship, it is difficult to calculate what exactly needs to be in place.

CHALLENGING SUCCESS: LIVING WITH DIFFERENCE

Now consider variations on family forms that may make relationships for some families more complicated. Interracial, interethnic, and interfaith marriages are on the rise. In the United States, individuals are five times more likely to marry someone of a different race or ethnicity than 50 years ago (one in six marriages is interracial).[44] Almost two in five marriages are now interfaith.[45] Same-sex marriage became legal across the United States in 2015. For many parents, a child's marrying outside of one's race, ethnicity, faith, expected gender, or class may present a challenge. These differences apply to some of the families in this book. Even if parents embrace their child marrying someone religiously, racially, or ethnically different from themselves, or someone of the same gender, as many do, members of their extended family may be less accepting and cause stress or conflict in the extended family.

* * *

The past helps shape the present. Yet, what may be most influential in the ultimate success of an in-law relationship is the determination to make it work. Family members have to accept, adapt, and even embrace the fact that the addition of new family members is inevitable and necessary for family growth. It is a balancing of the horizontal and the vertical nature of families. Horizontally, sons- and daughters-in-law have to manage relationships *within* or across their own generation—with their partner and with their siblings and siblings-in-law. Vertically, they have to manage relationships *between* generations—with their parents and parents-in-law. Mothers- and fathers-in-law have to manage, horizontally, their own marital relationship and the relationship with the other parents-in-law as they manage, vertically, the relationship with their own child and their daughter- or son-in-law. It is a simultaneous harmonizing of the past and the present with an eye toward a future legacy of support and love.

IN SUM

In 1911, the *Mona Lisa* was stolen from the Louvre and no one noticed for 28 hours. It was because of its theft and the search for it that Leonardo Da Vinci's painting became the most famous painting at the Louvre and, arguably, in the world. People had paid attention to it before but, once spotlighted and given a different context, people became more aware of it. Here we want people to become more aware of their in-law relationships.

As family therapists, we know that how open families are to new members and new ways of interacting will affect the success of the relationship. Parents, different from their predecessors who played a large part in spouse selection, will have to trust that their child is capable of making a wise decision both in spouse selection and in how to raise the next generation. When children convey their competence in these areas by their mate selection and their caregiving and childrearing skills across the lifespan, it is easier for the parents to trust and let them be. With a better understanding of the impact of in-laws, we can build even healthier, more functional relationships that can sustain families across generations.

CHAPTER 2
A Snapshot of In-Law Research

Stretching back to the 1960s, a limited body of research across multiple disciplines has been published on in-law relationships, but it has primarily focused on mothers-in-law and daughters-in-law. Women researchers seem particularly intrigued by the topic: We found virtually no U.S.-based articles written specifically about in-laws in that time period that did not have at least one or all female authors.[1] During this time period, social science has, with a few notable exceptions,[2] ignored fathers-in-law and sons-in-law and, specifically, how they manage their relationships with each other. One study referred to children-in-law but only studied daughters-in-law![3] A book focusing on learning to get along with one's in-laws had more than 140 references in its index on mothers-in-law, four on fathers-in-law, and five times as many references to daughters-in-law than sons-in-law.[4] What has been studied about these men's roles usually centers on caretaking of elderly parents and parents-in-law, the extent to which sons-in-law help their wives, and the extent to which daughters-in-law take care of their husband's parents. Thus, most of what we know from research is based on the experiences of women.

We begin our presentation of this research with a brief overview of research in seven areas that involve children- and parents-in-law. As we are writing this book for in-laws and clinicians, this review is not meant to be exhaustive and is not meant to cover all the research that has been conducted, some of which, because of its age, may not be as relevant today to changing gender and culturally embedded family roles. Excellent reviews of the literature appear in many of the resources we cite. In the United States, Karen Fingerman at the University of Texas Austin, Mary Claire

Morr Serewicz at the University of Denver, Christine Rittenour at West Virginia University, and Sylvia Mikucki-Enyart at the University of Iowa have done or are doing excellent research in the area. We encourage those interested in delving further into that research to read the most recent scholarship from these four scholars and others we have cited as women's and men's roles, including their extended family relationships, are constantly being reshaped in our dynamic society.

1. WHEN TAKING CARE OF ELDERLY IN-LAWS AND PARENTS, ARE THERE DIFFERENCES BETWEEN DAUGHTERS-IN-LAW AND SONS-IN-LAW?

In a word, yes, with some nuanced differences. We have already established that research reveals that women are more central in the kinkeeping of the family than men. Here we look at what happens with aging parents and parents-in-law, whose care often falls to the adult children and children-in-law. Such care may start at a later age for family members than ever before as baby boomers are staying in the workforce and living independently longer than previous generations.[5] When care does start, it can take a toll as the more time and resources a child spends with a parent in need, the less time and fewer resources he or she has with a marital partner and his or her children. The marriage may be affected but not always equally for husbands and wives. In one study of 132 middle-aged couples, husbands' and wives' filial obligation (the extent to which they felt they needed to help their parents) was measured and then correlated with marital happiness. When wives were found to give a lot of support to their parents but their husbands felt little filial obligation, the marriage was less satisfying for the wife, probably due to the husband's not being supportive of the time the wife was spending with her parents. Wives who viewed their husbands as being supportive of their own parents—his in-laws—reported higher-quality marital relations.[6] This is an example of how in-law relationships influence the marriage.

While this research pertains to parents, caretaking of in-laws also needs to be seen in the light of the extent to which daughters-in-law, more than sons-in-law, get involved with and feel an obligation for caretaking of both sets of parents. In a rare study that included sons-in-law, social work professor Judith Globerman[7] interviewed 10 sons-in-law, six daughters-in-law, and their spouses who had a parent with Alzheimer's disease. She found that sons-in-law saw themselves as reactive in assisting their wives in caregiving, helping out only when asked to. Daughters-in-law tended to take charge of caregiving, even of their parents-in-law. "[T]he daughter-in-law is sometimes involved in caregiving in order to help her husband manage his relationship with his parents . . . [This] suggests that women do kinkeeping because they know what to do, and they find it intolerable when it is not done right."[8] Sons-in-law tended to believe it was more expected of their wives than of themselves to do the caregiving and that they were not especially proficient at caregiving. When the sons-in-law did get involved, they did it more out of a feeling of obligation than affection, Globerman surmised. Note, once again, that this study was published in the 1990s and much has since changed about the expectations for these roles.

Ursula Henz,[9] a sociologist at the London School of Economics, in a more recent study analyzed data from 2,214 couples who participated in the British General Household Survey. Sons and daughters helped out their own parents similarly until the demands of caregiving became great. At that point, each spouse helped out the other but sons-in-law still did less caretaking than daughters-in-law. Similar to Globerman's findings, sons-in-law tended to take direction from their wives when it came to caregiving of both sets of parents. Their wives' time availability affected the extent of the sons-in-law's involvement, with their time in caretaking reduced if their wives were not working outside the home. One implication of the findings is that women—who feel the pull of family obligations more strongly than do men—are more likely to leave the labor market to do caretaking of the older generation.

A team from the Philadelphia Geriatric Center surveyed 252 co-resident daughters and daughters-in-law and their husbands to study caregiving patterns in the elderly. While sons gave more hours of caregiving to their own parents, daughters gave close to equal amounts to both sets of parents.[10] Noelle Chesley and Kyle Poppie, using data from a 1995 national survey of 2,085 U.S. citizens, parsed the type of support provided to parents-in-law. Women provided much more emotional support (such as comforting or listening to problems) to their own parents and to their in-laws than did men. However, when it came to helping with tasks around the house and with transportation, men and women were equally engaged with both parents and in-laws.[11]

An oft-repeated partial explanation for the potential differential roles played by women is that they are socialized to play a more nurturing role in the family.[12] In our research on siblings, we found that sisters play a much more central role in family communication, though there is some evidence that younger brothers are now communicating in patterns similar to their sisters.[13] As gender is related to caregiving of the elderly, it certainly needs attention in all generations, as well as when in-laws are not ailing.

2. DOES THE BIRTH OF A CHILD MEAN A SHIFT IN THE RELATIONSHIP BETWEEN THE CHILD-IN-LAW AND PARENT-IN-LAW?

The research is inconclusive on the impact of the birth of a child on the in-law relationship. More than 30 years ago, Lucy Rose Fischer, a professor in family studies, interviewed women in western Massachusetts and explored shifts in relationships between 33 daughters, 30 mothers, and 24 mothers-in-law. She found that once the daughter had a child, relations improved with the mother and deteriorated with the mother-in-law, creating more ambiguity between them. What typically annoyed daughters-in-law would be critical comments the mother-in-law made about how the child was being raised ("you shouldn't spank") or interactions the mother-in-law had with the child (offering a cookie). The daughters-in-law were also annoyed with critical comments about their home management and that their mother-in-law seemed to have no interest in them as a person. In addition, and not surprisingly, daughters-in-law expressed more ambivalence about receiving childcare help from their mother-in-law than from their mother, where the roles would have been more defined.[14] This makes sense given that the mothers raised the daughters, so they have shared parenting experiences, and are much more likely to hold similar parenting approaches and strategies, while mothers-in-law's approaches to parenting may be not only different but in direct conflict at times. Note that this is a 1980s study and thus the findings may be less relevant today.

More recently, Deborah Merrill conducted interviews with 53 daughters-in-law and 14 mothers-in-law related to some of the 53 daughters-in-law. She found no consistent pattern in the change in the mother-in-law/daughter-in-law relationship following the birth of the next generation. Many daughters-in-law said the birth made them feel closer to their mother-in-law, while others were resentful of the lack of help offered. In one example when things turned for the worse, a daughter-in-law recounted, in relation to the birth of her child, ". . . that her in-laws became intrusive with advice only once their grandchildren were born."[15] While these are the views of daughters-in-law, in a Midwestern study of 104 parents-in-law, having a grandchild was not related to any positive or negative feelings the parents-in-law felt toward their son- or daughter-in-law.[16]

In a recent Norwegian study, though, of both married and cohabitating parents, contact with in-laws was more frequent and more positive when there were young children. Couples who were cohabiting and childless had the least contact and the least positive relationships with the older generation.[17]

3. DO MOTHERS-IN-LAW REPORT THE RELATIONSHIP WITH THE DAUGHTER-IN-LAW IS BETTER THAN THE DAUGHTERS-IN-LAW REPORT?

For the most part, the answer to this question is yes. Ramona Marotz-Baden, a professor at Montana State, and Deane Cowan, a family therapist, surveyed 44 mothers-in-law and 55 daughters-in-law who were Montana ranchers and farmers. Mothers-in-law were more likely than daughters-in-law to report no problems in the relationship (34% of mothers-in-law and 17% of daughters-in-law). When problems arose, mothers-in-law were more likely to use communication to resolve problems. Daughters-in-law tended to ignore problems that arose rather than communicate about them. Ignoring the problem was the second most used strategy by mothers-in-law, while "taking time out" was the second most used strategy by the daughters-in-law. Avoidant strategies were used more by daughters-in-law than mothers-in-law. On a positive note, having the other family member "show respect" was the key feature in helping them get along with each other. Having similar values and goals was mentioned by both groups as another reason for getting along. Note this was also research from the 1980s.

Merrill also concluded that mothers-in-law have a more positive view of this relationship than daughters-in-law. Almost 60% of the daughters-in-law reported some conflict and 48% reported feeling ambivalent toward their mother-in-law; only 24% of the mothers-in-law expressed ambivalence, and a smaller percentage described conflict. Merrill posits that mothers-in-law need their daughter-in-law more as the daughter-in-law makes the social arrangements and, by extension, may permit greater access to grandchildren.

4. DO SHARED IDENTITY AND SUPPORT MATTER? MOREOVER, WHAT ABOUT THE DAUGHTER-IN-LAW'S MOTHER?

Absolutely they matter. Not surprisingly, as Marotz-Baden and Cowan report, when in-laws hold similar values and see themselves as part of the same family, it is good for the relationship. Christine Rittenour and Jordan Soliz surveyed 190 daughters-in-law, asking them about their communication patterns with their mothers-in-law.[18] Their participants were obtained through network sampling and students in undergraduate classes. When a mother-in-law and daughter-in-law shared a family identity, there was a greater likelihood of a good relationship. To help further cement a shared family identity, appropriate self-disclosure (too much of the wrong kind was not helpful) between the women and receiving supportive responses from a mother-in-law were linked to better relationships. As might be expected, exclusionary behavior by the mother-in-law (such as making remarks that made the daughter-in-law feel like an outsider to the rest of the family, not explaining family rituals, and devaluing the daughter-in-law's opinions), were not helpful. The perception of interference was also an impediment when it was experienced as a lack of support. Interference took the forms of criticizing the daughter-in-law's parenting or demeaning her as a wife.

Another way to look at shared identity and support is to consider how families communicate. Carolyn Prentice, a professor of communication studies, conducted in-depth interviews with 42 in-laws and looked at how involved families were with newlyweds as well as what impact the new in-law had on the family's communication patterns. She found that families communicated about their norms and routines both indirectly and directly. By indirect communication she refers to the family members continuing as they always had and anticipating the new in-law would feel comfortable assimilating because the family members trusted that their own family member would choose a partner who would fit in with the family's way of interacting. Direct communication was manifested when families sensed discomfort in the newcomer and family members felt they had to rationalize their own behavior. An example given was a situation in which a man asked his prospective father-in-law for permission to marry the daughter. The father shared his expectations that the son-in-law would participate in family events even though that participation differed from the son-in-law's interactions with his own family. This father was communicating directly about expectations rather than assuming (indirect communication pattern) that the son-in-law would fall in line.

Past personal and family history with in-law relationships also seemed to shape the approach that many interviewees took to their interactions. If parents had bad relations with their own parent-in-laws, they often veered from direct communication; they wanted to do the opposite with their children-in-law by not being too dictatorial.[19]

In the two-way street of family life, Prentice found that families had to adapt to the new in-law, co-creating a new shared identity. Sometimes families became more demonstrative emotionally as a result of a new daughter-in-law who liked to hug and be verbally expressive. In one example, though, an emotionally demonstrative son-in-law turned off a mother-in-law who was more emotionally contained, and the mother-in-law expressed surprise that her own daughter would be attracted to such an expressive man.

Disclosure from one family member to the next is often seen as a form of acceptance and inclusion. Disclosure is also related to greater relationship satisfaction, according to research by Mary Claire Morr Serewicz, who surveyed 98 triads consisting of the adult children couple and one of their parents. This was true for both the child-in-law and the parent.[20] Disclosure can take the form of talking about unsavory family history (though too much of this can be a turn-off given the family orientation of the receiver of the information), family traditions, and positive feelings toward a child-in-law.[21] Imagine coming from a family that does not share much and marrying into a family that shares a lot.

Values can also diverge about the discussion of taboo subjects. Too much disclosure can cause discomfort. Conversely, being able to bring up such topics can help to bring families closer together and a new degree of intimacy can be achieved.

As had been wondered, what does a daughter-in-law's relationship with her own mother mean for her relationship with her mother-in-law (we found no comparable research on fathers and sons)? Neither encouragement by a daughter-in-law's mother to be close with the mother-in-law nor a positive relationship between a daughter-in-law and her own mother were predictive of daughter-in-law/mother-in-law relationships. While these relational aspects are not associated, this question requires more unpacking. Rittenour and Soliz hypothesize that a strong commitment to one's family *may* be a barrier to identifying closely with one's in-laws. In addition, they note that children-in-law may feel they are being disloyal to their own parents if they are too close to their in-laws. At the same time, a weak identification with one's family may lead to greater closeness with one's in-laws. "[B]ecause much of the 'struggle' for daughters-in-law is associated with the tension of loyalty toward a mother versus closeness to a mother-in-law, the actual relationship between a daughter and her mother may be an important factor in a harmonious relationship with her mother-in-law."[22]

5. WHO DEALS WITH WHOM IN THE RELATIONSHIP? FOR A SON-IN-LAW OR DAUGHTER-IN-LAW, WHAT PART DOES HIS OR HER SPOUSE PLAY IN DEALING WITH THE SPOUSE'S PARENTS? WHAT ARE FAMILY SYSTEMS AND HOW DO THEY WORK?

Does a son-in-law speak for his wife when dealing with his parents or does he let her deal with them? Does a mother-in-law speak directly to her daughter-in-law or communicate with her through her son? We return here to the important matter of communication as it helps to influence many of the areas discussed. Patterns of communication vary, with no one model of communication working for every family. Along these same lines, Prentice found "the widespread practice of mediating the relationship between the newcomer and the family through the spouse, especially when dealing with problematic issues around routines."[23] This pattern of communication could evolve for a number of reasons, including (1) the newlyweds were rarely separated so there was little opportunity for individual conversations; (2) the newlyweds did not seem to want to have separate relationships with the family; (3) the new in-law felt socially awkward; and (4) past interactions involving the new in-law had not gone well. These reasons were given from the parents-in-law's perspective. Still, from the child's perspective, one newlywed said she felt her husband's parents had little interest in her as a person, so she stayed close to her husband when with the in-laws. Children-in-law may also be protected from in-laws by their spouse if the spouse views his or her parents as difficult to deal with or believes the parents-in-law are not supportive of their new child-in-law. While this practice avoids or reduces conflict, Prentice believes, it makes the in-law an outsider. Such three-way relationships are examples of triangles, as Murray Bowen explains (see Chapter 9), and can be both a symptom and a source of relationship problems.

Apostolou's research with a Greek-Cypriot population points out the role that sons- and daughters-in-law might play in trying to convince, or, as Aposotlou put it, manipulate the parent-in-law into a state of acceptance of the child-in-law. The research participants were asked what they might do if they loved someone but felt that their parents do not like them. The most likely tactic was the "I am right for your child" approach. Here the younger in-law is trying to convince the elder in-law that she or he would be a great mate and a good influence and will take wonderful care of the prospective spouse. The next most frequent suggested tactic is the "I don't deserve this" approach, where the goal is to convince the mate's parents that the prospective in-law does not deserve this rejection. As part of this approach, the mate is asked to intercede on the prospective in-law's behalf.[24]

In Marotz-Baden and Cowan's research on mothers-in-law and daughters-in-law, both groups tended to turn to their husbands for advice about getting along with each other. As mentioned, mothers-in-law said they were more likely to employ the strategy of communicating with their daughter-in-law than daughters-in-law reported they were likely to employ in dealing with their mother-in-law. Daughters-in-law were most likely to employ the strategy of ignoring any issues that arose with their mother-in-law. These are commonly used models of family interaction—communicate through the adult child and not with the in-law; ignore the issue; or deal directly with the in-law.

Dealing directly with the in-law may be best for families with an open style of communication and is consistent with a method that is central to Virginia Satir's approach to healthy family communication. An open model of communication may, of course, clash if one spouse comes from a family of indirect communicators while the other comes from a family of direct communicators. We return to this issue as a key component in Chapter 9 when we focus on improving in-law relationships.

The question of communication is embedded in the larger notion of family systems. We explore in the book the roles that spouses of both generations as well as the other set of parents play in the parent-in-law and child-in-law relationship. Quite simply, if a mother-in-law is struggling with a daughter-in-law, we need to consider where both of their spouses fit in, as well as perhaps their siblings and grandparents, and their wider social contexts (religion, culture, reference group, neighborhood, and so on). As one classic text explains, "The system model analyzes the behavior and psychological makeup of the individual by emphasizing the continuity of the influences that family members have on each other from the earliest life of the child through the present moment."[25] Family members influence and are influenced by each other, as family-based research avers. How exactly it plays out in relation to in-laws is what we explore further throughout this book.

Let us also consider Linchpin Theory here. Morr Serewicz explains that there would be no relationship without the choice made by the child as to whom to marry; the child selects the child-in-law for the parent.[26] So, to at least some extent, that daughter or son would always be an integral part of the intergenerational in-law relationship, the linchpin. Sometimes that role is more active and sometimes it is more passive but, symbolically, it is always there, as we explore in later chapters.

6. HOW USEFUL IS INTERGENERATIONAL AMBIVALENCE AS A LENS FOR VIEWING IN-LAW RELATIONSHIPS?

Not only is ambivalence used to look at adult child–parent relationships, but it is also helpful in considering in-law relationships. Ambivalence has been used to define the contradictions in our interpersonal relationships, the push and pull between setting boundaries and establishing intimacy.[27] According to sociologists Ingrid Connidis and Julie Ann McMullin, ambivalence between family members can exist at different times over the lifespan as families progress from a state of solidarity to one of conflict and back again. Ambivalence can also apply to a state of mixed emotions when one family member is coming to terms with the situation of another family member[28] that may not have turned out as he or she wished. Examples of this would be a parent who is disappointed with a child's career trajectory or is unhappy with the child's choice of a spouse yet wants to maintain a relationship with both the child and the spouse.[29] Ambivalence, like many states of discomfort, may not always have negative outcomes as it may be a spur to push someone to try and resolve a situation.[30] People often take steps to improve their relationships when they feel uncertain or uncomfortable with them.

Ambivalence between adult children and parents can carry over to the treatment of or feelings toward the parent- or child-in-law. Health can play a role in this scenario. When in-laws are in poor health, relations with them are more likely to be characterized as ambivalent,[31] which is hardly surprising. Relationships become strained as more caretaking of aging in-laws is needed. At the same time, as in-laws age, they are less able to provide financial or childcare support to their adult children.

In addition to the psychological ambivalence described in relation to interpersonal feelings, there is also sociological ambivalence, wherein ascribed societal roles may be unclear or in conflict with how a person, or family, wishes to act.[32] This concept places people in a social context and is similar to role ambiguity in that there are conflicting feelings about how someone should behave. Researchers Santos and Levitt describe in-law relationships as inherently ambiguous—they originate involuntarily through marriage and can be ended through divorce. They exist in a society where marriage supersedes family, leaving in-laws with no clear roles.[33] Sylvia Mikucki-Enyart, a University of Iowa communication researcher who studies relational and family uncertainty (in this context when parents-in-law have doubts about how to act, feel, and think when with their son- or daughter-in-law), found in her research that ambiguity between in-law generations is common.[34]

Women are reported to be more likely to experience ambivalence than men,[35] a fact that helps to explain some of our findings about the complicated and differing roles that women play when compared with men. Not surprising, adult children are more likely to experience ambivalence toward their in-laws than toward their parents—they have less shared history and the roles are less defined,[36] likely feeding the ambivalence that parents-in-law feel toward their children-in-law.

It can get complicated. If parents believe they have not launched a child well, they may fear the child will not take care of them as they age. They love their child but are also concerned about the child's future. The parents may then transfer that fear to their new child-in-law, further muddying the relationship waters. Of course, a wonderful child-in-law can have the opposite effect and help allay parents' fears about their own child. We heard from many parents-in-law who joked that they liked their son- or daughter-in-law more than their own child. Any doubts that parents-in-law had about their own child may diminish with the selection of a great mate.

Ambivalence can also derive from the child-in-law not getting the family he or she had hoped for when married. Jean Turner and colleagues conducted focus groups and semistructured interviews with 23 daughters-in-law and 19 unrelated mothers-in-law. A lens of intergenerational ambivalence was used to understand the mixed emotions inherent in these relationships. One of the interviewees described being attracted to her husband's family to replace the one she was raised in, while another described, rather sadly, always feeling like a second-class citizen with her husband's family. Many daughters-in-law had anticipated a better family relationship than they actually achieved after the wedding.[37] These experiences lead to in-laws having to learn how to accept something less than ideal, or far from what they had built their expectations up to. The father does not get the son-in-law he hoped for; the son does not get the father figure he wanted.

Judith Silverstein, in relating a case that exemplifies intergenerational ambivalence, shows how the lack of resolution between a son and his mother can triangulate in Jane, the daughter-in-law:

Jane had significant difficulty dealing with her widowed mother-in-law. Her husband had an ambivalent relationship with his mother: he loved her very much and was quite devoted to her, though they fought a lot. She . . . clearly had a sense of competitiveness with her daughter-in-law. Early in the relationship, before Jane and Fred were married, Jane met her mother-in-law and spent most of a weekend with her. Afterwards, her future mother-in-law, Marilyn, complained to Jane that she wanted to get to know her better and felt badly that they didn't have more time. Jane, on the other hand, thought that she had devoted quite a bit of time to meeting her future mother-in-law. She felt defensive and inadequate as a daughter-in-law. Marilyn tended to be critical in general and was particularly so of Jane, although Fred did set some boundaries and would not tolerate hearing his mother criticize Jane. Marilyn was temperamental, pouted frequently and expected to get whatever she wanted. When Fred wanted to spend time with his mother during vacations, Jane felt extremely competitive and jealous of their relationship. The more jealous she felt, the more Fred felt he had to defend his mother and this conflict became chronic. Numerous sessions in therapy were spent dealing with Jane's dislike of and competition with Marilyn. Jane was close to her own parents. Fred did not have a problem spending time with them or having Jane visit them for weekends without him. Jane seemed more dependent on Fred than he seemed to be on her. She was jealous of his time and was furious if he went anywhere without her.[38]

Silverstein's case nicely illustrates a number of potential in-law issues. The mother and daughter-in-law had different perceptions of what was needed from their first time spent together. Marilyn's tendency to be critical stung an especially vulnerable Jane, who felt she was competing with Marilyn for time with Fred. Fred was trapped in a no-win battle, which may have fed his own preexisting mixed feelings toward his mother. If Fred were more resolved in his relationship with his mother, he might be able to navigate the terrain between the two women in his life more easily. This is how such ambivalence between an adult and his parent can manifest itself, leaving a legacy of uncertainty for the next generation. These experiences require adjustments by all involved about previously held expectations when marrying into a family. An awareness of the ambivalence can be the impetus to try and improve the relationship.

7. DO CHILDREN-IN-LAW AND PARENT-IN-LAW RELATIONSHIPS CHANGE ACROSS TIME?

While these relationships can be classified into various life stages, so many other factors emerge over possibly a 30- to 40-year time span—from when people first marry and through the aging of in-laws—it is difficult to determine what changes over time. Morr Serewicz takes a broad view and considers these relationships as constantly in flux. Not only do relations change with significant life events (marriages, births, deaths, illnesses, job losses, moves), but even with minor events, like mood shifts, which can cause temporary tension in the relationship, and affect the outcome of research. Merrill found from her interviews that the biggest improvement in the relationship between mother-in-law and daughter-in-law came from the fact of being married, with 75% marking that event as making a difference. The majority who reported initial friction in their relationships resolved that acrimony later on in the marriage. In most cases, as people spend time together, they become more comfortable with each other. This was the case with many of those interviewed by Merrill.

Research conducted in Indianapolis approximately six months before and six months after the wedding and involving 60 heterosexual couples and the mothers of the brides and grooms points in two seemingly opposite directions: "Having more contact in general was associated with lower positive relationship quality and increased negative relationship quality after marriage . . . Yet individual contact [between the in-laws] was associated with more positive feelings about the relationship after the wedding."[39] The authors surmise that when the contact between the in-laws is coerced, it feels different from when the two in-law generations get together by choice. Further, positive feelings before the wedding were associated with positive feelings afterward.

Those two studies looked at changes from the beginning of the in-law relationships. Julianne Serovich and Sharon Price,[40] in analyzing a sample of 309 children-in-law couples with living parents-in-law and parents, divided the in-law relationship into three phases representing the typical lifespan: (1) the pre-child phase, where in-laws were in the role of parent to the adult children; (2) the child phase, where the children-in-law had at least one child and the in-laws were in the role of grandparent (see our earlier response about the impact of the child on the relationship); and (3) the dependent phase, where at least one of the in-laws was in poor health and was being visited by one of the children. Clearly such family life phases should evoke different emotions and needs from both children-in-law and parents-in-law. Interestingly, no differences were found across the phases in the satisfaction the children-in-law felt toward their parents-in-law.[41] The authors found that sons-in-law reported greater satisfaction (than daughters-in-law) with their fathers-in-law and also that sons-in-law viewed fathers-in-law more favorably than mothers-in-law. Daughters-in-law's views of each in-law were similar. The authors emphasized that while differences exist between the genders, the overall quality of the relationships was highly rated, and that perhaps in-law relationships are popularly perceived to be worse than they actually are.

Finally, with time, family members often move geographically closer or farther away from each other as they age and retire and as educational and employment opportunities arise. The result? Unclear. Living in close proximity to one's in-laws, as well as to one's parents, was found to be associated with greater feelings of ambivalence toward the in-laws in one study[42] but not in another.[43] Like much family research, ours included, the findings may vary as a function of the characteristics of the sample, how and when the research was conducted, and by the very nature of family life with its changing dynamics.

CONCLUSION

A range of studies helps us consider these complicated relationships, which are often rife with ambivalence and ambiguity. We are also left with a multitude of ever-evolving questions: How are the changing roles of women and men in families, at work, and across society affecting in-law relationships? How do these relationships vary from one culture to the next[44] or from one region of the country to the next? Understanding how these variables play out in families across the lifespan is daunting. Learning about them through a mixed-methods approach, incorporating both open-ended interview questions and multiple-choice survey questionnaires, is one way to gain perspective, but no one study and no mountain of research can encompass the idiosyncratic nature of the human relationships.

CHAPTER 3

Mothers-in-Law and Their Relationship with Their Daughter-in-Law

In the first chapter we described the historical and social challenges that mothers-in-law experience fulfilling their unique role. The context in which mothers-in-law operate today is vastly different from the past and varies from culture to culture and family to family. In this chapter we answer a series of questions by drawing on our research. From surveys and interviews with mothers-in-law, we are able to construct a picture of those relationships that work very well and those relationships that are highly troubled. We also explore those relationships where the mothers-in-law do not feel particularly close nor particularly distant from their daughter-in-law. These relationships on the surface are pleasant, yet may have some ambivalence and a significant amount of accommodation in them.

By hearing from those who feel that they are very close with their daughters-in-law, we learn how such relationships come to be and how they are sustained over many years. These close relationships provide a potential road map for others who feel less close or are struggling with their daughters-in-law. While some of the dynamics of these struggling relationships, such as problematic personality traits or an upsetting family history, are not easily changed, reading about the experiences of others may help to normalize a mother-in-law's own experiences and stimulate considerations of ways to modify what may feel like a stuck relationship. While we focus here on the mother-in-law and daughter-in-law relationship, to fully paint the picture of their relationship, it is necessary to gain the perspective of the daughters-in-law, which we provide in Chapter 4. The perspectives do not always match up. It is also vitally important to consider the roles that the mother-in-law's son and the mother-in-law's husband/partner may play in supporting or deterring this relationship.

Many mothers-in-law feel close to their daughter-in-law. To dig into this relationship, we need to look at the range of relationships that we found and what we learned from talking to mothers-in-law. On one end of the spectrum, we have the wonderful relationship described by this mother-in-law:

> She just does small things that are really nice. Like the other night I was sitting at a fundraiser and I got a text and I looked at it and it was from her. She texted me that she loved me. She makes me feel really loved and what else can you ask?

Elsewhere on the spectrum, we see a more cautious account of a relationship that is close, yet has required some accommodation. This mother-in-law has clearly dialed back her expectations from what she would have wanted the relationship to be:

> When they were first engaged, my son cooks, and he brought her over and we had breakfast together and I loved her right from the beginning. She asked if she could help with anything and I said, "If you like, you can make the fruit salad." So my son and I cooked the breakfast and I gave her the fruit. Well, when we sat down she had cut up all the fruit except for the orange. She had left the orange peel on in the salad, so that told me that she doesn't normally cook. Nothing was said then. My son and I just looked at each other. It wasn't until their engagement party a few years later that I thought it would be a funny story, a nice story for everybody. When I told the story, I could tell it upset her. It seemed like she was hurt by that. I thought she would get a kick out of it and think it was funny. But I knew then that I couldn't poke fun with her. She might take it more personally, so I don't do that anymore just because I want them to have a good relationship and I don't want to be a thorn in anybody's side.

And, of course, there are some mother-in-law and daughter-in-law relationships that do not work. Mothers-in-law in these situations can find little good to say about their daughter-in-law, have often struggled with the daughter-in-law from the beginning of their relationship, and regularly feel excluded. As one mother-in-law whom we introduce later told us in relation to her son, "She has an issue with our closeness. She does everything she can to keep us separate."

Just how complicated are these mother-in-law/daughter-in-law relationships? Even some mothers-in-law who have told us they are as close as they can be with their daughter-in-law add cautionary notes—they have to watch what they say to her. "I feel close," one mother-in-law, a retired therapist, told us. "I don't feel *real* close. I mean, I don't feel estranged or anything, but I don't feel like she's my daughter. I feel like she's my daughter-in-law. There's some little bit of something there or a lack of something. I don't know. There's a warmth but there seems to be real hesitancy."

So, big picture, we heard from mothers-in-law along a continuum with exemplary relationships at one end, to those who have to work a little harder than they might have wished to stay close at another point on the continuum, to those with virtually no relationship at the other end of the continuum. It is to the subtleties of trying to understand these complex and often dynamic relationships that we next go.

Singer and songwriter Joni Mitchell is described in a biography as being critical of pop music. Mitchell disparages pop for always wanting its happy songs to be played in major keys and its sad songs to be played in minor keys, a black and white treatment of music. Mitchell sees life, and music, as more gray than that portrayal and peppers her songwriting approach with suspended and unresolved chords as well as with progressions that combine both happy and sad.[1] Mitchell may also be characterizing the mother-in-law and daughter-in-law relationship. The relationship is not always played in a major key, even when it is happy; hopefully, when the relationship is strained, some suspended or major chords are added to the minor tones.

What follows are 10 questions that we believe are frequently on the minds of mothers-in-law and can guide understanding of their relationship with their daughter-in-law. We use the results from the surveys and our interviews in our responses.

1. ARE MOTHERS-IN-LAW CLOSE TO THEIR DAUGHTER-IN-LAW?

Simply put, the majority of mothers-in-law feel the relationship with their daughter-in-law works. To answer this question more fully, we looked at seven key items that capture the nuances in relationships and created a variable (a scale) to evaluate relationship quality. These included five positive statements ("My daughter-in-law and I have a close relationship," "I admire my daughter-in-law," "I can ask my daughter-in-law for advice," "I trust my daughter-in-law," and "I enjoy spending time with my daughter-in-law") as well as two negative statements ("I avoid my daughter-in-law" and "I have problematic conflicts with my daughter-in-law"). We chose these seven because of the range of circumstances that can exist between two people. A mother-in-law might admire but not be close to her daughter-in-law. A mother-in-law may enjoy spending time with a daughter-in-law but is leery of asking for advice for fear it could be seen by the daughter-in-law as the mother-in-law then being able to offer advice to her.

Approximately 67% to 80% agreed or strongly agreed with each positive statement while approximately 8% to 10% agreed or strongly agreed with the negative statements. Specifically: 33% strongly agreed they were close; 42% strongly agreed they admired their daughter-in-law; 29% strongly agreed they could ask her for advice; 37% strongly agreed they enjoyed spending time with her; 50% strongly agreed they trusted her; 5% strongly agreed they avoided her; and 4% strongly agreed they had a problematic conflict with her. We looked for high levels of agreement with the positive statements and high levels of disagreement with the negative ones to create a variable that allowed us to look at a number of other characteristics that were related to a *close* mother-in-law/daughter-in-law relationship.[2] We use this seven-item variable to answer the questions related to closeness between the mother-in-law and daughter-in-law. We use the term *close* as a shorthand for the aggregation of all seven aspects of the relationships.

The number of relationships where the mothers-in-law felt *close* to their daughter-in-law, but also admired the daughter-in-law; enjoyed spending time with her; could ask her for advice; trusted the daughter-in-law; did not avoid her daughter-in-law; and did not have a problematic conflict all greatly outnumbered relationships in which the two were not close! In addition to these items, three-quarters said the daughter-in-law was warm to them, two-thirds said their daughter-in-law was attentive to them, and over half of the mothers-in-law agreed or strongly agreed they shared similar interests with their daughter-in-law. These first two items, in particular, are an assessment of the daughter-in-law's efforts directed toward the mother-in-law and are important to include in further exploration of the relationship between the two and in understanding the role that the daughter-in-law can play.

While we use a scale of seven items to gauge the quality of the relationship, other responses may shed additional light on this relationship: Almost one in four answered they maintained emotional distance from the daughter-in-law; one in six answered they walked on eggshells around their daughter-in-law; and one in nine responded their daughter-in-law made them feel nervous. If the mother-in-law believes her daughter-in-law has struggled with mental health or substance abuse issues, as one in eight believed, their relationship was not as strong. The son's substance abuse history also was related to less closeness between the mother-in-law and daughter-in-law.

What might a mother-in-law and daughter-in-law relationship look like? We offer some in-depth, up-close, and character-defining examples of ones that are working very well, ones that are struggling, and ones that are satisfactory for the most part, although not particularly close or distant.

When Relationships Are Highly Satisfying

Evelyn

Evelyn is White, 62 years old, and the mother of four children. She is employed as a teacher. Her daughter-in-law, Allie, married her son 12 years ago and is Evelyn's only child in-law as her other three children are unmarried. Both her son and Allie are in their mid-30s. Evelyn feels very close to her own parents, remembers her parents were close with their in-laws (Evelyn's grandparents), and feels close with her husband's parents. We would predict from this intergenerational history that Evelyn would be close with Allie, continuing a trend across four generations. In turn, Allie is described as being close with her parents (as were most of the daughters-in-law in the sample). Such intergenerational warmth on both sides of the family often bodes well for the mother-in-law and daughter-in-law relationship.

Evelyn sees Allie as vital to her relationship with her son

> because she is the closest link to my own child and I need to be just as happy with her as I am with him. We *are* very close. She would call me very often when the children were little, almost daily. We like to get together to do things we enjoy in common, like crocheting [only 11% of our sample "strongly agreed" that they have similar interests as their daughter-in-law, which strongly predicts greater closeness]. We get together to visit the grandchildren although not as often as I would like to. [They live 15 miles apart; 49% of the mothers-in-law lived within 20 miles of their son and daughter-in-law; geographic distance was not related to relationship quality in our sample. This may be because of the ease of electronic communication for those who wish to remain in close contact or because, for some, geographic distance may help both to get along by staying out of each other's space.] We have frequent family meals, too. She was hesitant in the beginning about family meals because she was shy. But she loves to cook with us now.

When Evelyn was asked to describe a difficult event she and Allie experienced, she struggled to come up with a response:

> The only time we had a disagreement was on the issue of spanking. The two of them believe very strongly that it should not be done at all. That's not how I was raised and how I raised my children and I think the disagreement comes

from her side of the family. It didn't end up needing to be resolved. It was on one of her many phone calls when such a child did this, such a child did that and I said, "Well, if it reached that level, I would've spanked him," and she said they weren't doing that so we discussed it for a while and she is just firmly resistant to spanking.

Evelyn answered on the survey that she and her daughter-in-law had different parenting philosophies, as did one-third of the mothers-in-law we surveyed. Despite what could have been considerable differences around parenting approaches, Evelyn's relationship with Allie is not significantly affected.

Evelyn's family is highly inclusive, which, given the family history, would be expected, and it extends to Allie's parents: "We have multiple holiday get-togethers throughout the year and they include her parents. I invite them and they love it." Evelyn attributes her family closeness specifically to the situation she married into:

My husband is an only child and I was very well received by both of my in-laws. We did many similar activities before and after we married. The first Christmas we spent at my folks' house without them and my mother-in-law said she felt left out so in subsequent holidays we always brought my in-laws up to my parents' house.

Evelyn is further enthused about Allie because she thinks her son and Allie make a good team, one of the areas of cooperation we inquired about during the interviews:

They work very well together with maintaining the house and taking care of the children. It's not a categorized thing like "this is your job" and "this is my job." There is no defined "his" or "her" job. They have completely melded. I think we have definitely gotten closer and that may be because of having children. That brings a whole new level of discussion we can have. She was very shy in the be-ginning, not standoffish, but she would stand in the background. We lured her in eventually and she loves being here now.

Evelyn does not believe that Allie has interfered in any way with the close relationship Evelyn has with her son:

I couldn't possibly think of anything bad and nothing but positivity. I have seen over the years how much Allie tends to be similar to me. That saying that you marry your mother or you marry your father is so true. You can't get pushy.

I have always believed in being open and loving. No matter how long it takes, that party is going to warm up to you.

Fiola

Fiola is White, 69 years old, and a retired social worker. She and her husband live 500 miles away from their son and daughter-in-law, Judy, who are in their late 30s and have been married for nine years. Fiola and her husband have one other child, a daughter, who married before their son, Jared, married, so Judy was not the first in-law in the next generation. Fiola's parents divorced but she remained close to both while they were alive. She was close with her father-in-law and feels neither particularly close to nor distant from her mother-in-law. She believes her own mother also was neither close nor distant from her mother-in-law and that her father was close with his father-in-law.

This history is not as neatly lined up as Evelyn's and could potentially indicate that she *might* have a less close relationship with Judy, as she does not have as many strong familial role models for closeness. Yet Fiola, perhaps because of her social work training and because family history is not always predictive, works hard at relationships and at being inclusive. When asked if her experience as a daughter-in-law influenced her as a mother-in-law, she replied, "Not at all. I have not given any thought to how I wanted to be as an in-law. It's not something I ever put in a 'I need to learn about this. I need to understand this' box."

She feels very close with Judy and is keenly aware that Judy, unlike Evelyn's daughter-in-law, Allie, does not have a good relationship with her own mother. Such rifts can cause daughters-in-law to seek in their mother-in-law what they do not get from their mother. Fiola is sensitive to this:

> She's part of our family. It's as important as is my relationship with my kids. I was always comfortable with her and wanted to make sure she was as comfortable with us as possible and, you know, once you're in, you're in! You are part of the fam. I think our relationship has evolved because she has no relationship with her own mother. I'm not her mother. I've always been careful not to push myself on her just because she doesn't have a relationship with her mother but I want her to know that I'll be here for whatever she needs. When she got married, her mother played a very small role in the wedding but I didn't push myself in. I was, like, you guide us. We made it clear we were going to give her whatever kind of a wedding she wanted, so "you decide, this is all about you . . . we're there to do whatever you want." But now it's been a long time and we're pretty

comfortable with one another. I know when she's moody. I know when to give her space and let her be."

Fiola described how the level of acceptance from her and her family toward Judy, who was unaccustomed to such warmth, was difficult for Judy to handle:

Initially, everything was overwhelming for her, coming into our family . . . Jared was with her for maybe a few months, and then we were taking a family trip and he invited her to come, and we were just like, "Of course, great, welcome, and, what do you need? Do you want to go do this or do that?" and she just wasn't used to that, and so I think our generosity of spirit was overwhelming. It's just how we operate; it's no big deal. She's evolved in that now. Here's an example. For Shari's wedding, there was a big lavish celebration, so they needed clothes. So Judy said, "You know what? I went and looked at this dress and I would never think of buying myself a dress like this and then I thought, but Fiola says I should treat and nurture myself once in a while and if this makes me feel good, I've been working hard, then I should do that." She wore it and she said, "I'm so glad I got this because you taught me to value myself. I'm worth it." And so, that's nice.

As for Judy's mother, Fiola said:

Her mom is a really yucky person, was brutal to Judy. The short version is that while Judy was growing up, her father is Muslim, and her mother is Lutheran, and a lot of the family is in Tunisia. At one point, her dad wanted to take her and her brother to see the family and her mother worried that he was going to kidnap them. They ended up getting divorced and Judy's mother made it as though their father never wanted to be in touch with them and destroyed all his letters and changed their name. So she grew up like this. Her mother treated her brutally, verbally abused her, and she had to work through that for a long time. Jared was a steady person to help with that. But the mother, after the wedding, did nothing and then did some things that hurt Judy and they severed the relationship. She's never seen their children. So, it was a little bit tenuous for Judy . . . Could she trust me? Could she count on me? Was I going to be reliable? Was I going to disappoint? But Jared, because of the way Jared is, slowly brought her around. It's just been a very complicated, evolving relationship.

Fiola and Judy communicate a fair amount. Sometimes if Judy is free, she will call Fiola just to chat, leading to Fiola feeling very loved. Fiola feels comfortable confronting Judy on some of her behaviors, too:

Judy can be very moody in the morning. There could have been something that set her off and we don't know what it is. I'll just know to ignore it and stay out of her space. Or there might be things I might disagree about in how she handles the kids in that I might be a little more forceful. She doesn't like to be confronting, and I understand that because of from whence she's come. So we might disagree on that, but I don't get into that. When she gets moody, I might say, 'Did you eat? Did you drink? Because you know you get this way when you don't eat or drink enough.' And she'll say, "Golly, I was really awful, wasn't I?" and I'll say, "Yeah, you've been better. You were not great." So we do that and can laugh about it.

As far as expectations for their relationship, Fiola had few when Jared married:

We love who they married and everyone is incorporated in the family. As long as they're all doing good things and they're happy and productive in whatever they choose to do, we're not critical. There were no "shoulds." I'm not a "should" person. There was never the "Okay, now you should call us mom and dad" or "You should call us this many times a week" or whatever. Whatever it is, it is.

Like many relationships that are working, theirs has evolved over time:

She knows us really well now. We go away together as families a lot. She knows my stuff and I know her stuff. As I see compared to people who live in the same cities as their kids, we don't talk every day, sometimes she comes to the phone, sometimes not. It's all okay. As long as I allow them to live their lives however they choose, we have to continue to be welcoming and loving and let them guide the relationship. We don't feel or need to have any control.

Evelyn and Fiola represent just two of the highly positive relationships that mothers-in-law report. Many relationships are straightforward with the mother-in-law loving and accepting the daughter-in-law and feeling loved and accepted in return.

Culture

We wish to add here the cultural imperatives that some religions and cultures place on close family relationships. In some East Asian cultures, for example, when you marry into the family you are part of the family; the boundaries are more inclusive than in Western families. You are automatically accepted and there is no question about closeness or distance; you are like another daughter. Even being asked about the level of closeness can seem strange as the child-in-law is now family.

This next mother-in-law, Hania, living in the United States and born in Pakistan, provides such an example. When we asked Hania how important her relationship was with her daughter-in-law, Nayeli, she replied:

> Oh my gosh. The relationship is of the utmost importance. I am getting goose-bumps just thinking about her. We're just a second set of parents. Allah says it, too. I just think, how can you not love this child that your child loves? It's inconceivable to me. Nayeli and I have a very close relationship and it's so important to me. She just won our hearts. She didn't lean on her husband to build a relationship with us. She built the relationship one on one. She calls us "Amma and Abba" [Mom and Dad] and it irks me when daughters-in-law call their mother-in-law "Auntie." Your mother-in-law should be your second mother! When my son and Nayeli are visiting us, she tiptoes to our room and knocks on our door at night, and sits on our bed to make some small talk about work and whatnot. I love that. We're at the level of mother–daughter relationship. Her mother raised all of her kids so well. They're just such pure people.

The way the two met shines light on the role parents may play in arranging marriages:

> We were at an Islamic Society of North American Convention before we had gone to propose to her family and we saw her as soon as we walked in. She was walking out of the matrimonial convention with a booklet in her hand and I just snatched it from her and told her she wouldn't need that anymore. I really don't know why I did that [laughs], but I don't think Nayeli minded. We laughed about it later.

In the above examples of close relationships, there is little role ambiguity. To appreciate how lucky many mothers-in-law feel about their situation—and they often reference friends who are less fortunate than they are—we turn to those who are struggling.

When Relationships Are a Struggle

Geneva

Geneva is a 65-year-old divorced African American woman who recently retired from her job as a technician. Both her son and her daughter-in-law, Holly, had children from previous relationships that they brought into the marriage and have since had twins. Geneva has one other son who is not married. Quoted earlier, she is an example of a mother-in-law who is fed up with her daughter-in-law yet has to tolerate her to keep the lines of communication open to her son. As will be seen, Geneva's early upbringing would not have been predictive of the relationship that has developed, whereas Holly's might have been. Like a small number of the mothers-in-law in our sample, Geneva did not approve of the marriage:

> The relationship with Holly is not important at all because of her attitude. She has no respect of my love for my son. From the beginning, she took issue with the closeness between him and me. When he was in trouble with his house payments, and that's before he even married her, he came to me for help and then she has the nerve to get mad at me and tell me about helping my child. What woman wouldn't want me to help my child? If you have my child's best interests at hand, you would be glad I had the money to help him. Especially when you had to get pregnant so you could move in there so she has issues with our relationship. But that doesn't matter because nothing is going to change that. There's no relationship other than she is married to my son. I try to be cordial. Going back to my background and my family growing up, we were a close family. It was one big happy family. We have no relationship really. It's just that she's my son's wife. She's not a daughter to me at all.

When asked to describe a difficult event with Holly, Geneva remembered a birthday party she threw for her son:

> I'm paying for the party because his children wanted to give him a party. It wasn't my idea, and she confronts me that I should have told her about it. I did. I invited her and gave 10 or 15 invites for her side of the family. Her opinion was that how could I plan a birthday party for my son without telling her. His children wanted the party. It's always like that. She has an issue with our closeness. She does everything she can to keep us separate.

Geneva is aware that Holly's upbringing was difficult:

> She had a really traumatic childhood. In her household when her mother and father were together, he was violent. I think it's just a lot of things from her childhood that cause that, but she has an issue with my closeness with my son and if you go deep into it, she will keep her children as far apart from our family as she can. Only when she absolutely needs us to watch them, they're here. That has been an issue.

When pressed for a positive interaction with Holly, Geneva described how supportive she felt about helping Holly with their wedding plans and how Holly thanked her at the wedding for all Geneva had done. But then, when it came time for the traditional mother–son and father–daughter dance, because Holly's father was dead, Holly told the DJ to play fast music and everyone got up to dance. Geneva felt cheated out of the moment.

Whereas Evelyn saw good teamwork between her son and daughter-in-law, Geneva sees none:

> She is not any help to my son. None. He does everything. All she's done is move in the house and tore it up. The same furniture that we put in the house when he bought it is still there. She has brought nothing to the table but two babies. That's it.

While many mothers-in-law commented on how their relationship with their daughter-in-law has improved, Geneva sees no movement:

> Nothing has changed. I don't think it ever will because I think she realizes I know something. It's one thing when you are young and you get pregnant, but when you have a 15-year-old daughter and you're 30-plus and you're telling me your pills didn't work and you end up with twins, too? She did that and she knows that I know that. My son was by himself with his two older children when he bought that house so, of course, as his mother I'm going to make sure the house has curtains and different things. Nothing's changed! A woman her age moves in the house and she has nothing to bring? It's sad. The conversations I have with her are very superficial. I don't get deep with you if I don't trust you.

Alice

For another example of a difficult relationship between mother-in-law and daughter-in-law, we return to Alice, the 67-year-old White real estate agent whose quote begins the book. From her we hear great annoyance about the behavior of her daughter-in-law, Inez, because she is not available to Alice as much as Alice would like and because of some of her past behavior:

> While our relationship was important to me, it was shocking that Inez wasn't interested and that she didn't feel the same way. For a long time, I thought I must be doing something wrong and then I realized, nope, she just isn't interested . . . The beauty with me is now that I have my other daughter-in-law in my life I know that it can be what I hoped it to be.

Alice was close with her mother, was not particularly close with her father, and was not close with her own in-laws. Inez was the first child-in-law to join the family nine years ago; her other son was recently married. There are no children from their marriage. The relationship between Alice and Inez has never been strong and they live 2,500 miles from each other with little time together to work to improve it.

When asked for an example of a difficult situation, Alice recalled a dispute involving seating arrangements in a car on the way to a wedding when Alice's mother needed to be catered to:

Inez came in for my niece's wedding. My 93-year-old mother was there as well. We were getting in the car and I asked Inez if she would get in the middle and assumed she would agree. She said, "Ugh, no. I'm not sitting in the middle. No way!" and I thought, "Should I put my mother or me there?" Inez said it was because she gets carsick. I thought that was interesting because: A. I get carsick, I know what carsick is and B. I know enough to know that when you get carsick the best place for you is in the middle. The assumption that it doesn't matter if grandma is 93 and I'm 66 and no respect is involved and just "I'm not gonna do it." And then at the wedding we had to park and she ran out of the car and ran ahead and told my sister that she didn't want to sit at our table. She was so mad at me for asking her to sit in the middle. So the rest of the day she didn't talk to us.

Alice adds further context to the relationship:

Inez never answered an email, never talked to me on the phone, would never relate to me when she came in. She would come into town and sleep until 3 o'clock. She would never want to be with me if I offered to take her somewhere, do something for her, buy her something. No, no, no. I just couldn't get through and I didn't know what to do. Disappointing to me but she is not mean to me and I'm not mean to her. She does not keep my son from us and they have a strong marriage. I know people who have issues with daughters-in-law keeping their sons away. She does not do that at all. Our son has maintained a good relationship with us and he comes in from Arizona by himself more often than with her. So the relationship is just distant, literally, physically, and symbolically.

A couple's relationship with their in-laws is not always parallel. Alice's son is close with his in-laws: "Inez's parents are lovely and try hard and my son is used to having close extended family relationships and he gets along well with them. I want that and I'm happy for him."

Having established that Alice has a wonderful relationship with her other daughter-in-law, we asked what factors contributed to that relationship being so successful, while the relationship with Inez is so difficult:

> She wanted it as much as I wanted it. Inez didn't. I wanted a close relationship with my own mother-in-law, but she had five children and just wasn't that interested in having a relationship with me and I had to learn that. But I thought, when I have a daughter-in-law, I can show her that I want a good relationship! It doesn't matter whether you are a daughter-in-law or a mother-in-law, you have to *want* to have a relationship. My mother-in-law didn't want it, Inez doesn't want it, and now my newest daughter-in-law does and it's great because I actually believe I'm a good mother-in-law. I see other mothers-in-law that are intrusive and tell their children what to do and give unwanted advice . . . I'm not interested in doing that. I just want to love my sons' partners and have them be a part of a loving family.

Alice bounces back and forth between feeling included by one daughter-in-law and excluded by the other. Yet she appreciates the relationship that Inez, who is excluding her, has with her son. Here, we see ambivalence in what is a highly unsatisfactory relationship, whereas for Geneva there is no ambivalence—the feelings are all negative.

When Relationships Are a Mixed Bag or Are Neutral

Finally, many in-law relationships just *are*! Both mother-in-law and daughter-in-law get along, they accept each other, are not particularly close or distant, and have found a way to make the relationship work for the greater good of themselves and other family members, most notably the son/husband. Such relationships are not usually complicated. The women respect each other but are not each other's best friends. The mother-in-law may have other children and children-in-law and is closer to some than to others. She may feel that she has a strong relationship with her son and an adequate one with her daughter-in-law, which keeps her son happy enough. It is often the happiness she sees in her son that makes the relationship with the daughter-in-law work.

Doris

Having only one child might drive the mother-in-law to work harder on the relationship with the daughter-in-law. Doris, a 61-year-old, White, married business administrator, when asked about the importance of her relationship with her daughter-in-law, Kate, described the process that she and Kate are going through:

> With having only one child, that's our family. We refer to them as our kids, and that's our family. It's very important that we all get along. When you have a son and he gets married, he becomes part of another family. A woman in the relationship tends to make the major decisions. I had to kind of find my way in their relationship. We have to find a common ground. She feels comfortable around me and has to feel I'm not going to be critical.

To secure the relationship with Kate and thus maintain it with her son, Doris wanted to send a message about their respective roles:

> It was important to me to make it clear I'm not her mom. She has a mom with whom she is close. I think it became easier for Kate and Herb to define their relationship once they had kids. When they were first married, they were defining their own relationship. Because Kate's family doesn't live in this state, Kate had to find a way to make it work here [Doris lives 20 miles from Kate and Herb]. She is a very, very strong force. But I am, too, and I describe her as me, but on steroids.

Doris and Kate maintain distance from each other. Doris said their relationship was

> one of mutual respect. I think that she still doesn't understand that when we do things for them it's because we want to. Like when we pick the kids up from daycare, she's like, "Oh, thank you so much." It's not that big of a deal. That's what we're here for, we're the grandparents. It's getting more comfortable as time goes on. She still doesn't know how to accept kindness. I remember the first Hanukah together. We've always gotten our son eight gifts, so she got eight gifts. She was completely overwhelmed. Her family doesn't do gifts for birthdays or anything and what my son and Kate have decided to do is to emulate a lot of the traditions from her family. That's their choice. I don't call her a lot, I text her. I text my son, and I'll say "call me." Kate will call me if the kids want to do some type of crafts; she defers to me for all of that. As long as they have traditions and recognize their Jewish heritage, I'm happy.

Doris also discusses the impact of the daughter-in-law's mother on relations between the families:

> One of the issues, and I've come to terms with it, is her mother comes to visit for long stretches at a time. When she comes, they don't make any effort for us

all to get together. That's her mother's time with her and the kids, and we don't co-mingle. In my mind, let's all get together and be a family. That is not their choice. They say she gets so little time with the kids, but, when you add it up, she's there for 24 hours a day for 15 days. It's just coming to terms with that. I've talked about that with Herb. I'm not completely at peace with it.

Neither particularly close nor especially distant, Doris is doing what she can to maintain the status quo. Part of maintaining it is to not deal directly with Kate when issues arise:

I just talk to Herb. I don't feel that I can talk to her about conflict. Hopefully, it will change in the future. We, also, haven't ever spent long periods of time together. We're not the type to get lunch together. We don't do things together. Frequently, when I think, "Gee, I wish we did this," I step back and think, "Well, I didn't do that with my mother-in-law, so it's okay that we don't do things together." Plus, we both work full-time.

The opportunity for one-on-one time between the two women is constrained by their work lives, but Doris also realizes she has had no role model in her own history as to how the relationship could work. This, for her, makes success more challenging.

Lois

Sometimes there is a lack of personality fit. Lois, White and 55 years old, describes how she has to accommodate to her daughter-in-law of seven years—she admires her in many ways but has a hard time connecting with her:

My relationship in broad terms is very good but it is not near as easy as a relationship as some. Personality-wise, not as warm, not as inviting. I am often not sure where I stand, or what she thinks. I am drawn to people who are warm. I am off the charts with relationships and intimacy and she is more power driven, more detail driven, more work driven, and not as warm, but gifted and an amazing mom and those kind of things. I am a hugger and she can be much more stand-offish. Do I hug anyway or do I back off from who I am? If I walk into her house and she is talking or whatever, she won't stop. She will just keep doing what she's doing where I would stop and welcome somebody and so sometimes I am left thinking that is just rude. We just operate differently.

Personality differences may not always be quite as stark as in Lois's example but can still make accommodation necessary, as this next mother-in-law explains:

> It's always very pleasant but it's always on her terms every time we get together. When we are together, you know, I like her, I think she's a good person, she's a great mother, and I think she's a good wife but she's kind of picky with my son and too kind of rigid. It's not like anybody's fighting or saying anything, you know. We're not that type of people.

This final example of personality differences between mother-in-law and daughter-in-law was corroborated for the mother-in-law by her son (the daughter-in-law's husband):

> When I come to stay, my daughter-in-law's not a person you're going to sit and chat with for a long time. She's more "give me the short answer" to things, so when I'm with her, I let her lead with that and I'm careful. She might talk about some problems at work and unpack as much as she wants but I can tell she wants the short version from me. That's fine. At first, I took it personally. I thought, "Oh, she's not interested in what I have to say," and it wasn't that at all. Len [her son] said to me once, "I can't go into detail with her; she's like, 'Please get to the point'." So, I adjust.

Consistent with others' research, the majority of the mothers-in-law felt some level of closeness with their daughter-in-law. Some feel extremely close and some quite distant, with a large group in the middle who have figured out a way to make the relationship work in a satisfactory manner to maintain contact with their son and grandchildren.

2. I DID NOT KNOW MY DAUGHTER-IN-LAW WELL BEFORE THE WEDDING. WILL THAT MATTER?

About 40% of mothers-in-law agreed or strongly agreed that they did not know their daughter-in-law well before the marriage. Not knowing her well was related to less closeness.

Of course, not knowing someone well before marrying into the family can carry a variety of meanings. A mother-in-law may not have met a daughter-in-law because of geographic distance or because the marriage followed a short engagement. A mother-in-law may have met the daughter-in-law but feels she was difficult to get to know because she was quiet and shy, or emotionally withdrawn. This was the case with Yvonne, a mother-in-law, and Eleanor, her daughter-in-law:

> We first met Eleanor in a restaurant. My son didn't want to bring her to the house because our house is three times the size of the house she grew up in and it would have overwhelmed her. So we went to the restaurant and met her there, which I thought was kind of strange. They held hands under the table. She was very insecure and ordered the exact same thing that he ordered. There were so many signs that she was very insecure about meeting us and it didn't really get a whole lot better than that.

For some mothers-in-law it could also be that the mother-in-law thought she knew the daughter-in-law well only to find her to be very different after she married into the family. This is illustrated when mothers-in-law say things like, "She showed her true colors after they got married."

If they did not feel they knew her well, they were also less likely to approve of the marriage, as was the situation with 10% of the mothers-in-law. Not approving of the marriage was a significant predictor of later emotional distance between the two.

Stella was not on board with her son's choice of a wife, did not know her well, and now feels left out of their lives, replaced by her family:

> She's a very nice girl. She comes from a good, Christian family. She was homeschooled so . . . my relationship with her? I get along with her. She isn't what my first choice for my son would be, just because she doesn't have the drive and the outgoingness like he does. Before she got married, she really staked her claim on my son. I didn't like that. I feel like she could potentially hold him back because everything revolves around her. He loves her with all his heart. That's why I would never be ugly to her but he puts her on a pedestal and he'd rather not have the conflict with her so he just does whatever she needs. She stays home. She was in college when they got married and then she quit. They get along and have fun, but if it's not all about her, she all of a sudden has migraines.

Stella's son and daughter-in-law just returned to the United States after spending one year overseas:

> Now that they are back in the States I thought they would be more involved with us but she pulls him away for her family more and throws tantrums and fits and whines so that they're with her family all the time . . . even holidays. She wants to be with her family and he doesn't want any conflict.

While these last examples focus on relationships that are a struggle, many mothers-in-law we interviewed had no problem becoming close to their daughter-in-law once she entered the family even if they were different in significant ways and felt they did not know her well at the time of the marriage.

3. HOW MIGHT MY FAMILY BACKGROUND AFFECT MY RELATIONSHIP WITH MY DAUGHTER-IN-LAW?

Here we look at how the family history of relationships may play out in the mother-in-law and daughter-in-law relationship. We do so with caution as it is difficult to definitively connect one or a series of events in one's past to one's relationships in the present. Yet closeness can be learned; families show relationship patterns that continue across generations; nurturing in families can be handed down to future generations as part of a family legacy.

While we stand on the shoulders of those who came before us, if there are unhealthy experiences, like an estrangement from a parent or a significant battle with an in-law, positive events and intentional effort can intervene to reduce the effect of those experiences. In fact, people often work hard to correct in their present relationships the unhappy residue of their past relationships. Parents may try to provide emotionally for their child what they feel they missed from their own parent. In thinking about what a mother-in-law's history might mean for her relationship with her daughter-in-law (and remembering to factor in her husband/partner's behavior and her son's), we would add into the mix the daughter-in-law's history, which can play a key part, too, in how close the mother-in-law feels to her.

With these caveats, we wondered what a mother-in-law might have learned growing up from her own parents' relationship with their in-laws (the mother-in-law's grandparents). About half of the mothers-in-law believed their father and mother had a good relationship with both of their in-law sets. Observing a good relationship between generations would naturally provide a blueprint for how future generations can work out their relationship in a positive way. But if the mother-in-law's parents divorced, the parents were naturally viewed as not having a good relationship with their in-laws, the mother-in-law's grandparents. So not only might mothers-in-law whose parents divorced be less close with their parents, they may also have observed worse relationships between their parents and their grandparents.

About one-fifth of the mothers-in-law reported that their parents had divorced. A little more than one-fourth of the mothers-in-law were divorced or separated from the father of their son. The mothers-in-law reported about a third of their daughter-in-law's parents had divorced. Because we know so little about the nature of the divorce (whether it was agreeable or acrimonious) or when it occurred (in the mother-in-law's childhood or in her adulthood), we cannot safely draw conclusions about the impact of divorce on her family relationships. Others' research suggests that divorce causes distance between parents and adult children, especially fathers.[3] We do know from our interviews that if divorce does happen between the son and daughter-in-law, the relationship between the mother-in-law and now ex-daughter-in-law can continue for the welfare of the grandchildren, as this mother-in-law, Swoozie, told us:

> My younger son is getting divorced, so that really affected my relationship with that daughter-in-law because there is a lot of animosity going on. It's been really hard. I miss her and I think that she probably misses me, but it is just too hard for her to have a relationship with me. I saw her the other night when I brought my granddaughter to her house and she opened the door and put her arms out and said "happy birthday" to me. It made me hopeful that we're going to be able to see each other a little bit more and it won't be so hard to drop her daughter off because that was something that I was always worried about. I don't know how close of a relationship that we can have, but I'm hopeful.

People not only learn about closeness from their own family of origin, they also learn from their parents-in-law and can use that experience with their daughter-in-law, as in Dana's example:

> I remember my mother-in-law, who I really love, took me to the movies. My husband was out with his dad, at the time we were just boyfriend and girlfriend, and she called me and asked to go. I had to say yes, but I was uncomfortable because I didn't really know her that well. Now I feel like that was a turning point for me, so I did the same thing with my daughter-in-law. I called her and asked her to go to the movies, and then we went to dinner. It was really great. We got to know each other away from my son and husband and really began a nice relationship.

Finally, people also learn how to correct emotionally distancing. As one mother-in-law told us, "I was never close with my mother-in-law so I fought like tooth and nail to become close with my daughter-in-law and son-in-law. I wanted them to have something different and I wanted that too."

Growing up with intergenerational family closeness that feels comfortable can generate positive attitudes toward family, as we heard from many of those we interviewed. While divorce in the family-of-origin and strain with a parent-in-law may be related to emotional distancing in some families, many mothers-in-law took corrective steps to not repeat a cycle of distancing with their daughter-in-law.

4. MY SON IS MARRYING SOMEONE FROM A DIFFERENT RACE/ETHNICITY/RELIGION FROM HIM. MY SON IS MARRYING SOMEONE FROM A DIFFERENT ECONOMIC BACKGROUND. WHAT CAN I EXPECT?

Historically, marrying outside of one's race, ethnicity, or religion has been correlated with higher rates of marital difficulties, which can cause more struggles between parents-in-law and children-in-law. However, intermarriage has changed dramatically in the last 50 years as discussed in Chapter 1. Slightly more than one in 10 of the mothers-in-law reported on the survey that their son married someone of a different race or ethnicity. In our sample, interracial/interethnic marriage had no bearing on— was not statistically predictive of—the quality of those mothers-in-law's relationships with their daughters-in-laws.[4]

One 56-year-old White mother-in-law, Bonita, saw a great fit with her daughter-in-law:

> She's Native American with Spanish influences. I'm a sixth-generation Floridian and she's a sixth-generation New Mexican, back to when New Mexico was just a territory. Her great-great-great-grandfather built the first mission church in Albuquerque. She's Catholic and, while she's not practicing, I think she still has Catholic values which mesh well with my son because he still has some Mormon values, even though neither of them practice or believe in those religions. They are very complementary. Also, I have a lot of knowledge and sympathy about the Catholic faith. There are a lot of things I like about it, like the strong feminist aspect of some of the Catholic Church and charities. I've been with my daughter-in-law to a lot of the mission churches out there. So it's been something that's drawn us together more than separated us.

Even though the combination of differences in race, ethnicity, and religion meshed for her, a son's marrying someone from another religion was another story within our sample, where 17% reported an interfaith marriage. Nationally, since 2010, four in 10 marriages were between people of different religious groups.[5] Still, within our sample, interfaith marriage was related to a less strong relationship between mother-in-law and daughter-in-law. Marrying someone from a different religion could mean that any children who are born are raised outside of the faith or with less religiosity than the children's grandparents might want. For those very connected to their faith, this can be a concern. Sometimes, it is the level of religiosity that can cause a problem even within the same faith, as we learned from our interviews.

For example, Ellie described how her daughter-in-law became less enamored with religion and that caused distance between them:

> My son and his wife are struggling with their relationship with Christ and my daughter-in-law is struggling even more so. So even though we are able to have open conversations about anything and everything, talking about a relationship with Christ for her is a little bitter. I believe something happened some years ago, and she attributes that to Christians as people, as opposed to the people it happened with. So, that is where the struggle is that we have.

We also wondered what impact differences in economic class growing up would have. Marrying someone from a different economic class, as 23% of the mothers-in-law said their son did (split evenly between families where the son was more affluent growing up and families where the daughter-in-law was more affluent growing up), did portend a less close relationship. Class differences may mean that values around money are related to levels of comfort that the in-law families have with each other. Stella, who we introduced you to and did not know her daughter-in-law well before the marriage, is almost apologetic about the economic differences between her daughter-in-law's family and her own: "They keep on pinching . . . not a nice home. Nice people, don't get me wrong, but just economically very different from the way my son grew up."

Economic differences could result in, for example, discomfort around how much is spent on the wedding and who pays for it, the gifts that are given over the years, and the vacations that grandchildren are taken on. Differences could also lead to competition between both sets of grandparents and to how the mother-in-law views how the daughter-in-law is spending money.

Yvonne felt that her daughter-in-law, Eleanor, who came from humble roots, became comfortable too quickly with her son's greater affluence:

> She's become a tad entitled because she's fallen into a world that is much bigger than the world she was in before she met and married my son. We took her

on lots of wonderful vacations with us before they got married. And we raised our children very specifically not to feel entitled to anything. We didn't move to where the headquarters of the company were where the children of the other executives are all the worst spoiled brats who do not contribute to society in any way, shape, or form, so totally entitled. Our kids never read about what their dad earned or what privileges we had. They knew things were good because we had great vacations. They knew that they were loved. We just didn't give everything they wanted and we have two children who are very dedicated to giving back to God's world and we are very proud of them. But Eleanor seemed to catch the entitlement bug from what she's been given.

Differences between people can be seen as a strength for a marriage as new daughters-in-law bring new customs and cultures into a family, as Bonita reported. They can also, when it comes to religious and economic differences, be related to emotional distancing, as we heard from Ellie and Yvonne.

5. I AM EXCITED ABOUT BEING A GRANDMOTHER. WHAT CAN I EXPECT WILL HAPPEN WITH MY RELATIONSHIP WITH MY DAUGHTER-IN-LAW AFTER SHE GIVES BIRTH?

Many mothers-in-law with sons worry that after becoming a grandmother their access to their grandchild will run through their daughter-in-law and, if they are not careful in how they treat her, that access will be impeded. The research literature is equivocal about whether having a grandchild brings the mother-in-law and daughter-in-law closer or pushes them apart. As discussed in Chapter 2, having grandchildren does provide more reasons for contact, especially around childcare, which often brings the mother-in-law closer by dint of the contact. In other instances, the daughter-in-law giving birth pulls her closer to her own mother and subsequently makes some mothers-in-law feel excluded.

We asked, "Did you experience a change for the better, for the worse, or no change in your relationship with your daughter-in-law after she and your son had their first child?" An equal percentage (41%) believed the relationship with the daughter-in-law improved with the birth of the child as answered they felt little or no change in the relationship (41%) with the birth of the first child. The rest said that it was a mixed bag, getting better in some ways and worse in other ways (14%), or that things changed for the worse after the birth (4%).[6] About one-third of the mothers-in-law and/or their spouse reported they were providing childcare; about half of those providing childcare described it as a significant amount of childcare. Almost half of those providing childcare said the relationship had gotten better, over one-third said there had been no change, one in seven said it had gotten better in some ways and worse in some ways, and one in 20 said the relationship with the daughter-in-law had gotten worse.

Thus the birth, coupled with the provision of childcare, will usually be related to the mother-in-law feeling closer to the daughter-in-law or will not have a negative impact on the relationship. Of course, like much in these complicated relationships, other considerations are in play for both women that might affect their relationship:

a. Is this the mother-in-law's first grandchild?
b. Does the mother-in-law have other children who might produce grandchildren?
c. How close do they live to each other?
d. What role is the daughter-in-law's mother playing?
e. How often does the mother-in-law feel consulted or included?
f. What is the mother-in-law's son's role in providing access?
g. What is the role of the mother-in-law's husband or partner in childcare and in the relationship?
h. Does the mother-in-law feel "used" as a babysitter—for example, is she called at the last minute as a backup and is not fully integrated into the grandchild's life, as one mother-in-law felt?
i. Have the daughter-in-law and son been struggling for years to get pregnant and have finally succeeded, adding further joy to the experience for all family members, or is the pregnancy unplanned or unwanted?
j. To what extent do they agree or disagree in terms of parenting philosophies and practices?

Mothers-in-law we interviewed often feel that they do not have the same access to the grandchildren that the other in-laws have. They speak of having to maintain a delicate balance with their daughter-in-law, who often will seek advice from her own mother before going to her mother-in-law. They comment that their own daughters consult with them more about childcare than do their sons, who have turned over much of the childrearing to their wives. In a society where traditionally the father does not play as key a role in early childrearing, some fathers do not provide the same access to the grandchild that the mother can, and this places some mothers-in-law in what they feel is a tenuous position.

Sometimes both grandmothers are excluded, as was the case with Eleanor:

When Emmy was born, I had every new grandmother's dream of being needed to help take care of the baby. I was actually told by Eleanor, "I don't need your help." She actually said those words! She did not want us at the hospital when she was born; it was supposed to just be her and my son there. Her mother was told no one sees a new baby until they're four weeks old and her mother didn't go either. What was happening was that she didn't want anybody finding fault with anything she did. She didn't want anybody seeing her uncomfortableness or not knowing what to do next.

We wish to note that *not* having grandchildren can also cause distance to grow, as was the case with this mother-in-law, who saw the relationship between her and daughter-in-law essentially end:

I don't know what happened, but my daughter-in-law and my son have severed contact with me and my husband and my whole family. She's a lovely young woman. She's been with my son for over 20 years. I've always thought that we were very close, but I just don't know what happened. It's been very sad. It could have been that she had three miscarriages in a row, and that she is now unable to conceive. That was a very big loss for her. Maybe that's made it very difficult for them to have a relationship with us. Here's my daughter who has three children and is pregnant with a fourth and, of course, we're very excited about that, so maybe it's just hard for her to be around us.

This example could also present another dynamic that should be considered when an in-law or other family relationship suddenly changes for the worse. Maybe the emotional distancing had nothing to do with the mother-in-law and daughter-in-law relationship, though the mother-in-law may be looking at it through that lens. Perhaps this daughter-in-law was depressed after her third miscarriage and withdrew socially from other relationships, too.

A positive note was found that could help build the mother-in-law and daughter-in-law relationship: Over four-fifths of the mothers-in-law agreed or strongly agreed that their daughter-in-law is or would be a good mother.

6. I SOMETIMES FEEL LEFT OUT BY MY SON AND DAUGHTER-IN-LAW. MY DAUGHTER-IN-LAW SEEMS TO INTERFERE WITH MY RELATIONSHIP WITH MY SON. HOW COMMON ARE THOSE FEELINGS?

These are difficult feelings to have and can occur as a result of a variety of situations. Exclusion by a son and daughter-in-law can be a conscious decision on their part. The couple may be trying to distance themselves from family members in general or from specific family members. They also may be attempting to build a life of their own, feeling they need more time together, rather than actively trying to push people away. They may feel pulled in each direction from each set of in-laws and are avoiding that stress or conflict. Sometimes parents do interfere—according to their children and children-in-law—despite their honest and best efforts to not interfere. Events, parties, holidays, and vacations arise and branches of the family are not invited, either purposely or as an oversight. Sometimes exclusion is not intended to send a message but is the result of an oversight, misunderstanding, or miscommunication.

About one in four of the mothers agreed or strongly agreed with the statement "Sometimes I feel left out by my son and daughter-in-law." Almost one in five felt their relationship with their son was hindered by their daughter-in-law. As expected, there is a strong relationship between feeling left out and feeling the daughter-in-law hinders the relationship (a little more than half the time when a mother-in-law felt left out or hindered, she endorsed both). And, if the mother-in-law feels left out and/or feels the daughter-in-law hinders her relationship with her son, she feels less close to the daughter-in-law. We will return to the important role that the son can play in this relationship with our answer to Question #9.

The sense of being included or excluded can start even before the marriage, as this mother-in-law with a close relationship with her daughter-in-law told us:

> The wedding planning, she was sweet. When she got her dress she asked if I would come to the dress shop to see it. I came back again for one of her fittings. She kept me included, and you don't have to do that all the time for the mother of the groom. She took us all to the venue. She would show me her invitations. She was sweet in that way.

Inclusion, which breeds closeness, can extend to the birth of a grandchild, as it did for this mother-in-law: "She involved me in every way, even during labor! (Laughs). I was the one who walked out. I couldn't take it. She was very generous and her mom was very generous about that and I was included every step of the way."

In most cultures, mothers naturally, though not always seamlessly, cede the role of caretaker to their son's spouse or partner, as in this next example, where it slowly dawns on Johanna that what has unfolded is the normal course of events and it was not that she was being excluded, she had been replaced:

I have to tell you the funniest . . . well, it wasn't so funny at the time. After my son had the first surgery, we were all in the hospital with him. And he wanted something and my daughter-in-law and I both got up to get it. And she got there first and he didn't say to her, "No! My mother needs to do this." So I thought, Mm-hmmm, I see I am now no longer the most important woman in his life. And I had about 15 minutes of being really angry and jealous and upset. Then I thought, well, this is how you raised him. This is what this is for so that they build their relationship. I'm the mother in-law now. So I have my own position, which isn't the same position, so I was sort of trying to . . . OK, we're all adults and I have to figure out how to interact with an adult child because, you know, when you have a son and he's dating and the girl's all over him and they're kissing—ick, get away! But they were never like that. They were always very respectful. So it was just sort of getting the relationship from accepting the fact that I was being moved out of the way to now that's OK. I didn't lose my relationship with my son because there's another woman. I have a different relationship. But that was hard.

Feeling excluded can occur in relation to having grandchildren (see Question #5). Gertrude felt included until her daughter-in-law became pregnant:

In the beginning of the relationship, it was good with both here in college and they had plans to get married. We got along well. We traveled together, shopped together, and ate dinner together several times a week. Our problem started with the baby shower. She wouldn't let me help. It was just her friends and her mother who helped. It made me feel as if I wasn't a part of my grandchild's life and I wasn't part of the family. It was my son's child, so I should have been a part of every moment of my grandchild's life.

When asked what her son's position was in this, Gertrude gave an answer that also indicated how the daughter-in-law could be seen as interfering in the mother–son bond: "I spoke to my son about the relationship and he says that I am overreacting. He feels that I meddle in his relationship. He refused to speak with her on my behalf. Like I said before, it was good until she got pregnant; then it was over."

7. HOW MIGHT MY DAUGHTER-IN-LAW'S PARENTS AFFECT MY RELATIONSHIP WITH MY DAUGHTER-IN-LAW?

Parents want their child to marry into a wonderful family and have in-laws who are kind, loving, and supportive; will serve as good role models for future grandchildren; and have good values. In reality, what the parents get can be anything from that ideal situation to a very distant, troubled, or interfering set of in-laws for their child as well as for themselves. Some mothers-in-law feel that they and their spouse are competing with the other parents-in-law in terms of gift giving, spending time together, or nurturing grandchildren. The competition can come from the mother-in-law or the mother-in-law may feel the other in-laws are generating the competition, either of which can set all the relationships in a problematic direction and involve their children and grandchildren.

Few of these relationships are cut and dried. Feelings of ambivalence may arise. On the one hand, a mother-in-law may be happy her grandchild has another loving grandparent to go to with a bruised knee; on the other hand, the mother-in-law may resent that she is not the one who is giving the knee a kiss. Each set of in-laws has to figure out how to arrange their relationship with their adult, now-married children, with their children-in-law, and with the other set of in-laws and, of course, the grandchildren. If both sets of in-laws live in the same city, are they included in each other's events? If one set of in-laws is divorced, are both exes included with their new spouses or partners? If one set lives in town and one out of town, do they see each other when the out-of-towners visit the children and grandchildren, or would the out-of-towners, pressed for time, not want in-town in-laws included in their more limited time? What if one set is more affluent and is better able to give more time and money to the children and grandchildren? Having two sets of in-laws is a balancing act not only for the married children who may feel caught between the two (as we discuss in Chapters 4 and 6), but for both sets of parents-in-law as well.

If the mother of the daughter-in-law is more available, that can cause a mother-in-law, who may already feel she is walking on eggshells, to feel even more excluded around the grandchildren, as in this observation from a mother-in-law:

> Women kind of gravitate towards their mothers when there is a problem and the men just kind of go along with it, which was news to me. I had no idea. At first, that was tough because I was working and her mother didn't work, so her mother took care of the grandchildren, so that gave her more of an "in" with my son and his wife and also with the grandchildren. It was hard for me because

I was working five days a week. She got more time with the kids and they knew her better.[7]

During interviews we asked about the relationship between the two sets of in-laws. Many had known the other in-laws for years as their children came from the same community; a few had known the other in-laws longer than their married children knew each other. Some met them once or twice before the wedding and a few did not meet the other in-laws until the wedding and have had little contact with them since. The majority described the other in-laws in generally favorable terms, consistent with how their relationship with their daughter-in-law was described, with only a very few saying their relationship with them was poor. When the relationship is positive, it is often an inclusive one, as in this example: "I like her parents very much. They are really nice people. We see each other at holidays and sporting events and presently we still occasionally cross paths when the kids are playing soccer or whatever. Good people."

Some mothers-in-law expected the relationship to not be close and are thrilled when it is, as in the case with Francis: "Funny you should ask. It is great. I was just with her parents today. We met up for breakfast. I am lucky our relationship isn't shitty. Oh my gosh, I have known her (the mother) since she was 16 and we have done great. I would do anything in the world for her."

And, of course, the mother-in-law can like one parent and not the other, as in this next example: "I really like her mother. Her dad irritates the crap out of me. He's obnoxious and he doesn't work and his life choices have brought him to a place where he is dependent on lots of people. So I just try to avoid him as much as possible."

This next mother-in-law dislikes both parents. She accused them of not having a car seat for a grandchild, of not giving enough money to the adult children, and of lying about how much they had to spend on schooling for their daughter. "I avoid her mother at all costs. If they are at Guinevere's house, I'm polite. I don't bring up anything that is a disagreement. I just don't invite them over to my house."

Differences in culture can be a barrier for some couples, as for this mother-in-law: "I can't understand anything her dad says because his accent is so strong. He's Hispanic from Puerto Rico. Her mom is a nice person but just not my type. We don't message each other or talk to each other. We didn't even speak to each other at the wedding. We just don't have that type of relationship. She's weird."

Part of establishing a relationship with the other set of in-laws may mean figuring out how much of a parallel "mothering" role to play with the daughter-in-law. Many mothers-in-law recognize they are not their daughter-in-law's mother and do not attempt to play that role. But we also heard about daughters-in-law who needed their mother-in-law to play that role if they were not close with their own mother (and even if they were close). Some mothers-in-law were willing to play that role if needed.

What we found in our sample was that daughters-in-law who were viewed as being close with their own mother and father had a closer relationship with the mother-in-law. Thus, it may be that having a warm relationship with one's parents bodes well for having a close and loving relationship with one's in-laws, just as having difficulties with one's own parents may translate into difficulties with one's in-laws.

In-laws may also play an important role in the mother-in-law's son's life. About one in 10 of the mothers-in-law believe their son is closer to his in-laws than to her! This *may* be more likely to occur when mothers-in-law live far away and the son's parents-in-law live closer and are more engaged with the family.[8] One mother-in-law put it simply, and it was a reflection also of her not being included: "They prefer to spend time with my daughter-in-law's family." As might be expected, when the son is perceived as having a closer relationship to his in-laws than to his mother, the son and his mother are not very close.

8. DO MOTHERS-IN-LAW GIVE ADVICE TO THEIR DAUGHTER-IN-LAW? THERE IS A LOT I WANT TO SAY BUT I HOLD MY TONGUE.

Can a mother-in-law give advice? During many of the interviews, when we asked for any advice for how to improve in-law relationships, "Don't interfere!" and "Don't meddle" is what we heard most often. As Marlene replied when asked what advice she would give, "Don't give advice even when it's asked for—just stay out of it. If you see a way you can help, do it, but don't meddle. Don't do that. It's a no-win situation." Another mother-in-law put it succinctly also:

> Keep your mouth shut and your nose out of their business. Don't offer too much because it is between those two people. I felt that even when I felt harsh feelings towards her, I wouldn't say that to my son or the kids, and I am in favor of very healthy boundaries. I would say let go if you want to have a good relationship.

Another mother-in-law, adopting an approach that might work in some contexts, told us she tries to offer advice within a context that is neutral. She puts it out there but does not expect it to be accepted.

Many mothers-in-law would agree advice *can* be given when asked for but, if not asked for, should only be given with caution. The question is also how open the daughter-in-law is to receiving it. We asked whether the daughter-in-law was receptive to the mother-in-law giving advice about her appearance, her job or career, and her marital relationship. Fifty percent of the mothers-in-law said they do not offer advice on appearance. Of the remaining 50% who offer advice, 34% believed the daughter-in-law was receptive, 42% answered neutral, and 24% believed she was not receptive. As to being receptive about career advice, 47% did not offer such advice. Of those who offered advice, 31% agreed she was receptive to it, 50% were neutral, and 19% believed she was not receptive to it. As to the marital relationship, certainly a situation more fraught with minefields for all involved, 63% did not offer any advice. Of those who did, 31% thought the daughter-in-law was receptive, 50% were neutral, and 19% thought she was not receptive.

Willie has known her daughter-in-law for years, so it is quite natural for her to offer advice:

> I feel like we've always been close even before they were married. When her and my son had problems before they got married and she would have trust issues and whatever, she would call me and we would go meet somewhere and just sit in the dark at the restaurant and talk and she could cry and tell me. I would give her advice and stand up for her and say, you know, my child needed what he needed to do. I gave her advice knowing him and knowing her. It helped her. She was always very appreciative and we've always had that relationship.

Clarissa has a good relationship with her daughter-in-law and is in the camp with those who do not offer advice:

> I have known her for years and my relationship with my daughter-in-law is different now that she is an adult. I respect her as an adult so I don't tell her what to do. I'm open for advice. If I thought she was doing something wrong I would probably leave it alone unless she asked for it.

Allie, whom we described earlier, wondered if gender has something to do with the level of comfort when talking to an in-law. She struggled to articulate her thoughts but seems to be saying that she might feel more comfortable giving advice to a son-in-law about her daughter than to a daughter-in-law about her son:

> I think a mother-in-law with my own son is different than a mother-in-law with my own daughter. I think the mother-in-law for a son is tricky. It's sensitive and

I think that there's a possibility that I might be like questioning if I was intrusive by suggesting anything. I just think having a son is a much more sensitive issue with a daughter-in-law then if I had a daughter and I was relating to my son-in-law about her. I don't know if that makes sense.

As might be hoped for the well-being of the relationship, if the mother-in-law believes her daughter-in-law is receptive to her giving advice, she is more likely to feel they have a close relationship. If the mother-in-law feels her daughter-in-law is not receptive, she is less close with her. However, we do not know which comes first: Does the lack of perceived receptivity lead to less closeness or does less closeness lead to a lack of perceived receptivity?

One final fact needs to be added to the mix: Mothers-in-law who perceive their daughter-in-law as unreceptive to advice are also less close with their son. We end on this point to segue into the next question—the relationship with the son—which is a fundamental building block for the mother-in-law and daughter-in-law relationship.

9. WHAT PART DOES MY SON PLAY IN ALL THIS?

This is a key question in terms of the well-being of the mother-in-law and daughter-in-law relationship. One mother recalled jokingly that when she saw her baby son for the first time she thought, "I hate his wife already." The strength of the mother–son bond cannot be overestimated. In African American families, there is an old saying, "We raise our daughters and love our sons,"[9] a testament to the special place that this relationship occupies. When the mother's son marries, the mother has to adjust to the role she will play going forward just as the daughter-in-law may have to figure out her place in the mother–son dyad. As we could surmise from the mother of the newborn, the son has the potential to play a powerful role in facilitating relations between the two women and both are likely to take cues from him. If the son wants to remain close with his mother, his wife may be wise to assist him. If he is distant from his parents, his wife can join him in that withdrawn position, though she also may serve to help bridge the distance. A son who is distant from his parents, in fact, may be attracted to his wife because he believes she could help him maintain that distance or help him repair the relationship.

Whereas Question #1 speaks to a dyadic or two-person relationship (that of the mother-in-law and daughter-in-law), when we consider the son, we are looking at a triadic or three-person relationship, which could be a potentially dysfunctional triangle. Triadic relationships are not inherently dysfunctional; they can provide great closeness and comfort for those involved. But they can be dysfunctional when one of the three persons is interfering in the relationship between the other two. That situation may need to be resolved so that the two people can carry on an unfettered relationship.

While most mothers-in-law said they were close with their son, those who are less close to their son are also less close with their daughter-in-law. In this "chicken and egg" relationship, it could be that less closeness between the women causes the son to be less close with his mother as he forms a boundary around his relationship with his wife to secure the marriage. It could also be that because the mother feels less close with her son, she forms a less close relationship with her daughter-in-law. A third possibility, and pointing out the complexity of such triadic relationships, is that the daughter-in-law sees relationship struggles between her husband and mother-in-law and is reticent to develop a closer relationship with her mother-in-law than her husband has.

We asked the mothers-in-law on the survey what part their son played in the relationship between the two women. We received a range of answers from "he thinks my daughter-in-law is awesome so I do, too" and "he promotes our relationship" to "I can't talk to him without her permission." While on rare occasions the son was described as having a negative influence, two-thirds of the time the mothers-in-law believed his influence was helpful in promoting their relationship; the rest felt he had little to no influence on the relationship. What does it look like if he has little influence? One frustrated mother-in-law wrote, "He doesn't really do or say anything." Another bypassed her son by saying that he has no role and the mother-in-law deals directly with the daughter-in-law in order to see the grandchildren. A third mother-in-law said that her son stays out of the way and lets her work things out with her daughter-in-law.

Some of the qualitative interviews with mothers-in-law and with daughters-in-law also indicate that, in some families, the son is not relevant to the relationship. Some told us they loved their future daughter-in-law immediately and would have wanted to be close with her even if her son did not marry her, as this mother-in-law reported: "I liked her from the start; from the moment I saw her. I thought, 'wow, look at this woman, what is my son doing with her?' She is very kind, and intelligent. She clearly loved my son, and whoever loves my son, I love and accept in the family right away." Other daughters-in-law (see Chapter 4) felt hated before they even said a word and said that their husband never played a part in the women's relationship.

During the interviews, we asked the mothers-in-law if the daughter-in-law relationship was important to them and, if so, why. The reason given most often had to do with wanting to stay close with her son. For those with only one child, staying close took on greater importance. A positive daughter-in-law relationship is seen as the way to maintain this closeness and establish a relationship with a grandchild. It may also be that a positive relationship may increase the likelihood that the mother-in-law will be well taken care of as she ages, a caregiving role that some daughters-in-law assume in relation to their mother-in-law.

Further, when the mother-in-law believes that her son is happy with her relationship with his wife (the daughter-in-law), the wife and mother are closer. These positive interactions can occur simultaneously, another triadic relationship dynamic. The wife and mother are getting along, which makes the son happy, which further reinforces the women's relationship.

The son does not have to be in the middle of the relationship for it to be a sign it is going well. In some families, not having the son play the role of communications conduit between the women is related to better relations between the women. Specifically, the mothers-in-law who feel they can speak directly to their daughter-in-law about important issues, without first speaking with their son, are closer to their daughter-in-law. In essence, the son is not playing the intermediary. They have a comfortable relationship that he does not have to mediate, which minimizes the triangle dynamics.

Mothers will take the cue from their son and are acutely aware of where they stand even when they get along with their daughter-in-law. One mother-in-law abides her daughter-in-law because of her son's love for the daughter-in-law but on the survey indicated she was neither close nor distant. She described the relationship in this neutral way: "She loves my son; my son loves her. I'm happy that my son has someone who loves him and who he's happy with."

One mother-in-law indicated on the survey she feels very close to her daughter-in-law and recognizes her son's position in that relationship:

> You know, she's married to my son and you want to have a positive relationship with her because it's important to him and it's important to me. If I didn't have a good relationship with her, depending on what the issue was, it would be hard for him to be in the middle between the two of us. I think that it's probably pretty likely that the son would gravitate towards the wife if he had to choose a side because she's the one he's married to. She's the mother of their children, so he wouldn't have a great deal of choice there.

So, yes, in most but not all families, the son plays a key role—first as a linchpin in bringing the two together, and then as a central figure in how they maintain their relationship. He may subtly or overtly greenlight or impede their relationship by acceding to his wife's or his mother's wishes for more or less frequent contact.

10. WHAT PART DOES MY SPOUSE/PARTNER PLAY IN MY RELATIONSHIP WITH MY DAUGHTER-IN-LAW?

Just as the son usually plays a significant part in the women's relationship, husbands or partners can also play a central role. As part of a parental team and as part of a marital couple, each partner may modulate the other's behavior.[10] More than half the mothers-in-law said their husband/partner had an influence on her relationship with the daughter-in-law. This can take a number of forms. The husband may suggest to the mother-in-law positive ways to interact with the daughter-in-law. In fact, 12% of the mothers-in-law with a partner in her home answered that her spouse/partner thought she should work harder on her relationship with the daughter-in-law.

Dotty credits her husband with interpreting the daughter-in-law, Jenny's, behavior to the mother-in-law:

> My husband is a very easygoing person, and sometimes when he and I are talking he says, "Dotty, it's the way she was raised. Jenny doesn't understand." We have discussed how we don't agree with the way her mother or dad treats her. My husband will say, "That's the way she was raised." Jenny is the oldest of three children. When her mother left, she became the mother of the two brothers, and she brings that worldview into our family.

Not only might a husband be encouraging greater understanding or more positive interaction between the two women, but he may be serving as a buffer between them. He may do this by entering into a triad wherein both women communicate to each other through him. He also may position himself alongside the mother-in-law as a support to her and present them as a unit or team. As importantly, he may be helping with the provision of childcare and financial assistance. Offering such assistance could have been his decision, the mother-in-law's decision, or a joint decision. In a few cases, he is the primary childcare provider, as when the mother-in-law is still working or is otherwise unable to provide childcare.

In some cases, the daughter-in-law is closer to the father-in-law than the mother-in-law, and that positive relationship helps the mother-in-law feel close to the daughter-in-law. In this next example, Penny was asked how her relationship with her daughter-in-law has evolved. In her response, we see how the connection to the father-in-law has brought the mother-in-law closer:

> I would say that we are more relaxed with each other. I think the evolution has been more with her and my husband where she is comfortable asking his advice. My husband is a tax attorney so she has asked him about legal and financial stuff and it's very nice. She has that confidence and that security to take advantage of that and we very much want to offer. I think other people might reject advice and say, "Oh, you're just parents meddling," but she's been very open and was the one who kind of initiated, "Can you help me with this?" So we have been very grateful that we weren't considered meddling parents.

Another role the spouse/partner plays for the mother-in-law is to provide support and validation for behavior that the mother-in-law perceives in the daughter-in-law, which sometimes can be negative:

> She is the same way toward my husband as she is to me. My husband didn't really care as much as I did and did not get as upset, but he certainly saw that what she was doing was not made up in my mind and that she was not interested in having a relationship with either of us. My husband has been very sick and she has expressed no interest or concern for him. It's just who she is. He just doesn't care as much and I am the one to care.

As mentioned, almost one-third of the mothers-in-law with grandchildren replied that they and/or their husband were providing childcare. In addition, four out of 10 said they and/or their husband were providing financial support. We asked the question as "and/or" because the provision of assistance is usually a couple's decision and, if one parent-in-law is providing it, there is likely some sacrifice in terms of time or money on the part of the partner.[11] The provision of assistance does not only flow to the children-in-law: One in eight of the mothers-in-law said their son and daughter-in-law were providing them physical care or help (sons were more likely to provide it to their parents than daughters-in-law, though daughters-in-law did provide it), and a handful said their son and daughter-in-law were helping them out financially. Not surprisingly, the provision of physical help and financial assistance, regardless of who gives it and who receives it, is related to having a closer mother-in-law/daughter-in-law relationship.

Because of the possible roles that a husband or partner may play, factoring him into the relationship equation between the mother- and daughter-in-law is important. Such factoring can also assist in helping to understand the nuances of the family systems, wherein little occurs that does not affect another family member.

CONCLUSION

We focused in this chapter on the mothers-in-law's relationship with their daughter-in-law. We learned from Evelyn, Fiola, Geneva, Alice, Doris, and many others about the mixed bag these complicated relationships can be. To get a fuller understanding of how these relationships operate, not only does the social context related to gender roles and culture need to be considered but attention also needs to be paid to the influence of other key family members. From a family systems perspective, we emphasize that others have a significant part in shaping these relationships, and reading their respective chapters, particularly the daughters-in-law's, can help in understanding the experiences of mothers-in-law.

CHAPTER 4

Daughters-in-Law and Their Relationship with Their Mother-in-Law

Many longstanding narratives exist around daughters-in-law and mothers-in-law—narratives that may unfairly place both women into boxes, which do not reflect the true nature of their relationship. One narrative is that they are both vying for the affections of the daughter-in-law's husband, the son of the mother-in-law. Another is that the daughter-in-law is fending off interference from the mother-in-law who is telling her daughter-in-law how to raise her children, the mother-in-law's grandchildren. A third, and quite different, narrative is captured in the loving biblical story of Ruth and Naomi, where Ruth forgoes all to remain with her mother-in-law. To escape a famine, Naomi and her husband and two sons moved from Bethlehem to Moab. One of Naomi's sons, Mahlon, married Ruth and the other son, Chilion, married Orpah. (Yes, this is the Orpah after whom Oprah Winfrey was named.) After 10 years, Naomi's husband and both sons died. Naomi told Ruth and Orpah to start a new life in Moab as she was returning home to Bethlehem. Orpah left, though reluctantly. Ruth responded, famously, "Whither thou goest, I will go; and where thou lodgest, I will lodge. Thy people shall be my people and thy God my God."

Within any narrative, many nuances more accurately reflect the ever-changing contexts in which these created intergenerational family relationships unfold. Few daughter-in-law and mother-in-law relationships are as good as that suggested by Ruth and Naomi or as black and white as those suggested by the more troubled ones depicted in in-law jokes. In this chapter, we look at how daughters-in-law get along with their mother-in-law. Given the centrality of women in families, an understanding of this relationship is paramount—it is the women who are likely the most powerful in connecting family members and in setting the tone for the relationships. This is not to say that the men are not pivotal; they often are. But, in some families, they are largely bystanders, as some of the interviews reveal.

Just as we wrote in Chapter 3 from the mother-in-law's perspective, there is often ambiguity from the daughter-in-law's perspective when she interacts with her mother-in-law. That is especially so when roles are not clearly defined. It is common that when someone is not clear how to act, she feels uncomfortable. The many evolving and conflicting themes in society around women's roles can get played out in the mother-in-law/daughter-in-law relationship. For example, the mother-in-law and daughter-in-law will have different perspectives based on their own family history on what defines a good wife and mother. There might be incongruent views shared about the daughter-in-law staying home with children or working outside of the home—or about the father being a stay-at-home dad or grandparents providing childcare if they are available. Role ambiguity can lead to the daughter-in-law feeling ambivalent about her mother-in-law's involvement. Perhaps the daughter-in-law wants assistance with childcare from the mother-in-law, but does not want the mother-in-law to take that as an invitation to comment on her parenting abilities. Maybe the daughter-in-law recognizes how important the mother-in-law is to her husband/spouse, but does not enjoy her company when the two of them are alone. These relationships can generate confusion and mixed feelings.

The big picture is that slightly more than half of the 351 daughters-in-law we surveyed strongly agree or agree that they are close with their mother-in-law. Four in 10 live within 20 miles of their mother-in-law, although that does not necessarily mean they spend a huge amount of time together; less than one in 10 spend 20 hours a month or more with her, including in-person and other forms of electronic communication, while almost four in 10 spend one hour or less a month in contact. In resurveying the daughters-in-law one year after the initial survey, we did find that while there were no significant changes for the overall sample, one in 10 changed for the better and one in six changed markedly for the worse.

The majority agree to statements indicating their mother-in-law is kind, warm, and available to them. We heard things that harken back to Ruth and Naomi, like, "My father-in-law passed away and so my mother-in-law lives with us now. She is very supportive, very friendly, it's very genuine. She's great and we have a great relationship." And "I see her as a mother figure, not as an in-law." We also heard from many daughters-in-law that their mother-in-law was important to them because she was both important to their husband and because having a cohesive family unit was of great value. For these reasons, even if they do not feel especially close to their mother-in-law, the daughters-in-law try to make the relationship work.

Ultimately, we talked to daughters-in-law with extremely close relationships with their mother-in-law, those who have highly strained relationships with their mother-in-law, and those whose relationships are workable but are neither very close nor distant. This last group consists of women who, although they get along with and feel affection toward their mother-in-law, recognize that family is important, wish to keep their spouse happy, and value the grandparent contact that their children have. To these ends, they make the relationship work.

What follows are a series of questions and answers that we see as key to understanding how these women's relationships operate and the role that other family members play. Our attempt is to shed light on this often complicated and misrepresented relationship.

1. ARE DAUGHTERS-IN-LAW CLOSE TO THEIR MOTHER-IN-LAW?

To answer this question more fully, we need to use more than one item on our survey—"My mother-in-law and I have a close relationship"—and combine a number of items to get a more complete picture of relationship quality. To assess relationship quality, we constructed a variable from seven survey questions similar to ones we created for the other in-law groups. Along with the question about being close, the variable includes the following four other positive statements and asks for levels of agreement from strongly agree to strongly disagree: "I admire my mother-in-law;" "I can ask my mother-in-law for advice;" "I trust my mother-in-law;" and "I enjoy spending time with my mother-in-law." The variable also includes two negative statements, "I avoid my mother-in-law" and "I have problematic conflicts with my mother-in-law."

Some daughters-in-law gave all responses that indicated a highly positive relationship, while a few gave all responses that indicated a highly negative relationship. For others, though, mixed feelings emerged in the relationships. For example, a daughter-in-law may admire her mother-in-law for what she is doing in the work world, but at the same time not feel close with her. A daughter-in-law may feel close to her mother-in-law but avoid asking her for advice about childrearing. We use this created variable and the term *close* to measure *relationship quality* as we look at a number of other variables to explain this complex relationship.

Approximately 50% to 62% agreed or strongly agreed with each positive statement while 13% and 22% agreed or strongly agreed with the negative statements. Specifically, 18% strongly agreed and 35% agreed they had a close relationship, 23% strongly agreed and 34% agreed they admired their mother-in-law, 23% strongly agreed and 33% agreed they could ask their mother-in-law for advice, 22% strongly agreed and 34% agreed they enjoyed spending time with their mother-in-law, and 23% strongly agreed and 39% agreed they trusted her. To the negative statements, 6% strongly agreed and 7% agreed they had problematic conflicts while 9% strongly agreed and 13% agreed they avoided their mother-in-law. Neutral responses appeared between 15% and 25% of the time and responses that disagree ranged from 13% to 28% depending on the statement.

While these numbers help to draw the big picture, we use the interviews to illustrate how these relationships operate, first by presenting the positive ones, then the negatives ones, and, finally, by presenting examples of those that offer a more mixed picture.

When Relationships Are Very Good

Lenny

Lenny is a 58-year-old African American office manager, married for 40 years and with two children. Her mother-in-law has been a widow for the past five years. When asked how important her relationship with her mother-in-law is, Lenny told us something that we have heard from other children-in-law about the parental role that in-laws play:

> We're very close. She means a lot to me. I see her as a mother figure, not an in-law. My mother-in-law is someone that I can always talk to knowing it's going to stay between us. I don't talk to her about my married life but, if I did, we are so close that she would support me even though I'm married to her son. I had an awesome relationship with my father-in-law also.

After the father-in-law's death, Lenny's mother-in-law moved out of state, 100 miles away, which meant that greater effort had to be made for Lenny and her husband to visit her: "She wants the same kind of time that we gave her here, and for us to drive up to her and it's not feasible because we're so busy. So sometimes she'll get a little sad that we don't spend more time with her."

Death of one in-law often means a shift in the relationship with the other. While acknowledging the disappointment her mother-in-law feels, Lenny does not feel any less close with her:

> She and I have mother–daughter talks. When she comes into town, I will try to spend time with her so we can just be with each other by ourselves. When I go to her house, she doesn't want to go out anywhere anymore. I try to sit there and spend time with her, even though I want to say "Let's go out somewhere." We do a lot of girl talk. Like when I call her, I may not have something to talk about. I'll just call to see how she's doing. We could be on the phone for an hour having girl talk. I'm talking about my day and we're talking about things we want to do, like the holidays, and we'll be at her house for Thanksgiving. We don't have to have anything to talk about; we just talk.

The daughter-in-law and mother-in-law bond has also gotten stronger over the years. Like other daughters-in-law we interviewed, Lenny does not credit her husband for this—the two women have achieved this on their own. It may be because they have known each other for so long: "I met my mother-in-law when I was eleven years old. After I got out of school, my husband and I married and my family already knew his family. But we didn't really build a close relationship until after that."

Lenny descends from a line of close relationships: Her parents were close with their own parents and with each other's parents, setting the stage for the family bonds that Lenny has with her in-laws. She offers advice to other daughters-in-law:

> See her as a second mother so that you can talk to your mother about something and then you can talk to your mother-in-law and feel like you're getting motherly advice. I love my mother -in-law just as much as my mother. I call her mom, but I know she's not my real mother but I can talk to her just like I'm talking to my mother. When I married her son, I went to her and told her, "I'm gonna call you mom because, as far as I'm concerned, you're my mother." We have kept that relationship ever since.

The boundaries between the women are clear:

> She knows that no matter what my husband and I go through, I am not going to pressure her to give her opinion and I'm not going to call her, downing her son. At the same time, her son is not going to call her downing me. It helps our

relationship, because she knows she doesn't have to deal with that. Even if we are going through something, she'll never find out.

Sunny

Sunny is a 25-year-old White graduate student who has been married three years to an African American man. They have a one-year-old child. Sunny's in-laws are divorced and her parents are married. The in-law relationship is very important to Sunny because

> My husband was mostly raised by his mother and her side of the family, so he's really close with her. He actually has a tattoo of her name on his arm as a sign of respect and honor. That tells you where she ranks in his life. Having a good relationship with her is important to my husband, so it's important to me.

Sunny has minimal contact with her father-in-law, who lives farther away than her mother-in-law, who also lives in a different state: "With my mother-in-law, I would say we have a really close relationship. We text each other. We don't need my husband to relay messages. She checks on me all the time to see how I'm doing. It's as if she's my biological mother." Sunny is also close with her own parents who are, in turn, close with their parents and in-laws.

Having a child has brought Sunny and her mother-in-law closer:

> I've always talked to my mother-in-law, but now it's even more just because she inquires about my son. He's her first grandbaby so she's really interested. My father-in-law, I don't feel like it affects our relationship because he has grandchildren from another marriage . . . My son is his fifth grandbaby and he's not the first boy . . . so I don't really feel like it's that impactful on our relationship.

Despite the great interest on the part of the mother-in-law in seeing her only grandchild, it is not always smooth sailing:

> My son doesn't see my husband's side of the family that often because they are over 400 miles away. With my family, they are only 80 miles away and we frequently visit them. So my son is closer with my parents and, whenever we visited my mother-in-law, she was hurt by the fact that he didn't want to go to her, that he cried whenever he was around her. I tried to explain to her that it's not

her, that he doesn't see her and she's like a stranger to him. She didn't really want to hear that and so that was difficult.

Sunny's husband's relationship with his father, Sunny's father-in-law, is instructive because of its reverberation on Sunny's marriage:

My husband always says that he tries to be the kind of husband to me that he wished his mom would have had with his father. He keeps that in his mind whenever we are argue. I really want my father-in-law and husband to have a good relationship, but when my father-in-law says things to my husband like, "You don't do everything you can to help me," it enrages me. I think, "How can you try to give my husband advice when he's in a successful marriage and you were not?" At the same time, I want them to have a good relationship, so I'm torn. [By comparison], my mother-in-law constantly tries to make sure that we're doing okay as a couple and individually.

Sunny does not feel that racial differences have affected the in-law relationships (see later in this chapter for more on interracial marriage) because of how active her husband has been in supporting her:

He has been really instrumental in starting those connections and speaking positively about me to both of his parents. To my knowledge, he's never vented to either of them about me. Maybe there are things in our relationship that aren't perfect, but he's never talked to them about me, painting me in a bad way. I think that's key because their opinions about me are obviously greatly influenced by him.

Ria

Our final example comes from Ria, a 35-year-old woman engineer who was born in India and has been living in the United States for three years with her husband of six years who was also born in India. They have no children. She is very grateful for the relationship with both her in-laws:

Unlike popular belief, I have been fortunate to get married to a spouse with lovely parents. I think most times they even surpass my parents in all they do for us. My mother-in-law's family was very matriarchal as her father passed away when the kids were quite young. Since my mother-in-law's mother ran the house, women get a lot of respect and choice. My father-in-law is very progressive as well. Everyone in the extended family loves them and looks up to them for advice.

What further enhances the relationship is the respect Ria feels:

> My in-laws are very non-interfering in our household, which is something I really appreciate. We consult them but the ultimate decisions lie with us. My spouse and I are family-oriented and we love them. My mother-in-law is also very close to my mother. They keep in touch on phone and WhatsApp. They are different in their ways of house management, but they are both nice and connect well even when they disagree.

The geographic distance—the in-laws live in India—poses challenges for Ria and her husband:

> I must say that having them over for five months was difficult and a big adjustment. We did not realize how used to having our own space and time when we are alone we became. Even though she pampers us when she visits, sometimes they want attention and we are too tired to offer it. [For the sample of daughters-in-law, 40% lived within 20 miles of their mother-in-law; geographic distance was not related to the quality of their relationship.] But this is more an issue with us than them. The good thing is there is dialogue in the house for everything and I do not have to speak behind her back. I love that I can be upfront with her as she can be with me.

Ria's in-laws were sad about the move to the United States for work but have not tried to make them feel guilty. Ria believes that while there is a cultural imperative to have children and live close to one's parents, her in-laws have not tried to impose restrictions. Ria is not surprised by this:

> I knew my mother-in-law before marriage. She is a great person, not just for her family but for others remotely related to her. I have made zero adjustments post marriage—clothing, behavior, and the choice to have or not to have a child. In fact, I am more open with my in-laws than I ever was with my parents. All of this became more apparent when we four started living together post-marriage and also how understanding they were when we had to move out. I love how progressive they are.

Whereas many daughter-in-law and mother-in-law relationships have ups and downs, this one has had no major hiccups. On a scale of 1 to 10, the worst Ria reported it has ever been was an 8. Ria took responsibility for it being as low as an 8, saying, while laughing, that she thinks her mother-in-law would have preferred a daughter-in-law who liked to gossip more and was more of a homemaker than Ria. Ria also thinks it will never be a

10 "because there will always be a generation gap and because I think she would love it more if I called her more. However, she is so sweet and never brings any negativity up. If this is an 8, it is only lacking something on my side which has nothing to do with culture or my feelings for her. I think even with your own spouse, you need a certain space."

Ria pointed out that everyone has differences with their own parents so it would be natural to expect some differences with one's in-laws. "The key to any relationship," Ria advises, "is respecting the other person's point of view and being honest. I feel it is imperative to set the tone from Day One so they do not feel that you are suddenly a different person."

All three of these daughters-in-law have clear boundaries and there is little, if any, ambiguity about roles. Lenny puts up no barriers in trying to establish and maintain a relationship with her mother-in-law, despite the 100 miles of distance. Her husband does not play an ongoing role in their relationship. Contrast this with Sunny, who believes that her husband's support of her with his parents has helped them grow closer but who also has a direct line of communication with her mother-in-law. Ria married into a family with an admirable mother-in-law with whom she also has an open line of communication. Ria's mother-in-law is highly supportive and non-interfering. All three mothers-in-law live at a geographic distance yet they are able to maintain a very close relationship.

When Relationships Are a Struggle

George Martin, the musical producer for the Beatles (often seen as the "fifth Beatle" due to his contributions to the music), was very close with his mother when growing up but was separated from her during World War II. After both son and mother reunited, he met and married Sheena— whom his mother could not stand, in part because Sheena came between George and his mother. George's mother never accepted Sheena and even, at one point, chased her around the house with a knife because of Sheena's perceived interference in a family matter.

We have heard similar tales of daughter-in-law and mother-in-law strain, though none resulting in reactions so extreme. Some of the daughters-in-law we interviewed who had poor relations with their mother-in-law have bridged this divide and grown closer over the years after early issues were resolved or put aside. Other daughters-in-law continue to keep their mother-in-law at a significant distance.

Closeness comes in many packages. This first example of a highly strained relationship between a daughter-in-law and mother-in-law places the husband/son squarely in the middle of what appears to have been an unhealthy and overly close relationship between mother and son. Over time, though, the relationship improved; but if we had interviewed Monica 12 years ago, the story would be quite different.

Monica

Monica, who is White and age 61, works at a car dealership in the Midwest. Married for 18 years with no children, her husband is four years her junior, her mother-in-law 20 years her senior. This is Monica's second marriage and her husband's first.

> For the first eight years of my marriage, my husband was married to his mother. I don't mean just in the vague way that he put her first, which he did. But she would make inappropriate sexual remarks about him to me, to us. The weird thing is that this didn't reveal itself until after we got married and, suddenly, I don't know what happened to her, all this shit came up. They would go off together on daylong dates to which I was not invited. On Mother's Day, most normal people go to brunch. No. He and his mother would go on a date from 9 in the morning until 9 at night. For her birthday, they would go on a daylong date. For her 60th birthday, they went on a long weekend to New York. The two of them! My girlfriends heard about this and were like, "What the fuck? Are you kidding me? You need to put a stop." I tried to talk to him about this so many times, in so many ways, using diplomatic language. When somebody's irrational and he's otherwise a rational person, but about this stuff, forget it. For eight years, I struggled with this and thought if this had been my first marriage, I would've left. But it isn't and I had already had one marriage and been through one divorce. I couldn't face another.

The turning point came when Monica told one of her husband's friends that her mother-in-law said that she liked to see her son in Speedos and not in baggy bathing suits. When her husband heard what his mother had said, he decided to talk to her. According to Monica, he told her, "'Mother, conversations about my bathing suit and my attire are completely inappropriate and not up for discussion.'" Her mother-in-law received the message:

> It hasn't stopped her 100% from making inappropriate remarks, but they're less appalling and obnoxious. Over the years of marriage, I kept trying to keep the peace. Finally, this past July, we were at the beach together, and she looked at me and said something that was an abject lie. I called her on it. I looked at her

and said, "That is a crock of shit. I have never done any such thing. That is bull-shit." She was stunned. Everybody was stunned. I had never done that. I have never barked at her and it felt great. I am not letting this shit happen again, never. I'm not putting up with it.

Monica recognizes how important the relationship with her mother-in-law is:

It's his mother. I don't care what anyone says, in-laws are important. I've watched other couples break up because of their parents. The thing is, other-wise I like her. She's an interesting woman, fun, and a great conversationalist. She's traveled a lot and is well read. But she has this weird relationship with her son and my ire was always directed at my husband. It was his responsibility, not hers. She's messed up in this weird psychosexual thing. But it was his responsi-bility to put the marriage first, not hers. It was his responsibility to lay out those boundaries, so that's why I never held it against her in the way I held it against him because it was his responsibility. But he was letting her dictate the terms.

This unhealthy mother–son relationship took many years to develop. As Monica tells it:

When my husband was 14, mother and father were having marital problems. Apparently, his father was having affairs, and so his mother, rather than confiding in a friend about it, would take him on these long walks and confide in him. Her 14-year-old son! To say that's inappropriate is putting it mildly. As an adult, he could not see that there was something wrong with that. I would say, "Don't you see that she had no right to burden you? That she has this twisted relationship where she looks at you like her boyfriend? Don't you see anything wrong with that?" And he said, "No, I don't see what's wrong with it." You could not talk to him about this. When I first met my husband and we started dating, he said something I thought was so sweet and calculated to get to every girl's heart. He said, "I would do anything for my mother." I remember thinking, "He's so sweet!" He could not see it. Now I assume he sees it, but we don't talk about it.

Monica is clear about what she wants from the relationship with her mother-in-law:

It's not my responsibility to be her friend. I want to have a good relationship with her—but get your own friends! I'm happy to do things with her, but I'm not interested in being buddies. You don't have to love your in-laws or think they're the greatest people in the world, but you have to have a decent relationship with them. Otherwise, it will poison your marriage. I knew he wouldn't have my back. "Let it go," his advice to me was about his mother, is his way of sweeping it under the rug. Of course, there are things you need to let go. But this serious shit, I should've put my foot down a lot sooner. I guess I was afraid . . . it did bring us to the brink of divorce.

Tara

Tara is a White, 35-year-old mother of three children, ages three, seven, and 10. She is a senior in college and has been married for 11 years. She does not consider her relationship with her mother-in-law to be at all important. Her father-in-law died a few years ago after divorcing her mother-in-law when Tara's husband was seven. Tara was close with both her parents (her mother died a few years ago) but neither of her parents were particularly close with their in-laws, Tara's two sets of grandparents. Tara and her husband have figured out a way to minimize their in-law struggles—they have parallel patterns of interactions with them. A common approach, each spouse deals with his or her own family.

A typical precipitating factor of an emotionally distant relationship between daughter-in-law and mother-in-law occurs when the daughter-in-law does not feel initially accepted:

My mother-in-law had a lot of problems with our relationship early on, so we decided that it would be best that my husband deals with his family and I deal with mine in order for our marriage to be good. When we decided to move in together her immediate reaction was "Why would you move in with *her*?" She was very condescending and mean to me, so that set the tone for the rest of our lives. It's basically all on him and I limit my interaction with her as much as possible because it's just not a good relationship. She is overbearing and opinionated. If you don't do things her way then you are wrong or you're an idiot. I had a hard time hearing all this negative stuff from her. It came to a boiling point with Dave and me and we would fight about his mother, which was never good. So we had to decide how to handle it, and that's the communication we chose to do.

This has worked well, given the nature of the relationship:

He's the gateway between me and her. I don't pick up the phone and call her and she doesn't call me. There's no attempt to talk for any reason unless she's in my house and, even then, it's very surface like "Hi, how are you doing?", just pleasantries. In short, my relationship with her is very turbulent and tumultuous.

When there is conflict between two generations, the third generation (the grandchildren) can get pulled in. Not in this case:

> I try to keep my negative relationship with my mother-in-law away from my children and maintain peace for their benefit. Presently, there is no interaction as we had a big fight six months ago. Since we aren't talking, they aren't interacting with her. Since they are young, they would not have a relationship with her without us so there is no contact and it's very deliberate. Prior, if she said something snarky to me, I wouldn't respond so it would never escalate in front of them. I bit my tongue and, when she left, I would talk about it with Dave after the children went to bed. I never talked badly about her in front of them.

We wondered what had happened that caused the contact to stop. What we heard from Tara was about an event that some families could get past while others, where there was already a tenuous relationship, would find it hard to ignore: "We were at my children's dance recital and she made disparaging remarks about some of the children dancing on the stage. My husband asked her to be quiet, which caused an uproar. They argued and she stormed out of the recital and made a huge scene. My husband and I haven't talked to her since."

The separation that Tara's husband, Dave, was willing to endure with his mother was all the more poignant because Dave's father abandoned the family after he and Dave's mother divorced. His father tried to re-establish a relationship years later but Dave was not interested. Dave's experiences with his father may have shaped his early marital interactions with Tara through Dave's desire to stay in close contact with his mother:

> Early in our marriage his mother had a really negative impact on our relationship. Dave and I would fight because of things that his mother would say to me. She would say something and I would take it out on him, so we had to learn how to not do that because it's not his fault and it's not healthy. That went on for the first five years we were married. Then a big blow-up with me and his mother ended with him kicking her out of the house. That was when a lightbulb went off in his head and he realized his nuclear family was more important than her, and that was when we figured out how to handle all of this.

Unlike Monica, Tara had a sense of what she was getting into when she married: "I agreed to marry Dave knowing how she is, so my advice would be to understand the family dynamic before you get too far into it. We really let her negativity affect us for a long time. We could have saved ourselves a lot of time fighting if we realized that earlier."

Amelie

Whereas Monica and Tara are relating to a mother-in-law with boundary and personality issues, this next daughter-in-law has a mother-in-law with a disease. Amelie is White, 51 years old, and a social worker. Married for 27 years and mother to one child, her parents are married, as are her in-laws, who live 80 miles away. The relationship with both her in-laws has been at an arm's length since its inception:

> They are both in recovery and were when I met them. They were alcoholics and drug addicts. My mother-in-law had issues with using prescription medication and she's been, as far as we know, sober for a while. The best way for me to describe both of them is that they never want to get too deep into a relationship. It is very surface-y, as would be typical given their history.

It is hard to know to what extent the addiction kept Amelie at a distance from them and if they would have been close if not for it: "I think the best way to describe it is we are very different and I haven't taken the time probably, even after all these years, to get to know them. When our son was younger, I was hopeful maybe that we could try to build some type of relationship. But it never really went that direction."

Amelie married her husband a few months after they met and she did not know her in-laws at all by the time of the wedding. Her son was born shortly after that, and differences in parenting philosophy further kept the two sets of in-laws from forming a bond: "We're not close and we're not getting deep into a relationship. It essentially has not changed since it began."

Amelie and her husband have reached out to them to offer assistance as they age (both are in their 70s) and they have refused:

> My mother-in-law will get angry if I offer to help too much. She will get really upset. It's sad to watch someone who is so closed off, who clearly could benefit from physical assistance. Like, could I help you over the curb. But also the emotional resistance. We bring my mother here a couple times a year so that she can get a change of scenery. We've offered a visit to my mother-in-law but she just can't fathom that idea. She's so closed off she can't think about that.

Amelie has kept her distance also because her husband shared some of his mother's past behavior:

I know things about her. She probably knows that I know about them and keeps her distance. She will openly tell you that she's in recovery, but it's not like she would delve into the severe depression that she had when we were first married. She has had electroconvulsive therapy. She's also been inpatient several times, but it's not anything that we would ever talk about. She is one of the most private people I have ever met.

Amelie does appreciate one attempt her mother-in-law made when Amelie and her husband were in a low period themselves:

My husband and I have had marital difficulties and, at one point, we actually separated about three years in. She came over to the house to try to talk with us and see if there was anything she could offer. That was huge. Another time I had surgery and she came over to make sure I was taken care of and to make dinner. Those are two highlights that I go back to, but it's more of a doing than a trying to actually connect on an emotional level.

Amelie and her own family of origin are accustomed to operating on a much more open and transparent level. Her mother-in-law's way of dealing with things is the opposite:

I feel a little bit like I've been pulled into the game that my husband's family plays that everything is just fine. It is a mentality where we all play as if everything were fine until it blows up in your face and then you deal with it. So, stepping into a family that is so closed off, so private, secretive, and so forth, has been something I had never experienced in my life.

Luckily, for Amelie, her sister-in-law, married to her husband's brother, experiences the family in the same way: "We are a great support to one another. I've talked to her about her feelings, which have been hurt many times by things that our in-laws have done. She and I have talked about it so many times that we are not going to change that. You just have to let it go."

Boundaries in family relationships are complex and tricky. With Monica and Tara, we see extremes in terms of a lack of boundaries. Both mothers-in-law say, and at times do, whatever they want without a filter. Amelie's mother-in-law is the opposite; she has a closed boundary and does not let anyone or anything in. As a result, she is not emotionally available and does not allow Amelie to know her.

When Relationships Are Mixed

Not all relationships are particularly close nor especially distant and tension-filled like the six we have just described. Many are mostly pleasant and uncomplicated, and only occasionally cause the daughter-in-law to grit her teeth and tell herself to keep quiet in the service of maintaining family harmony. Sometimes that means understanding what can be changed and what cannot be changed as well as just accepting the good with the bad.

Gabriella

Gabriella, age 30, was born in Spain. She has been married to a native-born American for two years. They have no children. She has a master's degree and works in the travel industry in the United States. Her in-laws live about an hour's drive away. Her parents live in Spain. Gabriella does not feel she has a close relationship with her mother-in-law:

> It's a formal, respectful relationship with her. She is my husband's mother, and that's it. The relationship with my father-in-law is friendlier. I believe he really likes my husband being with me because I am from Spain, and so he is more like a friend to me. My mother-in-law is more correct, formal, and distant. I guess it is her personality too; she is colder and quieter, whereas my father-in-law is a warm person. He jokes where she is more introverted. My mother-in-law sees me as the one that took her baby.

Like many daughters-in-law with mixed relationships, this one revolves around her husband: "It is important for my husband. He is much closer to her than I am because he is her son. My husband likes me to talk to her when we visit. We try to see them on the weekend for a couple of hours. They don't ask us to come over for dinner or to eat with them; they are not that type of American family."

Like some international marriages, contact between parents-in-law is limited:

> The only time both sets of parents met was at my wedding in Spain. My mother loves everybody, and opened her arms to them. Even though there was a language barrier, and a lot of silence (laughing), my mother is the type of person that will try to make herself understood with her gestures. She opened her house to them, and entertained them. She hugged them when they left. However, there has been no contact since.

The relationship between Gabriella and her mother-in-law has been slow to develop, in part because of her mother-in-law's reticent style:

> When we were dating I was going to their house most weekends, but I did a lot of hiking and meeting up with friends, so I did not see her as frequently as I do now. Their schedule is very busy, too, as both work. At first, we did not talk much. It was more her asking me questions such as, "What are you doing here?", "Why did you decide to come to the U.S.?", and "Why are you with my son?" Now we have more of a mutual conversation. We talk about work, our homes, etc., but she doesn't ask me how my week was. That never happens. She doesn't even ask her son that. She never goes into detail about anything. They don't like being in anyone else's business.

It is hard to know to what extent the formality between the two women is cultural and was initially more difficult because of a language barrier:

> Since we married, my relationship changed with her. She saw how happy her son was. Also, my English has improved and I can communicate better with her than before. Sometimes she cannot understand what I say. At first it was shocking for them; someone from another country, with an accent, that wasn't using the same words that they were used to. She did not talk much to me but now, with my language improvement, we communicate better.

There is not only a language barrier; Gabriella faults her mother-in-law for some of her past behavior:

> My in-laws split up years ago. Everybody has problems, my family too, but I think there was a big impact when my mother-in-law left her home and abandoned her kids. I don't know why she left. She was having problems with her husband and instead of sitting down and trying to resolve it like my family would have, she just took off. Then she came back, left with the youngest child, and then returned. How can a mother leave her children? She gave birth. She has a bond with her children, so leaving her family to me is a big difference. Also, when we talk about money, my parents worked their entire life, and built what they have today. They live comfortably now, which is the big difference from my husband and his family. They live paycheck to paycheck. They spend everything. They are not educated, and do not know how to save, how to maintain good credit and stay out of debt.

Gabriella believes she and her mother-in-law have become closer with time: "We know each other better now than we did before. Each year it gets better. I care for her and my father-in-law. They are my husband's parents, and if anything happened to them, it would devastate him and, of course, upset me. Polite and respectful, it is a formal relationship, but I'm happy with it."

Darlene

Whereas Gabriella's relationship with her mother-in-law has never been one of extremes, Darlene's relationship with her mother-in-law, Franny, had some significant bumps in the road before settling into stability. Bumps still exist with her sisters-in-law. Darlene, White and age 58, has been married for 36 years and has two adult children. Darlene and her husband own a small store in the suburbs of Richmond, Virginia, where the interview took place. Both sets of parents were alive until the last few years, and Darlene described her own upbringing as quite loving. Now only Franny remains from the older generation. In talking about their relationship, Darlene describes what we have heard about other in-law relationships: Once a marriage occurs, the child-in-law immediately becomes part of the family, even though she may have felt very much the outsider before the wedding:

> Franny did not want us to get married, absolutely not. I was not her pick. She physically fought me getting married even on the wedding day. We were ready to walk down the aisle and she tried to talk my husband out of it. I never knew why. I was the only one he ever dated. Maybe stealing the baby [he is second of three children and the only boy]. Then, as soon as we got married, she often told his sisters she was closer to me than to them. His sisters didn't like that.

Why someone is not initially accepted can be due to racial, religious, or socio-economic differences. That was not the case here:

> First time I came to the house, I was 17, my sister-in-law looked out the window and said, "I don't like her," I was told. It is still that way today. I think they are very clannish. I am Christian. I am White. It would be different if I were a Black Jewish kid. They fought me from Day One. Same economic class, too. Once we got married, it all went away. There have been times, though, when Franny and I can go at it. She has some goofy ideas and I try to let things go. My cousin converted to Judaism and Franny could not imagine why she didn't need a blood transfusion to get rid of the Christian blood. That is her ignorance. That was such an ignorant, stupid way of thinking. We can strongly disagree and we can get through it. Our battles are usually not political but social. "You are going too

left," she might say to me, though anyone knowing me would see I was right of center. I can have a politically tough argument with her and we can still respect each other.

While they have reached a truce, to get there they had to, from Darlene's perspective, overcome some significant differences ranging from child-rearing approaches to basic decency:

She raised her kids in the 1950s, the old school way, so she would not under-stand that my kids are sheltered and it is a very different world than hers when kids could just go out and play. She always thought I was too protective. But our worst moments came when I had my first miscarriage. She couldn't understand what a miscarriage was. She was horrible. We had been trying for 20 years and we thought we couldn't have children, so when I got pregnant, we told everyone, which was a big mistake. "Well, what did you do to cause the miscarriage?" she said, which you don't tell a grieving mother; "you must have done something wrong." Then she told everyone that I imagined the whole thing, that I must have had a hysterical pregnancy that was a figment of my imagination. That infuriated me. It was her ignorance. She wasn't doing it to hurt me, even though she hurt me very much. She can't process what she hasn't experienced. My hus-band was so mad at her, but I said it was just a case of the stupids.

Like some of the other husbands we have described, Darlene's husband took a hands-off approach to the relationship between the women: "He is like, 'that's just her.' He has never come to my defense or to her defense; he is neutral. I don't attack her. We just call it a case of the stupids. It is great unless you are the victim. It is really her ignorance, and she is not trying to hurt you. That is how I have learned to deal with her."

Darlene is now capable of having a relationship with Franny within cer-tain boundaries and because Darlene has changed:

I can call her any day, any time. She is 90 and wobbly, but she would do whatever she could for me. I am blessed to be married to my best friend. If Franny and I have one bad conversation in a year, I can compartmentalize it with her. I am much more tolerant as I get older. It is getting grayer as we age and things are not as black and white.

Gabriella and Darlene have come to realizations about their mothers-in-law and their capabilities: Gabriella's mother-in-law is not emotionally accessible and Darlene's has a "case of the stupids." Yet they maintain the relationships while not considering themselves emotionally close to them.

They each accept the relationship for what it is and do not make it a major issue in their marriage, for the sake of their marriages.

While we can report that a majority of daughters-in-law feel close with their mother-in-law, it is in the attempt to define closeness that we see the nuances in how the relationships work. We now turn to other questions that arise in further understanding the range of relationships between daughters-in-law and mothers-in-law.

2. HOW MIGHT MY FAMILY HISTORY AFFECT MY RELATIONSHIP WITH MY MOTHER-IN-LAW?

The old cliché "the apple never falls far from the tree" implies that family history has a way of repeating itself. We hear this in "Like father, like son," and "Like mother, like daughter." People often wonder if families with significant disruptions, relocations, and health issues produce a next generation with a similar imprint just as they wonder if narratives of academic strength, athletic prowess, or emotional warmth will produce a next generation with a similar record.

Family theory supports the notion that interactional styles and behaviors are learned from one's family of origin and may repeat across generations. When describing their own parents' relationships with their parents-in-law (the daughter-in-law's grandparents), 51% of the daughters-in-law believed their mother was close with her in-laws while 61% believed their father was close with his in-laws. Daughters-in-law who believed their mother had a good relationship with her in-laws were closer with their own mother-in-law. Daughters-in-law who believed their father had a good relationship with his father-in-law were not necessarily closer with their mother-in-law. It may be that watching a mother navigate her relationship with her mother-in-law was instructive in how the daughter-in-law could have a good relationship. Being close with one's own mother or father, as most were, was not related to being close with one's mother-in-law.

From interviews, we saw that coming from a family where a lot of warmth was felt and shared has a strong influence on the daughter-in-law and how she navigates relations with the older generation. Kelly, a White 60-year-old textbook sales representative, has an exemplary relationship with both her mother-in-law and her daughters-in-law. But what makes her rare perhaps is that she also has a great relationship with her ex-mother-in-law. She and her first husband divorced after 20 years of marriage when he left for his secretary, as trite as that may sound: "His family thought he was a jerk for cheating and then a jerk for losing me," Kelly said. Kelly had been a breath of fresh air in his family. Her husband was one of four boys and the family was very emotionally contained. "I am a hugger and come from a family of huggers," she told us. "His family had never said 'I love you' to each other and after hanging around with me for a few years, they all started to be able to do that."

After the divorce, Kelly thought it was extremely important for her two children to have contact with their father's family, even though their father increasingly absented himself from them. She made the effort and it paid off. Now, 15 years later and remarried, Kelly stays with her ex-mother-in-law whenever she travels on business to Boston. Her earlier experiences of closeness with her family of origin have paid off for her in many ways. Now, with her two sons married, she is extremely close with her daughters-in-law: "Family was very important to me growing up and all the members remain very important to me now." She is an example of how early experiences in one's family can affect both older and younger generations and how one member of a family can have a positive impact on potentially problematic situations.

3. MY HUSBAND IS A DIFFERENT RACE/ETHNICITY/ RELIGION FROM ME. HE COMES FROM A DIFFERENT ECONOMIC BACKGROUND. WHAT CAN I EXPECT FROM MY MOTHER-IN-LAW?

Researchers have noted that homogamy, marriage between people who are similar in important cultural ways, promotes initial attraction and greater marital cohesion. For example, it has been reported that if a couple's race, religion, social class, or educational levels are the same, they will be more likely to share values as well as social network connections.[1] These similarities would likely also lead to greater ease when interacting with in-laws. At the same time, we are in a period of greater intermingling than ever before as people travel more, live farther from home, and interact with people different from themselves. These factors can lead to greater accept-ance of "others" joining the family than in previous generations. But how does this translate to in-law relationships?

In our sample, one in six of the daughters-in-law, like Sunny and Gabriella, were married to someone of a different religion and one in seven were mar-ried to someone of a different race, according to how they responded to specific questions on the survey. Perhaps reflecting recent social changes and greater acceptance, neither interfaith nor interracial marriages were predictive of the relationship quality between daughter-in-law and mother-in-law. Growing up in different economic circumstances than their husband/spouse, as one in three daughters-in-law did, also was not related to relationship quality. It may be that children who marry outside of their faith, racial group, or class were more likely to be raised by parents who were open to such differences.

One daughter-in-law, a Latina, felt embraced by her White mother-in-law, found her to be curious about the Latin culture, and said her mother-in-law wanted her grandchildren to speak Spanish. Despite some daughters-in-law feeling accepted, this does not mean that in some families there are not some disruptions with intermarriage, as these next two cases illustrate.

Lauren, a 35-year-old White psychologist, has been married for nine years to a man from Guyana. She said this about her mother-in-law: "My husband shared with me once that his mom made some comment about his not dating Whites or not dating White Americans because the cultural difference is too great and it would be too much of a struggle."

In another example, a 28-year-old Latina, Lora, married for two years to a biracial[2] man, had this to say about the differences in culture:

I don't have the best relationship with either one of my in-laws. In broad terms I think it is just their perception of me taints how they treat me and, in turn, I treat them that way back. I am not going to play too nice if I am being treated meanly. With my mother-in-law, the disconnect in our relationship comes from cultural expectations and sort of how she conducted herself in her household with her sons. She comes from a very male-dominant environment, and she conducts herself as such where she is super-submissive to the men in her life. While I found that I was able to submit in certain areas in my marriage . . . I also found that I am very opinionated and uncompromising in certain areas within my marriage and how I parent my sons versus how she does it. My father-in-law is married to a woman who is a specific way. His son is not married to a woman, me, who is that way, and so I think that he has opinions on that, which he has shared with me, that have caused us not to speak for extended amounts of time. We don't get along because we don't see eye to eye and we do not have the necessary conversations in order to do so. My mother-in-law is Vietnamese and one can only assume and, forgive me if I'm ignorant, that she was born and bred to serve their men in a way that Puerto Rican women are not. So while Latinos as a culture tend to be very homey and accommodating, loving, and family and all this stuff . . . there are limitations to what we will do. Ethnically and racially we just don't maintain our values the same way.

While differences between people based on identity seem to have grabbed the headlines in the last few years as justifications for division, within our total sample, an intermarriage did not affect intergenerational relationship quality, while for some it was a plus and for others a hurdle.

4. HOW WILL MY RELATIONSHIP WITH MY MOTHER-IN-LAW CHANGE WHEN MY SPOUSE AND I HAVE OUR FIRST CHILD?

Much has been written about how the birth of a child affects the relationship between the daughter-in-law and the mother-in-law. The research is of two minds: In some cases, the birth brings the women closer together while, in others, the birth brings the daughter-in-law closer to her own mother to the detriment of her relationship with the mother-in-law.[3] Of course, births happen in context. Sometimes children are born before marriage; other times the couple has struggled for years to bring a baby to term, as we heard from Darlene. For some, the pregnancy can be easy and for others, such as Darlene, it can be fraught with worry. When the son is an only child or the only one of his siblings to have children, the arrival of the next generation takes on special meaning. With the birth can come new challenges: financial strains; childcare needs; and possible clashing parenting philosophies that can manifest themselves immediately or as the children reach new developmental stages, when parents and grandparents can be tested by a sulking adolescent. A daughter-in-law may be able to accommodate or ignore in-laws she does not particularly care for before a child arrives or when the child is easy to care for, only to find herself feeling the need to shield the child from the grandparent in the later years, as we heard from Tara.

To understand the impact of having children, we looked at the daughter-in-law/mother-in-law relationship quality following the birth and at other times. For the daughters-in-law in our survey, nearly two-thirds had children from the marriage to the mother-in-law's son.[4] For over one-third, the birth was the first in the family. We asked about any changes in their relationship with their mother-in-law since the birth of the first child: 36% believed there had been little or no change in the relationship; 26% believed there had been a change for the better; 30% believed it had changed in some ways for the better and in some ways for the worse; and 9% believed it changed for the worse. From some we heard a description of the impact of the birth similar to what this daughter-in-law said: "I think we've gotten closer since the baby. I don't think we are extremely close. I mean, nothing has really changed in the past nine or 10 years. I think it spiked at marriage and again at Lily's birth. The big events bring us close." Another daughter-in-law was less sure of the impact of the birth for her but indicated it may have mattered to her mother-in-law: "No change on my part. I don't think that it was the birth of the child that produced the change in our relationship, but she may think differently about me now that I've produced a grandchild."

When looking further into the daughters-in-law who said there had been no change in the relationship, we see some who have a close relationship as well as some who do not have a close relationship. For those who already had a good relationship, the birth may have further solidified something that was working, and for those who were not close, the birth may not have enough of an effect to change the relationship.[5]

It is important to note, and perhaps surprising, that overall daughters-in-law with children report poorer relationship quality with their mothers-in-law than daughters-in-law without children. Why might that be? We think it is linked to parenting philosophy. Only 25% strongly agreed or agreed that they had the same parenting philosophy as their mother-in-law, with 52% strongly disagreeing or disagreeing that they have the same parenting philosophy. As expected, when parenting philosophies differ, the relationship is not as positive and daughters-in-law are more likely to say that the birth of the first child did not improve the relationship. While having a different parenting philosophy than the mother-in-law is related to having a less close relationship with the mother-in-law, it is not related to having a less close relationship with the father-in-law. It may be that the parenting philosophy of the father-in-law is less well known to the daughter-in-law. It could be that a mother-in-law is more likely to assert herself in parenting the grandchildren in a way that feels like interference to the daughter-in-law. It may also be that, if the father-in-law holds a different parenting philosophy, it has less of an interpersonal impact on the daughter-in-law by nature of his style of interacting with the daughter-in-law. Men tend to be more laid back in this relationship than women are and may have a less hands-on approach to grandparenting. Thus, any differences may not bump up as strongly against the daughter-in-law's approach.

We also asked whether the mother-in-law and/or father-in-law provide childcare. About one-quarter of the daughters-in-law receive childcare assistance; almost half of that group consider the amount of childcare assistance they receive to be very significant. When childcare is provided, the daughters-in-law report a better relationship quality with the mother-in-law. Childcare assistance occurs more often when the daughters-in-law believe they have a similar parenting philosophy as their mother-in-law. Of course, the daughter-in-law and son would be more willing to receive childcare and the grandparents to provide it if they share parenting philosophies. It could also be, however, that in-laws providing childcare may lead to increased shared thinking about parenting.

Sometimes problems in the relationship can emerge even before the birth of the child. This 43-year-old lawyer, Quinn, described such an interaction with her in-laws:

> While I was pregnant and we had been out shopping, I had seen a switch plate cover that was a Noah's Ark design. I was not looking for anything specific with that pattern. I thought it would be cute for the baby's room. She said, "Let me buy it for a baby gift." I have never been big into everything matching. I had already bought a lamp, bumper pads, and various things for the baby's room. A month later, I received this big package in the mail. She had been down the month before and knew I was decorating. By then I had completed the room and had it the way I liked it. The package arrives with a rug, bumper pads, crib sheets, light covers, lamp, and curtains with a Noah's Ark theme. It was ugly and I hated it, but she had spent a lot of money and she had bought everything to complete the baby's room based on the one little switch plate. I did not know how to react. I was very hormonal because I was about to give birth and here is my mother-in-law trying to take over *again*. I felt trapped because she had spent a lot of money and was expecting me to use the stuff and I did not want to disregard the fact that she just made this huge investment.

At that point, Quinn put her foot down and, in so doing, the relationship was set back:

> I did not want the baby's room decorated in this hideous pattern, so I confronted her. I said to my mother-in-law that we needed to talk and it was going to be a difficult conversation but I have to address this for the sake of our relationship and the sake of the kid. I explained that I kept a few of the items she sent but I was going to have to return the rest of the items. They are not what I want for the baby's room. I was not trying to be selfish or disrespectful and I appreciated what she had done for me, but this was my child and my house and it was too much. I felt like she was trying to take over. "Everything I do," I told her, "you do not approve of or you think I am doing it incorrectly. I will listen to your advice but I have to be able to make my own decisions, particularly in my baby's room. In my own home, I have to have the final say." This was the first of many conflicts, but over time, there have been less. Each time I have stood firm without going out of my way to be disrespectful. My parents-in-law do not like my assertiveness, but they respect it. It is somewhat weird, but they seem strangely impressed by it.

For Ida, a pregnant 37-year-old who has been married for two years, it already feels like the birth will separate the two women further:

She has been the worst! She doesn't really ask me how I'm doing. She doesn't even care how I'm doing because I haven't had the easiest pregnancy. She doesn't call me about it, nothing. Everything is through her son, who she sees once a week for two hours. She isn't really involved with me being pregnant. To outsiders, she is excited and can't wait to have her grandchild but has nothing to do with me. I just think she dislikes me so much she doesn't want it to be about me. I'm just a carrier of her legacy.

When no strong connection is forged between grandchild and grandmother after the birth, some daughters-in-law are disappointed: "I would say when our son was younger I was hopeful that we could try to build some type of relationship. It never really went that direction. We definitely have different ideas on parenting and different ideas about relationships. So, I don't think we have ever been able to bridge that gap."

Another daughter-in-law, Shari, echoed this disappointment:

She's really not involved. We have a kid now and, if the world were perfect, I would want my child to have a relationship with her grandmother. I guess there's a part of me that's irritated and angry that she doesn't show any interest, but I also feel like it's better this way, to just not have her involved, because, even if she was, she's not the person I would feel comfortable leaving my child with.

Having a child when the relationship is strong gives family members increased opportunities to spend time together. "It caused us to have more communication," this 30-year-old told us. "Before kids, we would maybe go over there on holidays and whatever, but, once we had kids, my mother-in-law wanted to be very involved. She would be over for birthdays and would come around more for them so, yeah, I would say it was just an increase in communication and we saw each other more often. They make her day."

Wendy, age 49, described how, even though the two women were close already, the birth brought them even closer. This relationship takes on special meaning for the mother-in-law because she is out of touch with one of her other children:

That was her first grandchild and grandchildren are extremely important to her. The fact that I trusted her to spend time alone with her—I stayed at home with my daughter at first and didn't let anybody watch her except her and my parents. I gave my mother-in-law the opportunity to develop a relationship with my daughter. When my daughter got older, I sent my daughter to her to spend a month in summer so she could continue to develop a relationship.

When the daughter-in-law feels close to the mother-in-law, as in this final example from Cora, everything the mother-in-law does gets framed in a positive light:

> I remember when the kids were about two or three, my mother-in-law told them that no one should be kissing them in the face because of germs. So when the kids got home and we tried to kiss them, they were like, "Oh, no. Grandma said nobody should be kissing us in the face." I was definitely shocked, but my husband and I explained to them that grandma is right and no one should kiss you in your face, but we're your parents so we're going to kiss you and grandma will have to be okay with that. If there is ever a time that I disagree with something she did or said to the kids, I never throw her under the bus in front of the kids.

5. HOW MIGHT MY PARENTS AFFECT MY RELATIONSHIP WITH MY MOTHER-IN-LAW?

The answer to this question has many interlocking components to it, which, from a family systems perspective, need consideration. The short answer is—it depends! For example, if the daughter-in-law is an only child, she will loom larger in her parents' life than if she has siblings. And, if she is an only child, the amount of time, financial support, and physical and emotional care her parents may need from her may affect her availability to be with her in-laws. (Similarly, if her husband/spouse is an only child, her mother-in-law may have a stronger interest in the relationship.) Regardless of her sibling status, if the daughter-in-law has not set appropriate boundaries with her parents before she married, then she and her husband may have difficulty doing that with the in-laws as a married couple. These factors, in turn, can affect the daughter-in-law's relationship with her mother-in-law, who may watch her son pulled into the vortex of his in-laws. If the daughter-in-law's parents are divorced, then she and her husband may have to split time with two, three, or even four households (if her parents are divorced), thus further pulling them both away from the parents-in-law. If her parents live closer to the grandchildren and have a stronger relationship with them, then the mother-in-law may feel left out.

Also to be considered is whether the two sets of parents are in competition with each other, as sometimes happens. If so, then the actions of the daughter-in-law's parents, giving more financial and childcare assistance, taking them on better vacations, or providing gifts that are more lavish, can fuel the competition.

Many in-law sets become close after the marriage and join each other for holidays and family events. Sometimes the two sets of parents grew up in the same community and knew each other even before their children starting dating. Longstanding relationships between people with shared histories can positively affect the daughter-in-law and mother-in-law relationship. Of course, preexisting contact between parents can also make family matters rather uncomfortable, as seen in this next example:

> Our in-laws' relationship is awkward. They did not want my husband and me to be together given that my mom had an affair with his dad when we were kids and that's how I met him. There is a lot of bad blood. It was something everyone wanted to put behind them and we were like, "Nahh" (laughing out loud). We were in love, so sorry for everybody.

According to the daughters-in-law, being close with their mother or father was unrelated to having a high-quality relationship with their mother-in-law. For daughters-in-law, the vast majority strongly agreed or agreed they were close with their mother (79%) and their father (72%). It is a common belief that if one is not close with one's parents, in-laws can fill that void. We would have expected that a lack of a relationship with parents could pull a daughter-in-law closer to her in-laws. But we also could have expected two other scenarios: (1) that a very close relationship with her parents could preclude a daughter-in-law from having emotional space for her in-laws, or (2) that being close with her parents taught her about being close with other parental figures. All three expectations could apply and pull the pattern in different directions, causing our overall survey responses to not show a particular trend.

While no trends emerged, here is an example of how the relationship with the mother does affect the relationship with the mother-in-law and can make things dicey. Carol is a White, 29-year-old school social worker, married for five years and with no children. What she describes is a potential tug-of-war or triangulation involving both mothers that eventually resolved itself:

> My mom and his mom consider each other friends now. They call each other and talk without me being around. It was a process leading up to it, though, because I am an only child and my mom can be a little, I don't want to say territorial, that's kind of a strong word. But she wanted to make sure my mother-in-law

knew that she was my mom and don't come over here and go too far, especially around the wedding. We went dress shopping and my mother-in-law asserted her opinion and my mom just kindly put her in her place. My mother-in-law got the hint. She never meant anything bad by it. She just was excited about it. My mother-in-law would say, "Oh, I love that dress," and my mom would be like, "Uhh, no." My mom knows me better because I am her daughter. Certain parts of wedding planning were a little stressful. My parents-in-law wanted to be super-involved and my parents thought that this was their only shot. My mom knew they had another child and this was her only chance. Ever since then, it has gotten progressively better. As I have talked to my mom about how difficult holidays were, she was more open to the idea of sharing us a little bit. I am married now and I cannot expect him to be with my family only for the holidays. We have to give and take a bit.

Seeing parents and parents-in-law getting along is usually a good sign for the relationship between the daughter-in-law and the mother-in-law. Specifically, when the daughter-in-law believes her mother-in-law is supportive of her relationship with her own parents, and even has her own relationship with her parents, it is a sign of a strong relationship with her mother-in-law.

Jealousy, though, involving the in-laws and the parents is a bad sign for the daughter-in-law and mother-in-law relationship. We found that the daughter-in-law and mother-in-law relationship was worse, as would be expected, when the daughter-in-law believed that her mother-in-law was jealous of the daughter-in-law's relationship with her own parents or when the daughter-in-law believed her mother-in-law was jealous of the relationship her son (the daughter-in-law's husband) had with the daughter-in-law's parents. This would be more likely to occur when the mother-in-law compares herself negatively, for whatever reason, to the daughter-in-law's parents and feels she cannot "measure up."

Jealousy involving both sets of in-laws can work the other way, too. When the daughter-in-law reports a good-quality relationship with her mother-in-law, she is more likely to perceive her own parents are jealous of the relationship she has with her mother-in-law. In other words, for some of the daughters-in-law, being close with a mother-in-law can be unsettling to the other set of parents. Of course, like many of our findings, this could be a chicken-and-egg situation in the other direction—when the daughter-in-law has parents who tend to be jealous, she may develop closer ties to her mother-in-law.

Having a strong relationship with a mother-in-law, however, does not always upset parents. Hopefully, that is what they want for their daughter, as in this next example, where the daughter-in-law, mother-in-law, and mother have all struggled with addiction:

> My mother-in-law runs an AA group at a prison. The fact that she's in recovery is also something that I admire. Actually, this is something that I realized just now. I always wanted my mom to stop drinking and she didn't, so it's kind of like . . . My mom's gotten a lot better, but my mother-in-law to me, I don't know how my mom would feel about this, my mom doesn't seem jealous that I really like my mother-in-law. She seems happy for me. It's very complicated. I think she's happy I'm married into a family that she likes and it gets me away from her extended family because they're crazy. I think her being in recovery is a part of it because I don't drink anymore. I always wanted my mother to quit and she never quit. And my mother-in-law is not only in recovery but she's made a healthy life-style out of it. She's just transcendent. I just really like her. I feel like the ways I like her, I'm like, "I could be like that."

While many mothers and mothers-in-law have a relationship, the relationships can be nonexistent *between* the in-law sets, as is Gabriella's situation where the two sets of parents live 3,000 miles away from each other. It is not that there is animosity; it is that they do not seem at all interested in each other or, in Gabriella's case, do not have any need for contact. One daughter-in-law told us, "Outside of wedding preparations and the occasions when the grandkids are at one grandparent's house versus the other and there are conversations with regard to pick-up or drop-off . . . there isn't a relationship."

Inevitably, even if it is not easily measured, the way the daughter-in-law integrates the two mothers into her life sends a powerful message to them both. The relationships will rarely remain static. As one parent or parent-set ages and needs more time and effort from the daughter-in-law and her spouse, the other set may receive less attention. Attention can never be divided evenly, nor do families have an infinite amount of time and resources.

6. WHAT PART MIGHT MY HUSBAND PLAY IN MY RELATIONSHIP WITH HIS MOTHER?

The role of the husband in the relationship between his mother and his wife must be considered, as his choice of spouse is what brought these two women together as family. While Darlene is an exception in that her husband plays almost no role between Darlene and her mother-in-law, many of the daughters-in-law talked about the importance of being close with their mother-in-law because she is meaningful to her husband. A daughter-in-law ignores her spouse's role at her peril, especially if the notion of family is important to her and others in the family. Writ large, the husband usually plays one of two roles: Either he can be the conduit between the women, with communication flowing through him, or he can encourage a separate relationship to occur between them—one in which he is not intertwined. Whichever way the communication flows, his role should not be underestimated.

To understand the husband's role we asked, "To what extent does your husband influence your relationship with your mother-in-law?" Two in five (41%) responded that he had a very positive or somewhat positive influence and slightly less than half (48%) responded he had little or no influence. The rest (11%) said he was a somewhat negative or very negative influence. For an example of a positive influence that a husband can have, Rikki told us about the teamwork that she and her husband demonstrate and the message that it sends to their in-laws:

> I think having him [husband] stand up for me. Us working as a team improves because when your in-laws see you working as a team, that will make them understand that you two are together and you're meant for each other. If they see that you're having a confrontation and never get along, then probably that will influence the way things go between you. It's good for any parent to see their kid and their spouse getting along.

This teamwork was echoed by Sunny, whom we use as an example of someone who gets along well with her mother-in-law and who said that her husband never "vented" to his parents about her. A different daughter-in-law put it this way: "We have always supported each other and we are a united front against outside influences. We address others together." These women have husbands who stand beside them and put a clear boundary around the relationship, which not only strengthens their own relationship but also defines, by extension, their relationship with their mother-in-law.

Showing a united front can look different from one family to the next. Some daughters-in-law have husbands who actively defend them by inserting themselves in the middle of the relationship, as with the example from this 37-year-old married for 10 years:

> I learned that I need to let my husband be the one to deal with his family and to kind of back off and not get involved with them because things had gotten so bad that I couldn't let go of the negative comments and judgments his mother had towards me. By shifting the responsibility to my husband in dealing with her, I don't hear them anymore, so they don't affect me as much.

This 33-year-old daughter-in-law also argues for leaving the heavy lifting to the husband when dealing with his family: "I think having your husband involved in creating and defining the dynamics of the relationship is important. He deals with the direct conflicts and I get to do the more background stuff and sometimes the more fun stuff, like taking her shopping."

Naturally, if the daughter-in-law believes her husband is close with his parents, she will want to make the relationship with them work for her husband's happiness. Sixty-nine percent of daughters-in-law believed their husband was close with his mother and 63% believed he was close with his father. (We consistently found that the adult children are closer with their mother than their father and that they perceive their spouse to be closer with their mother than their father. These differences in perceptions about closeness to each parent are discussed in later chapters.) With the majority of daughters-in-law holding such a belief about their husband's relationship with his parents, it would be expected that she, too, would want to be close with them, especially considering that almost 90% strongly agreed or agreed that they were happy with their marital relationship. Whatever the daughters-in-law are doing seems to be working; nearly three-quarters of the daughters-in-law believe that their husband is happy with the relationship she has with his mother, and only one in eight agreed their husband thinks they need to work harder on their relationship with their mother-in-law. Connecting the dots, then: When the daughter-in-law has a happy marriage and believes that her husband is happy with the relationship that she has with her mother-in-law, the women's relationship is closer.

Ideally, family members should be able to interact with each other without feeling they are walking on "flypaper." But that does not stop a number from getting that flypaper feeling. Almost one in four daughters-in-law sometimes feel caught between their husband and their mother-in-law, and one in five feel uneasy about their husband's relationship with his mother. We can harken back to Monica's story of the intense relationship between her husband and mother-in-law to have a clear example of how both of these feelings might develop. Almost one in six feel their mother-in-law interferes in their marriage. George Martin's wife, Sheena, would definitely say her mother-in-law did that when chasing her while wielding a kitchen knife.

Discomfort about the relationship can derive from a daughter-in-law feeling that her husband is too close to his mother, as we also saw with Monica, and as we see in this next example from Carla, a White, 35-year-old nurse with two children. Married for seven years, Carla had heard how resilient her mother-in-law was after a divorce from her husband's father:

She remarried one other time when my husband was younger and that didn't work out. Ever since, she lived on her own and did a whole bunch of different things occupation-wise. She took care of the house, landscaped the property, and had tenants that lived there. She seemed to be in control of everything. But under the surface she is not in control of much of anything.

When Carla first met her husband, she was impressed by how caring he was:

My husband had a really close relationship with her and I thought, "Wow, this is great" . . . Almost like best friends. But the more I got to know, they really were like an emotional support for each other. My husband's brother is very successful. He is very analytical in his thinking. My mother-in-law and my husband are more emotionally driven. My brother-in-law didn't need her, while my husband is the one who needed her around. So he turned into the person who never left her.

Carla described her husband as a mama's boy before mother and son reversed roles and his mother became dependent on him:

She tries to present like she really doesn't need him. If she is struggling with something, he will say, "I'll just do it." And she will be like, "No. No. I don't need you to do it." But she does need him to do it, so their relationship is strange. My relationship with her is unstable just because of fluctuations that have occurred so often. She's very insecure. She's very sensitive. She's very needy.

As Carla's husband gained a bit of emotional distance from his mother, it became easier for Carla to deal with her. That distancing between mother and son also helped to strengthen the boundary around Carla and her husband's marriage and reinforced how the husband's behavior can have a direct effect on the women's bond.

7. WHAT PART MIGHT MY FATHER-IN-LAW PLAY IN MY RELATIONSHIP WITH MY MOTHER-IN-LAW?

"He is active in my children's lives but in a different way than my mother-in-law. He isn't as emotionally invested in them as she is. He and I have a polite, courteous, and positive relationship, but we aren't close at all. I don't do things with him and the kids like I do things with my mom-in-law and the kids." While this daughter-in-law is describing the role many fathers-in-law (and fathers) play in a family,[6] in any one family, the father/father-in-law may be the more central and emotionally available figure. From the interviews, we saw many examples of a better daughter-in-law/father-in-law relationship than daughter-in-law/mother-in-law relationship. One daughter-in-law told us, "I'm closer to him than to her. I don't know why. I just feel closer to him—he's easier." As a result, the daughter-in-law sees both her in-laws more. We have heard of other situations where, because of this cross-gender closeness, the mother-in-law has more contact with the grandchildren. In effect, the father-in-law's closeness enables the mother-in-law to have greater contact and a higher-quality relationship.

Almost 40% of the daughters-in-law stated they felt closer to their mother-in-law than their father-in-law; the rest either disagreed with that statement (35%) or gave a neutral response (27%).[7] Even when the father-in-law is the less actively engaged in-law, he may influence the mother-in-law in her relationship with the daughter-in-law by coaching her on how to act and by being an intermediary between them as a way to reduce tension. He may be helping with childcare or with financial support, which can further cement the relationship between the daughter-in-law and mother-in-law and allow greater contact. When the father- and mother-in-law work as a team, they are usually more fun to be around. The father-in-law's behavior influences his wife's and vice versa, which, when positive, makes interactions with a happy couple more pleasant for the daughter-in-law.

It should be noted that, in cases where the father-in-law is absent or not emotionally available, the mother-in-law's availability as a parent and grandparent takes on increased importance. In this way, it is his absence that influences the relationship.

8. WHAT HAPPENS WHEN MY MOTHER-IN-LAW IS CLOSER TO ANOTHER CHILD-IN-LAW THAN TO ME?

No one likes to feel as if she is not liked as much as someone else. When a daughter-in-law feels she is less well liked than another child-in-law, it may be because she entered the family later, has less "chemistry" with her mother-in-law, lives farther away, or is raising grandchildren in a way that makes the mother-in-law uncomfortable. It could be that her spouse is not as well liked and so she suffers by association, or, on the other hand, her spouse is the "favorite" child and therefore she gets an unwelcome level of scrutiny and judgment. Being of a different race, ethnicity, or religion has historically been problematic with family relations,[8] although this did not prove to be the case in our sample. At the same time, there can be a good deal of closeness between the daughter-in-law and the mother-in-law yet the daughter-in-law believes the mother-in-law just happens to be closer with another child-in-law.

Feeling less liked than another child-in-law is common. One-third of the daughters-in-law believed that their mother-in-law was closer to another child-in-law than to her. Consistent with that belief, daughters-in-law who had that feeling felt less close with their mothers-in-law than those who did not hold that belief. Of course, some daughters-in-law may not mind being less close, especially if their husband/spouse feels less close and they do not like their mother-in-law. They may not mind being the less favored if that frees them from spending time with the mother-in-law.

As we dig deeper into the responses, we find that if the daughter-in-law feels her mother-in-law is closer to another child-in-law than to her, that may be symptomatic of other significant problems that may be afoot. For example, she is more likely to be unhappy with her marriage and is less communicative with her husband about her feelings toward her mother-in-law. She is more likely to feel that her mother-in-law hinders her marriage, that she sometimes feels caught between her mother-in-law and her husband (triangulation), and that her husband wants her to work harder on her relationship with his parents. These feelings are interrelated and it is hard to say they start at any one point. In other words, having a weaker marriage may be related to, but not caused by, feeling less liked.

We wondered if not being the first in-law to marry into the family could be related to not feeling closer than another child-in-law. It was not. Not being the first one to bring children into the family was also unrelated to feeling closer to the mother-in-law than another child-in-law. The distance that the couple lives from the mother-in-law was also not related to feeling favored.

In sum, when a daughter-in-law feels less liked than another child-in-law, it appears in our data that may be a symptom of other issues in the marital relationship.

9. I HAVE DIFFICULTY BALANCING TIME BETWEEN BOTH SIDES OF THE FAMILY. IS THAT TYPICAL?

Time is the coin of the realm for couples. The couple, particularly when they are starting out, have to negotiate how much time to spend with each side of their family, how much time to spend alone as a couple, how much time to spend with their couple friends, how much time to spend with their own friends apart from the couple, and how much time to spend alone. If children are present, another important demand on time is in the mix. Expectations about time management can vary greatly. In some cultures and for some families, there are few boundaries between the immediate family and the extended family; in collectivist cultures, as soon as you marry you become part of a wide family network. In other cultures, the expectations are that newlyweds will set out on their own and be more independent.

Today, it is less likely than ever that family members will be living near each other when children reach adulthood, although, according to the Pew Research Center, there are significant state-to-state variations in mobility. Alaska is the state that is least likely to hold on to its residents, whereas Texas is the most likely.[9] Not only do some couples struggle to balance time when their in-laws live nearby, they struggle when they have to travel to visit, as did Lenny, whom we quoted earlier in this chapter. Finding time may be especially difficult if the couple is in the "sandwich" generation— the phase of life when adults feel squeezed between taking care of their children and their aging parents.

One in four daughters-in-law in our survey believe they and their husband have difficulty balancing time between both families. This struggle can take many forms. If the daughter-in-law and her husband want to spend time with her parents, does she have to spend the same amount of time with his? If one set of parents is divorced, does that require spending time with each parent that is equal to the total time spent with the married in-laws? What if one set of parents needs the couple more than another set? What if one set of in-laws is helping (childcare, financial support) more than the other set? What if grandchildren enjoy visiting one set of in-laws more than the other? How does travel time for a visit fit into the equation? Does an only child need to spend time with her parents more than a child who is one of many siblings?

From our analyses, some commonalities emerged among the daughters-in-law who have trouble balancing both families. As expected, they are younger and have been married for fewer years, consistent with what we know about newly married couples. It takes a few years of life experience and marriage for some couples to figure out what their boundaries are and how they will include both sets of in-laws in their lives. Less happily married couples are more likely to struggle with this balancing act.

Couples also have greater difficulty balancing demands when the daughter-in-law feels the mother-in-law interferes in her life, when the daughter-in-law feels the mother-in-law is manipulative, and when the daughter-in-law feels the mother-in-law is emotionally needy. All these feelings evoke the worst stereotypes of mothers-in-law, yet they are true for about one in six daughters-in-law in this sample.

Living a distance away from the mother-in-law matters too, with the greater the distance, the greater the difficulty in balancing the demands. Balancing is also more problematic if parenting philosophies differ between daughter-in-law and mother-in-law.

Then there is the matter of jealousy that we discussed in response to a previous question. If the daughter-in-law perceives her mother-in-law as being jealous of the daughter-in-law's relationship with her own parents (as 13% did) or the relationship the mother-in-law's son has with the daughter-in-law's parents (as 19% did), balancing the two sets of in-laws is more difficult. But it is not only on the mother-in-law's side that problems may arise. Both sets of parents are more difficult to balance if the daughter-in-law perceives her *own* parents as being jealous of her relationship with her in-laws (as 9% did).

Sometimes a history of substance abuse or mental health struggles can make family interactions more difficult. We found here, too, that a history of substance abuse or mental health issues (as reported by about one in four of the daughters-in-law) as experienced by the daughter-in-law, her husband, or her in-laws (i.e., almost anywhere in the family system) is related to greater difficulty in balancing both sides of the family.

The amount of time also is related to the balancing act daughters-in-law confront. If the daughter-in-law believes she is spending either too little time (as 19% did) or too much time (as 8% did) with the mother-in-law, she struggles with balancing her time with both sets of in-laws. Finding the "sweet spot" in the amount of time spent with a mother-in-law is clearly important to the daughters-in-law.

CONCLUSION

We have described the many variations in these complicated daughter-in-law and mother-in-law relationships. While the majority of daughters-in-law have a good-quality relationship with their mother-in-law, variations exist and nuances are manifold. There are those with marvelous, loving, and unencumbered relationships and those who keep their mother-in-law at arm's length and want little to do with her. Some daughters-in-law are unclear about their role in relationship to their mother-in-law and struggle to define it while striving to be supportive of their husband. Some work to have a good relationship with their mother-in-law because of their husband's commitment and because they believe that grandchildren need grandparents. Others see limitations in their mother-in-law and accept that they may never have a great relationship with her; they are emotionally secure enough to accept her for who she is. And most experience multiple versions of these various types of relationships at different times in their married lives.

For those interested in experiences of daughters-in-law, a close reading of Chapter 3, on mothers-in-law, will be instructive of their perspectives. In Chapter 8, we describe how these relationships vary across gender (i.e., how the men's relationships differ from the women's) and how the context of these intergenerational relationships is framed by different perceptions of how close daughters-in-law and mothers-in-law really are.

CHAPTER 5

Fathers-in-Law and Their Relationship with Their Son-in-Law

Over 100 years ago, in most cultures, it was the father who "ruled the roost" by fulfilling a patriarchal role. Today, while men are still the primary breadwinners in most families, men's roles are slowly blurring with women's in the family just as women's are blurring with men's roles in the workplace. Men are doing more childcare and housework and women are more likely to be in management and professional positions and earning an equal or even greater share of the family income. Fathers are less likely to be the sole breadwinner and more likely to be driving a child to the pediatrician or soccer practice than their fathers were. They also, with the exception of some religious communities, have less influence about whom their children marry.

As the vestiges of male and female stereotypes are still extant, the father-in-law and son-in-law relationship continues to operate in the context of what it means to be both a father and a man in our culture. A father is likely to hold expectations for himself that he may have learned from his father or from other influential men in his life. He is also likely to hold expectations for the man who marries his daughter if she is heterosexual (see Chapter 7 for gay and lesbian in-law relationships). He may carry, for example, expectations for the way his son-in-law treats his daughter, the way the son-in-law raises their children, and the way he performs as a provider and in the workplace. It is important to note that the expectations for men in families are not universal; they may represent, on the one hand, traditional values and, on the other hand, contemporary values. In their 2010 book *Red Families Vs. Blue Families: Legal Polarization and the Creation of Culture*, Naomi Cahn and June Carbone offer a picture of American families that includes those who adhere to a traditional approach where the man is the head of the household (red families, predominantly found in the Midwest, the Bible Belt, and rural neighborhoods) and those who adhere to an equity model between spouses with shared roles (blue families, found in urban centers and on the east and west coasts). We also see that clash of values in the movie *Meet the Fockers* where Ben Stiller, as the future son-in-law, does not meet the expectations of his father-in-law, played by Robert DeNiro (a former CIA operative), of what it means to be a man—Stiller plays a nurse in the movie. Fathers-in-law whom we surveyed and interviewed came from across the United States and from almost every state. They may hold very different expectations for a son-in-law consistent with the community in which they live. We interviewed fathers-in-law who have very open and meaningful conversations with their sons-in-law apart from the women in their lives and fathers-in-law who leave such communication to the women. As one father-in-law joked, "I will call him and he will call me and be like, 'Happy Father's Day' and then we are like, 'Here's your mother' (laughs). That's about it."

In addition, the expectations for a son-in-law are likely based, at least in part, on the father's own intergenerational history of balancing work with family demands.[1] Being a father also can mean different things based on one's family background, including race, ethnicity, and religion. Some fathers give greater valence to spending time at work in loving support of their family, while others give greater valence to spending time with family.

We can add one more expectation to what the father-in-law may hold for a son-in-law: what he learned from his parents about interacting with others. As an example, take Pete, a White, 54-year-old minister, who learned from his father how women were to be treated. What he sees in his son-in-law grates on him:

> My son-in-law was raised differently than our daughter was raised. Nothing major; just little things. I was brought up in a home where courtesy, manners, treating my mom with respect, and opening her door because my dad told us to. He trained us a lot with that and I don't see that stuff in my son-in-law as much as I would like to. When we see a lack of manners, it's not something that hurts us. It's just sometimes we wish was different. The little things, like crossing a busy street, without showing concern for his wife. He will go ahead and cross where I was brought up to watch out for that kind of stuff. It's not one event but it's just little things like that we notice that we wish were different.

Being a father and husband, as noted, is entwined with what it means to be a man, and therefore is also often tied to what it means to be masculine. Masculinity has traditionally centered around control, strength, success, and reliability,[2] qualities that a father-in-law might value in himself and might want to see in a son-in-law. Men tend to feel more comfortable around men who exhibit their same level of masculinity.[3] When there is a sense from the father that his son-in-law fits the father's version of masculinity, the relationship may go more smoothly. Some of the successful father-in-law and son-in-law relationships that we found centered on the two men being friends with each other, appreciating each other's company, and sharing similar interests. We heard from fathers-in-law who enjoyed going for beers with their son-in-law, talking sports, or being active in the same way, as epitomized by this next example: "We have a good time together. He goes hunting with me. We watch football. He gets along good with my sons. He is an all-around great guy." So the son-in-law may not only be good father/husband material, but he may also match up with the father-in-law's expectation for manhood and, as portrayed in this last example, fit in well with the other men in the family.

THE FATHER–DAUGHTER BOND

The linchpin in the father-in-law and son-in-law relationship is, of course, the father-in-law's daughter and his relationship with her—just as the son is the linchpin in the mother-in-law's relationship with her daughter-in-law.[4] It has been hypothesized that a daughter having a positive and healthy relationship with her father paves the way for her successful intimate relationship with another person.[5] For many fathers and daughters, a positive relationship can be manifested in the father protecting his daughter. For example, this father talks about what it is like as a father to see his daughter with someone else, the son-in-law:

> My concerns about my daughter are different from my wife's concerns about our daughter. My wife was concerned about how judgmental I was going to be because this is the guy who was going to step in an essentially take my place. My wife and I used to joke when the kids were little about how I used to say to my daughters when they asked, "When can we date?" and I would say, "When I'm dead." I would joke about it, but I think my wife always would say, "You're going to be a tough one to get by." So I think that when she saw the way I welcomed

Earl and how I've gotten along with him, that was a great relief to her. She was always concerned about what standards I was going to hold the guys to.

If the relationship is good between the father and daughter and she has a happy marriage, the path will be smoothed for a good relationship with the son-in-law. If the father has a good relationship with the daughter, he would be more likely to approve of her mate selection and to do whatever he can to make his relationship with the son-in-law work. Of course, it may be easy to approve of the son-in-law if the father and daughter are close as she is likely to be attracted to a spouse who will fit in well with the family and would help preserve the father–daughter closeness. Thus, with a good father–daughter bond the table is set for a good father-in-law/son-in-law relationship.

If the father–daughter relationship is strained, however, the father may even warn off his potential son-in-law about his daughter if he feels that she is going to be difficult to live with. Singer Eddie Fisher, perhaps reflecting on his own unsatisfactory marriage to Debbie Reynolds, reportedly told his son-in-law, singer Paul Simon, when Simon asked for advice about his relationship with Fisher's daughter Carrie (of *Star Wars* fame), "Who told you to fall in love with an actress?"[6]

The key point is that fathers usually have conscious and unconscious expectations about the man who will marry their daughter. These expectations are based on the social context in which he is living and his own history with his family of origin. They are also based on his experiences in his current family—including his wife and any other children they may have—and his perception of the kind of spouse with whom his daughter would be happiest.

While we focus on the men's relationship, to understand them fully, it is necessary to gain the perspective of the sons-in-law that we provide in Chapter 6. Like the women's in-law relationships, the intergenerational perspectives do not always match up. It is also important to consider the role that the daughter and wife of the father-in-law play. We wish to emphasize that we do not believe an understanding of men's roles in the family should be gained by using a lens that is constructed for women's roles any more than women's roles should be viewed through a lens by what works for men. Yet, one important distinction emerges from the interviews. The father-in-law, because his daughter is the mother of the grandchildren, is more likely, than a mother-in-law who has a son, to have greater access to grandchildren. In many families, and despite the increased sharing of parental roles and remembering the red family/blue family paradigm, women spend more time with and raising children, largely determine access to them, and therefore often function as social managers in the family.[7]

In general, many fathers-in-law feel close to their son-in-law and describe qualities and behaviors in their sons-in-law that they view as positive: He treats their daughter well; he is a good parent and treats his own parents well; he has good work habits; and he shares in childcare and housework and makes a good team with the daughter.

Given the range and complexities of these relationships, we draw on survey data and in-person interviews (which tended to be shorter than the interviews with the mothers-in-law) to illuminate the nuances. What follows are 10 questions that we believe are frequently on the minds of fathers-in-law and can guide understanding of their relationship with their son-in-law.

1. ARE FATHERS-IN-LAW CLOSE TO THEIR SON-IN-LAW?

Because a single question on a survey is insufficient to measure the variety of relationships that exist between in-laws, as we did with the mothers-in-law, we created a variable by combining seven items on our survey that looked at the quality of the father-in-law/son-in-law relationship from a number of perspectives. Five positively framed statements were included: "I am close with my son-in-law;" "I admire my son-in-law;" "I can ask my son-in-law for advice;" "I trust my son-in-law;" and "I enjoy spending time with my son-in-law." Two negatively framed statements were also included: "I avoid my son-in-law" and "I have problematic conflicts with my son-in-law." We chose these seven because we believe they reflect the range of interactions and feelings that can exist between the two men. A father-in-law might trust his son-in-law but not especially enjoy spending time with him. This could be a qualitatively different relationship than one where he both trusted his son-in-law and enjoyed spending time with him. Similarly, a father-in-law could have problematic relations with his son-in-law but still feel that he could ask him for advice. As it is rare that there is not at least some ambivalence in relationships, with this variable we aggregate a series of questions that try to capture the ups and downs.

Approximately 68% to 80% agreed or strongly agreed with each positive statement while similarly approximately 85% disagreed or strongly disagreed with the negative statements. Specifically: 19% of the fathers-in-law strongly agreed they were close with their son-in-law (53% more agreed), 32% strongly agreed they admired their son-in-law (47% agreed); 23% strongly agreed they could ask their son-in-law for advice (44% agreed); 26% strongly agreed they enjoyed spending time with their son-in-law (54% agreed); 46% strongly agreed they trusted him (39% more agreed). For the negatively framed statements, only 1% strongly agreed they avoided him (only 2% more agreed) and 1% strongly agreed they had a problematic conflict with him (2% agreed). We looked for fathers-in-law with high levels of agreement with the positive statements and high levels of disagreement with the negative ones as exemplars of good relationship quality with a son-in-law.[8] We use this seven-item variable measuring relationship quality to answer a number of our questions related to closeness between the father-in-law and son-in-law. However, we use the term *close* only as a shortcut to describe the feelings that the father-in-law has for his son-in-law. We realize one adjective cannot fully capture such a multifaceted and often dynamic relationship.

In addition to the high levels of positive feelings evidenced by their responses to the survey statements we just reported, a number of other items also reflected good feelings between the two men. More than two-thirds said their son-in-law was attentive to them and three-quarters said the son-in-law was warm to them. In addition, almost half of the fathers-in-law agreed or strongly agreed they shared similar interests with their son-in-law (which predicts better relationship quality). These response rates are remarkably similar to what mothers-in-law reported about their daughter-in-law.

While sharing interests, being attentive, and being warm are positively framed, we also included other, negatively framed items: one in seven agreed or strongly agreed that they maintained some emotional distance from their son-in-law and more than one in five were neutral in their response to that statement. Very few fathers-in-law, only one in 33, indicated they walked on eggshells around their son-in-law, with one in 12 giving a neutral response. One in 25 felt their son-in-law made them nervous, with one in 11 giving a neutral response. What we take from these responses is that very few fathers-in-law have extreme difficulty with their son-in-law; additionally, when including the neutral responses, we see that a significant minority neither agree nor disagree with some of the feelings we were exploring, reflecting neither great comfort nor discomfort. If the father-in-law believes the son-in-law has struggled with mental health or substance abuse issues, as one in 12 reportedly had, our data show that can hinder the quality of the relationship. A few fathers-in-law reported their daughter had struggled with substance abuse or mental health issues and they were less close to those daughters.

Moving away from survey responses, which can usually only offer a broad-brush perspective on relationships, we want to provide a deeper dive into fathers-in-law and their son-in-law. To do this, we have chosen a few cases that illustrate outstanding relationships, a few that are highly problematic, and a few that are in a gray area, often characterized by neutral responses, that have some level of comfort but are neither especially close nor distant.

When a Relationship Is Highly Satisfying

Phil

Phil is a 64-year-old, African American, college-educated engineer who is retired from the military. When asked about the importance of his relationship with Geoff, his son-in-law of three years, he answered, "If you want to have a successful family, you want the son-in-law to fit in just like your kids. To me, the son-in-law is just an extension of your kids ideally. Just like it's very important to have a good relationship with my daughters, I ought to have a good relationship with my son-in-law."

This next comment from Phil exemplifies the earlier discussion about what many fathers want for their daughter—someone who will care for her, care for the couple's children, and be a good provider. And he adds another standard by which some fathers-in-law judge their son-in-law:

> I like the way Geoff looks after Sarah (Phil's daughter) and the way he looks after his kids. As far as career goals, he's working hard and he seems to be a person that's looking ahead. He has a good relationship with his mother, and that's one of the things that I admired him for. I judge people by how they treat their parents. If you're not going to treat your parents well, you're probably not going to treat your spouse well. I don't know all their business, but what I see looks good.

We also hear from Phil his impression of what a man's role should be in a marriage:

> They communicate all the time. When one goes somewhere, they call each other so they know where they are at. They do the housework together inside and outside. She helps outside, he helps inside. When he comes home, he takes care of the babies and she goes where she gotta go. They do everything together. They plan financially together.

Phil learned a great deal from his relationship with his own mother-in-law:

When I married Mildred, her father had already died, but her mother and I were real close. That relationship gave me a guide because, when you have a close relationship, things go so much better. It was a guide for me because, if you experience good things, then it's going to lead you down that path to do good things for other folks.

Phil interacts directly with Geoff without having to go through his daughter, Sarah:

We've made Geoff feel like part of the family. When they got married, we said, "We gonna treat him like we would treat the girls." He's our son now, so we include him in things and make him feel comfortable. He doesn't have to be with Sarah now to ask me stuff. He'll bring up subjects and call me. I'm comfortable with him and he's comfortable with me.

Robert

Robert, a White, 58-year-old financial advisor, describes his son-in-law, Mark, in glowing terms even though his relationship with him has gone through some rocky periods:

Mark is a teacher and, from an educational perspective, he's very well rounded. We have similar traits, values, and characteristics that foster our good relationship. He's very mature. He understands things financially. He's very analytical. As far as being proud of what he's done career-wise, he has taken jobs that are a lot of responsibility. As a result, he is quite successful. I see him marching up the corporate ladder due to his hard work and dedication.

While Robert describes a very close relationship with Mark now, it has not been without significant challenges. Mark had a substance abuse problem that he has since overcome:

We were very supportive and Mark was very proactive after some unfortunate situations where he realized he needed help. He immediately checked himself into AA, where he has since graduated. Through our support, through our daughter, Jenna, and her support, he has moved forward in life and is completely clean. He never drinks. That was the toughest thing my wife Sherry and I have helped them through. They did a lot themselves but they relied heavily on us. He's come a long way and he's doing great. We each went to a meeting that he had requested so we could get a feel for the atmosphere. That proved to him that we really cared. Once that was done, our relationship has become even stronger. Even though it was very negative, we learned a lot from it and now we are all better off.

In his description of Geoff, Robert also talks about the importance of his son-in-law being good father material: "He will be better equipped to make critical life decisions as he becomes a new father. He'll be able to tell his children that life isn't always easy and that there are obstacles that you overcome. I'm proud of how much he's grown and overcome such a serious problem in today's world."[9]

Two different fathers-in-law with different paths to what they each consider a very close relationship with their son-in-law. One has been smooth sailing all along and one has seen his son-in-law, with the support of his daughter, overcome adversity. Both admire their son-in-law and like the interaction they observe between their son-in-law and daughter. Such observations reinforce for the fathers that their daughters are with good men. Other fathers-in-law, as we show with this next group, do not enjoy such comfort.

When Relationships Struggle

Harry

Harry is a 60-year-old, divorced African-American retired military man who works in human resources. He has a strained relationship with his 33-year-old son-in-law, Derrick, who currently lives 25 miles away: "He's lazy. He doesn't have the mentality that I think a young man should have when he got married and took responsibility." Harry, in returning to the earlier point about paternal expectations for a son-in-law, assumed his daughter would marry someone like himself who would be a good provider. He finds it hard to respect Derrick and had to chastise him at one point:

I was deployed, and he was staying in the household, and he was not tidy. I couldn't deal with it at the time, but I sent him an email and let him know what occurred to me, pictures that were sent to me, that he wasn't being clean the way I keep things in my home. He responded to it, "Oh, you know me, Mr. R. I'm keeping everything straight." But I have pictures to show that he wasn't.

Harry added that, to avoid direct conflict with Derrick, he addresses his daughter about Derrick's behavior rather than confronting Derrick himself.

Harry found it difficult to describe a positive event in relation to Derrick. "Sometimes he tries," Harry told us. "But not as much as I think he should in reference to trying to do the right thing by taking care of the household." Harry is unsure how well his daughter and Derrick work as a team: "She's like me; she's a go-getter. She wants to make sure the I's are dotted, T's are crossed, taking care of the household and trying to do the best she can do to live right. He's not taking care of the bills but she is right there picking up the slack."

As an accumulation of what he has observed, and in line with Harry's view of what a husband should be and do, the relationship has deteriorated over time: "He's not stepping up being the man he's supposed to be."

Abram

Abram is a White, 64-year-old retiree. When asked if his relationship with Brian, his son-in-law, was important, he said, "It's not important to me. He's not my kind of person. He's somebody who makes my daughter happy, that's all." Abram understands and accepts that his son-in-law puts his own family of origin first but is not happy with that prioritizing:

> In terms of my family, he's an integral part. So if I'm doing something and I want the whole family to attend, I would want Brian to attend. There was an occasion when he was angry and he pulled himself away. This was during a wedding of one of my other children and he decided he didn't want to be part of it. He refused to be part of the pictures and it made a hole in the wedding service. It's hurtful if he's not part of the family. On the other hand, he has his own family and his family is his family. His loyalties are his loyalties.

Cultural differences can sometimes pull people together in excitement about learning anew about others. For Abram, the cultural differences in their two Jewish families is difficult to bridge:

> Our relationship is almost nonexistent because we had enough friction in the past because my ways and his ways are not the same. Brian was raised in what we would call a Persian household and . . . I was raised in a Polish household. We have different ways of behavior and he's an orphan on both sides [he was abandoned by his father and his mother died]. My understanding is that he was taught to behave in different patterns than I was.

Abram recounted a story about his wife preparing a meal for the whole family and putting an ingredient in a soup that Brian did not like. Since then, Brian brings his own food to the house: "He refuses to eat in our home except for pizza, which he buys himself, which is grossly insulting to us because we feed the world. And he knows that he's doing that to us. But what can I do? The attitude that causes him to be so angry is something he has to work on."

Abram grudgingly admits that the differences between them are more his problem than his daughter's: "He makes my daughter happy, lovely for my daughter. I'm very happy for them and I feel that my daughter is blessed with such a relationship. They are hard to find and he's the parent of my grandchildren."

They live 200 miles away from each other and do not have frequent contact, which Abram believes is for the better: "If we were close together, we would be killing each other."

In addition to noting the happiness in his daughter, Abram views Brian as a hard worker and, when asked to recall a positive event, noted the care that Brian helps provide Abram's mother-in-law (his daughter's maternal grandmother), who lives near his daughter and Brian: "I talk to my daughter constantly. I talk to my grandchildren constantly. Even to the point I help them with their homework. But he [Brian] is who he is." Abram has six other children, five of whom are married. He has good relationships with most of his children-in-law but a problematic one with a daughter-in-law. Abram struggled with his own in-laws, too.

Like Harry's and Derrick's, the relationship has not improved with time. When asked how comfortable he would feel talking about a range of potentially sensitive topics with Brian, many were off-limits (e.g., issues in his family, work issues, money issues), which may make Brian not feel included in the family. Abram has resigned himself to its current state: "It is strained. I will say that keeping distance at this point in my life is the smartest thing I can do because if I try to push, I will get resistance." Abram offers the following advice. "In Yiddish, we'd say the three *shins*. *Shvigin*—be silent. *Shaychen*—send them gifts. *Shtelen*—do not undercut him."

Neither of these men have the respect for their son-in-law they would like to have, but Abram can at least find some positive attributes in Brian in relation to Abram's daughter. Both have seen their relationship deteriorate and their sons-in-law are not playing the roles in their families that they should—Derrick is not being the provider and Brian is not willing to include himself in Abram's family and continues to separate himself by bringing his own food.

In addition to these two cases, we have also heard from fathers-in-law with other significant rifts with their son-in-law. In one case, the daughter, at the son-in-law's strong encouragement, converted to her husband's religion, increasing the emotional distance between all concerned. In another, a son-in-law was unfaithful and marital separation was occurring between a son-in-law and daughter at the time of our data gathering.

When a Relationship Is a Mixed Bag or Neutral

While these are examples of very close and very distant relationships, the majority of father-in-law and son-in-law relationships fall somewhere in the middle, with good or neutral feelings that accompany a certain amount of acceptance for what the relationship is, and a certain amount of accommodation from the father-in-law's perspective to his son-in-law. What we are trying to capture is that many fathers-in-law have found a way to make things work in order to stay close with their daughter and, in many cases, to stay close with their grandchildren.

Randolph

A 65-year-old African American man, Randolph, describes what such a satisfactory relationship looks like:

> My relationship with him is very important in the sense that he's married to my daughter and is the father of my granddaughter. They mean the world to me, and I want them to be happy. Having a good relationship with my son-in-law is important because it makes them happy. Would we be friends if he wasn't my son-in law? Probably not. He's just not really the kind of guy that is into talking deeply about stuff. We talk about superficial stuff. We talk sports, and watch games together if we're in the same house. But I probably wouldn't spend time with him just the two of us.

This is not the only father-in-law from whom we heard this. Another echoes this sense of distancing because of having little in common: "He's not the kind of guy who wants to sit down and have a beer and watch sports. He's an engineer so he can help out with the cars and that kind of stuff, but he's just not 'one of the guys,' I guess you can say. I guess I just don't have a lot to talk to him about."

Sometimes a father-in-law believes it just takes time, as in this next example from the father-in-law quoted earlier about his unhappiness with his son-in-law's manners. Here, Pete expressed some sadness that the relationship is not as good as he had hoped it would be:

> Yeah, we get along. We appreciate and respect each other. I think there will be opportunities for us to continue to grow closer. I have found I can't force that and I think he feels that, too. It's just, you know, they have been married five years, so there are still experiences that come up that we are learning about each other. I think I pictured it to be a bit different. Not having any sons of my own, I think I was picturing us to be a bit closer. More of a bonding that I think can happen. It just hasn't happened quite yet. That's not anybody's fault. I think it just takes time.

Marty

Another example of a satisfactory or neutral relationship is offered by Marty, a 62-year-old White man. Marty noted he felt close with his son-in-law and enjoys being with him yet explains it this way when asked how important their relationship is:

> Well, it's really not that important. He's not really a part of my life. He just lives so far away. I just don't see him very often. I see him twice a year. It's not because of any negative thing; we're just in different worlds. Whenever I'm with him, I love talking to him. We have good conversations about stuff. It's just that he's super-busy and I'm super-busy. Their life is very social. They go out a lot to party and go to bars and stuff and I'm just older. If they had a baby everything would change because we would go see the baby. It would just be a whole different thing and they would probably change their lifestyle too. I really enjoy the guy, I like being around him. We have great conversations about politics and all kinds of stuff.

So, yes, fathers-in-law seem happy with the relationship they have with their son-in-law. We wonder if, by nature, the men are less hyperbolic about relationships in general and may understate the highs as well as the lows. They may use a standard for closeness that is different from the mothers-in-law and thus their responses, as we show when we compare them in Chapter 8 with the mothers-in-law, are more modulated, consistent with how men modulate their feelings in general.

2. I DID NOT KNOW MY SON-IN-LAW WELL BEFORE THE WEDDING. WILL THAT MATTER?

Slightly less than 40% agreed or strongly agreed that they did not know their son-in-law well before the marriage. The feeling of not knowing a new family member can lead to understandable concern about how well he will fit into the family. As would be expected, not knowing a son-in-law well before the wedding was related to not having as close of a relationship.

Doug was one of those who did not know his son-in-law well but was able to bridge that divide as he came to appreciate his son-in-law and because Doug trusted his daughter's judgment:

> Because they married of their own choice, we were not able to know him much earlier than the marriage, just in one or two meetings. I saw in him the traits you would want to see in a young man: honesty, willingness, hard work. Of course, there were worries since I did not know him earlier and how things would turn out after the wedding. But I knew that my daughter is very responsible, so I had respect for her decision. I knew that it wasn't a whimsical decision.

Fathers-in-law who felt that they did not know the son-in-law well were less likely to approve of the marriage, the situation with only 5% of the fathers-in-law. One father-in-law told us he made a mistake by telling his son-in-law he had not approved of the marriage and it hurt their relationship for years. As also would be expected, not approving of the marriage was a significant predictor of having a less close relationship with the son-in-law.

Anecdotally, and unique to a father's traditional role in many a family, fathers-in-law reported favorably about the relationship with their son-in-law if the son-in-law asked for his approval for the proposal of marriage or if the son-in-law notified him that a proposal was forthcoming. In those ways, fathers often felt they were included by the future son-in-law. It was also a way to bridge a gap if the father-in-law felt he did not know the son-in-law well.

3. HOW MIGHT MY FAMILY BACKGROUND AFFECT MY RELATIONSHIP WITH MY SON-IN-LAW?

Naturally, it makes sense to wonder if a past family pattern or event will be repeated in the future as family history so often is. Here we look at a multitude of relationships, both intergenerational and current, and how they impact the father-in-law and son-in-law relationship. While "what is past is prologue," as Shakespeare wrote in *The Tempest*, and family history is often replicated in some form, still, lives are complicated. Many events can intervene to reduce the power of any single occurrence, like a divorce, and can motivate someone to rise above their own history. Patterns of interaction can be a part of such an intentional positive family trajectory. Loving and supportive relationships in older generations can set the stage for supportive and accepting relationships in younger generations just as an intolerance for difference or a pattern of emotional distancing can be part of a family's legacy.

To learn about the fathers-in-law, we start with their own history. Of those who had an opinion about the quality of their parents' relationship with their own same-gender in-laws,[10] approaching two-thirds believed their father and mother had a good relationship with both. That positive history was related to the fathers-in-law having a better-quality relationship with their son-in-law. In addition, fathers-in-law who had a good relationship with their own in-laws also had a better-quality relationship with their son-in-law. Thus in capturing four generations, growing up with parents having good in-law relations (with the respondents' grandparents) could be connected to fathers-in-law getting along with their in-laws and then getting along better with their son-in-law.

But if the father-in-law's parents divorced, the father-in-law was less likely to be close with his own parents. Parental divorce with the accompanying upheavals has been known to cause emotional distancing between parents and children, and this sample was no exception. A father-in-law whose parents divorced, as one-seventh did, also witnessed the expected emotional distancing between his parents and his grandparents. In a nutshell, in our survey, if the father-in-law's parents divorced, it meant two generations of reported distancing (i.e., less closeness with his parents and less closeness between his parents and grandparents).[11] About one-fifth of the fathers-in-law are divorced or separated from the mother of their child. We are hesitant to draw further connections between this history of divorce and the current relationship with the son-in-law as we do not know when the divorce occurred. If it occurred when the daughter was young, it might have a different impact on the family than if it occurred when the daughter was an adult or even already married.

Consistent with what we do know about family well-being, those fathers-in-law who have or had a good relationship with their parents-in-law are more likely to have a good relationship with their son-in-law. It could be they learned from their own experiences how to make it work for the next generation.

Whatever the findings, they do not apply to everyone. People may stay close with in-laws after a divorce for a variety of reasons, including to maintain a co-parenting custody relationship and to make drop-offs between grandparents and grandchildren easier. It could be there was not great animosity between the divorcing couple; for the welfare of the children, family members are getting along. Some parents keep contact with their ex-in-laws because they believe their own child was at fault for the demise of the marriage. This father-in-law told us about his relationship with his ex-in-laws: "Oh, we got along. They still treat me like I'm married to their daughter. So nothing changed about that. It has always been a positive no matter what the circumstance was."

4. MY DAUGHTER IS MARRYING SOMEONE FROM A DIFFERENT RACE/ETHNICITY/RELIGION FROM HER. MY DAUGHTER IS MARRYING SOMEONE FROM A DIFFERENT ECONOMIC BACKGROUND. WHAT CAN I EXPECT?

Historically, a marriage between people of the same race, ethnicity, and religion has a greater chance of success. Couples and their extended families often feel more comfortable with people similar to them. Traditions and lifestyles are more likely to be congruent. Yet Americans today are more likely than ever before to marry someone of a different race, ethnicity, or religion, a sign that greater acceptance has arrived.

In our survey research, less than 5% of the fathers-in-law's daughters married someone of a different race or ethnicity. Fathers-in-law whose daughters intermarried did not report a more distant relationship with their son-in-law. Anecdotally, from the interviews, we did hear stories of struggles with acceptance based on race, on language barriers between people born in different countries, and with varying cultural expectations. Some of these resolved with time as the generations got to know and appreciate each other.

Thirteen percent married someone of a different religion or spirituality. While not significant in relation to relationship quality, there was a very strong trend toward an interfaith marriage being related to a lower quality of relationship between the father-in-law and son-in-law.[12] Sometimes religious differences are felt most strongly and can cause relationship issues when grandchildren (the daughter and son-in-law's children) are raised in a different religion from the father-in-law.[13]

For this father-in-law, whose grandchildren are being raised in a different religion from his daughter, he focused comfortably on the values behind the religion:

> I was concerned when they first talked about getting married because he was Jewish and Charlotte and our family have been Christian for generations. I thought he might put pressure on her to convert. But Cal's not a very fervent Jew. He does observe all the holidays, but he's never, to my knowledge, put pressure on Charlotte to convert. Their child's being raised Jewish. It's a great religion for promoting ethics and good living. I think he exemplifies that from what I can tell in his life.

As for socioeconomic class, 20% of the fathers-in-law said their daughter married someone of a different economic status growing up (more often than not, the father-in-law reported his daughter's status was more affluent than the son-in-law's). Socioeconomic differences were not a predictor of the quality of the two men's relationship. This does not mean that some fathers-in-law easily accepted the differences. An example of such a father-in-law is provided by Sol, 87-years-old:

> He's a great provider for her and my granddaughter, Sarah. So I like him for that reason, but I really think that my daughter could have done a little better. So I would say our relationship is neutral. I've known him for 31 years, so it's gotten to a point where we both kind of accept each other, but in the beginning it wasn't the greatest relationship. Not to sound cocky or anything, but we come from a fairly wealthy family and he didn't necessarily grow up the same way, so there were some differences in how I hoped that my daughter's marriage would be and . . . I mean, he does take good care of her, and eventually I learned to accept it, but in the beginning we would argue over small things like about the wedding or about how much money they were going to spend on certain things.

This next father-in-law commented on his greater affluence and how his son-in-law impressed him with his success:

> One of the reasons that I came around to him was he ended up getting a very good government job so he was able to support my daughter in a way that I didn't necessarily see that he was going to be able to do based on his upbringing. His family lived in a poor area of Columbus and his parents were teachers. They just didn't have a lot of money going into it, but he did end up being able to support her, so that helped me feel better about the financial aspect.

Overall, family background differences may negatively impact in-law relationships, though families can also grow by being exposed to other family cultures. In an increasingly complex world, the ability to navigate differences and embrace them, as many families do, is an important keystone in family members' growth and in-law relationships.

5. I AM EXCITED ABOUT BEING A GRANDFATHER. WHAT CAN I EXPECT WILL HAPPEN WITH MY RELATIONSHIP WITH MY SON-IN-LAW WHEN MY DAUGHTER GIVES BIRTH?

"Definitely a change in the relationship, in that I became more grandpa and less father-in-law. It's really a change for the better just because I respect them both so much and what good parents they both are." Becoming a grandfather is an important milestone for men who enjoy seeing their children as parents, who love the notion of family, and who take pride in seeing their legacy carried on. One of our faculty colleagues, who became a grandfather, recently recalled his own grandfather sitting at a family event with all of his 12 grandchildren around, raising his arms over the brood and saying proudly, "Mine!"

Little research has explored what happens to the relationship between the father-in-law and son-in-law with the birth of a grandchild. Like so many other aspects of in-law relationships, more attention has been paid to women, and traditionally more family childrearing is undertaken by women. Because of the mother's often primary parenting role, her parents usually have greater access to grandchildren than mothers-in-law, who often have to rely on their son to facilitate access to grandchildren.

In one preliminary study we conducted, where we looked at fathers-in-law with satisfactory relationships and fathers-in-law with unsatisfactory relationships with their son-in-law, we found that those with highly satisfactory relationships all had grandchildren. In looking at their experiences, they strongly approved of the way their grandchildren were being raised by their daughter and son-in-law. One of our conclusions from that study was that fathers-in-law are highly invested in how their grandchildren are raised. We speculated that this factor is more important to men today than it was to earlier generations who were themselves less engaged as hands-on fathers.[14] So while fathers-in-law are not necessarily fully engaged in caring for and helping to raise the grandchildren, that childrearing is done well is important to and monitored by the fathers-in-law we surveyed and interviewed.

We asked the fathers-in-law how the birth of a grandchild affected their relationship with their son-in-law. Half of those with grandchildren believed the relationship experienced little or no change with the birth, 40% believed it improved with the birth of the child, 9% said the relationship got better in some ways and worse in others, and only two fathers said things changed for the worse. If childcare is being provided by the father-in-law and/or his wife (as it was for 38% of those with children), it does not affect the father-in-law and son-in-law relationship.

Other positive parenting signs emerge from our research that could bring the two men closer: 85% agreed or strongly agreed that their son-in-law was or would be a good father. One remarkable example comes from Mel, a 62-year-old White man, who believes that his son-in-law Russ is not only a great father but also a great person:

> Russ is the best thing that ever happened to Mary. Russ has been with Mary for 10 years now. He has a son from his first marriage and all get along well. Russ and Mary have my beautiful granddaughter and she rules the roost. They are a great family and Russ is welcome in my house anytime. Mary dated every loser in the world, it felt like. She dropped out of high school, was drinking all kinds of things, getting into trouble. I thought I was going to lose my little girl—and then she met Russ. Then a few months after they met, Mary got cancer and almost died, but Russ never left her side. He went to work, cared for his son, and every day and night he stayed by my girl's side. It saved my little girl's life, and I could not be happier. When they had their daughter, it was a great day. After the cancer we didn't think that we would have any grandkids from Mary, so little Sara is our miracle grandbaby.

We wondered if the relationship between Mel and Russ had always been good. In his answer, Mel shares the family-wide impact that a good son-in-law can have:

> It really started out great and first I thought, "Wow, please, Mary, don't lose this guy" as soon as I learned he had a job and didn't drink or do drugs I thought, "Man, I hit the lotto." I know Mary put the bar pretty low in the beginning, but Russ really is a great guy. He is like another son to me. Russ came in and was a model for Mary. Someone she loved was an actual living and breathing good guy. He evolved the whole family. I love my sons, but even now my middle son lives at home at 34 and my oldest was just released from prison. My sons love him, too. They are so relieved for Mary because I thought for a while they were going

to kill some of the guys that Mary dated. My sons are good people and they are getting better, and Russ is an amazing father and husband.

When we dug into the interviews with the mothers-in-law, a theme emerged of mothers-in-law feeling that they have to tread carefully with their daughter-in-law, walking on eggshells, in order to have access to the grandchildren. We did not see a similar theme in the fathers-in-law interviews because, as we hypothesized, they most likely have more access to their grandchildren.

What we did see, as discussed elsewhere, was some attention on the part of fathers-in-law to the way that their grandchildren were being raised. Michael, age 65 and White, is an employee assistance manager with a master's degree. His son-in-law, Greg, and daughter married five years ago. When asked about the importance of his relationship with Greg, Michael answered, "Extremely important . . . my wife and I were just talking about how we view him as a son, comparable to the relationships I have with my daughters."

This is a highly satisfying relationship, Michael believes, because of his son-in-law's maturity. In his description, we learn a bit more about how men with similar interests and perhaps sense of masculinity get along with each other:

> We relate to each other as two men. It might have to do with the fact that Greg is older. I will give an example. He and I and my other son-in-law go to football games together, baseball games together, and I think he relates to me as just another one of the guys and I relate to him that way, too. Often I look at him more as a friend than as my son-in-law. It's because we carry on like friends. We share a similar sense of humor and he has a very quick mind. I don't want to say peer-to-peer relationship, but it's probably closer to that than it is the traditional father in-law/son in-law relationship.

Less than one-fifth of the fathers-in-law reported their son-in-law had a different parenting philosophy. For Michael and Greg, part of growing closer after becoming a grandparent is that their differing parenting approaches were brought up by Michael as a potential issue. Parenting approaches are often embedded in the overall relationship:

> I think he perceives at times that I might not parent in the same way that he does. It's not that my wife or I criticize their parenting, but I think he senses that his approach is a little different than mine. That may come from the fact that he has heard from my daughter how we raised her and I get a sense that he

probably thinks, "I'm doing things a little different." I can think of an incident where our one grandchild was carrying on one day and we were at dinner at their house and I made a comment like "the meltdown might be coming" and I think, the way Greg looked at me, he interpreted that I expected him to do something about it, and that really wasn't it. I was just trying to say, "Let's ignore her and she will eventually stop."

Differences in parenting philosophy can be conflated with other philosophical differences. One father-in-law who is strongly opposed to handguns in the house has had to adjust to a son-in-law who grew up around guns and wants a gun in the house. With the birth of a grandchild, the father-in-law believed the risk of accidents occurring increased as his son-in-law believed the necessity for a handgun in the house also increased as he wanted to protect his family.

For another father-in-law, different parenting approaches were related to other issues he didn't admire:

> In the beginning, the way he wanted to raise Denise so strictly. Especially in a lot of the ways that he wanted her to act and eat was a problem. Certain things I thought were too rigorous and also the same with how he treated my daughter. He had a specific career plan for her and himself and he really wanted to stick to it. He wasn't really flexible.

Differences in parenting style traditionally have been contentious for mothers-in-law and daughters-in-law.[15] Now, with fathers and grandfathers more engaged in parenting, it could be a new arena not only for intergenerational connection but also for intergenerational strain.

6. I SOMETIMES FEEL LEFT OUT BY MY DAUGHTER AND SON-IN-LAW. MY SON-IN-LAW SEEMS TO HINDER MY RELATIONSHIP WITH MY DAUGHTER. HOW COMMON ARE THESE FEELINGS?

From our research, few fathers-in-law feel left out (one in 10) and very few fathers-in-law (one in 15) feel their son-in-law hinders their relationship with their daughter. In the rare event a father-in-law feels left out, he is likely to blame his son-in-law for hurting his relationship with his daughter. Holding these feelings does not bode well for having a good relationship with the son-in-law.

We wish to note that these feelings are not common for men. It may be because fathers are not overly concerned with inclusion by their daughter and son-in-law and the daughter tends to be closer with the mother, so a mother-in-law feeling left out does not seem that unusual. As is shown in the chapters on sons-in-law and daughters-in-law, both reported being closer with their mothers than their fathers. While this paints a picture of fathers and fathers-in-law being less close with others in their families than mothers and mothers-in-law, the fathers-in-law may not experience this as exclusion. Fathers- and mothers-in-law may be "left out" to the same extent, but men may not experience it that way as they had different expectations about what and when they would be included.

One of the few fathers-in-law who did feel excluded told us tersely: "They go out to do a lot of fun things without inviting me to go with them." Two reasons we heard for being excluded centered on the health of the parents-in-law, either that of the father-in-law or mother-in-law, and differences in finances, where parents-in-law did not have as much money as the children-in-law and were not being included as guests.

7. HOW MIGHT MY SON-IN-LAW'S PARENTS AFFECT MY RELATIONSHIP WITH MY SON-IN-LAW?

As we discussed in the chapter on mothers-in-law, parents want their child to marry into a loving family with kin who will treat their child well and assist with any grandchildren. In most cases, parents will be at the wedding and, if the two families are compatible and geographically close, will get together at birthdays, anniversaries, funerals, graduations, and other signal events. When children get along well with their parents, the odds of the two sets of in-laws getting along well increases. Because of these potential shared events, everybody getting along can make life easier, especially for the married children who brought them together. Geographic distance can shape the relationships (43% lived within 20 miles of their daughter and son-in-law), as the in-laws who live closer are more likely to spend time with the couple and, if there are children, be engaged in childcare and thus have a different relationship with the couple, and their grandchildren, than the more distant in-laws.

During the interviews we asked about the relationship between the two in-law sets. Most descriptions were quite positive. This father-in-law lives very near his son-in-law and daughter and describes a compatible relationship:

We get to see [the other set] when they are in town. The father is a bit stand-offish and his mother is warm, friendly, and loving. Our son-in-law is closer to his mother, but he gets along great with his father. They are actually divorced,[16] but they still come together for family events. We see them a couple of times a year, and they're coming for Christmas.

A second father-in-law, who lives a few hundred miles away from his daughter and son-in-law, greatly appreciates the inclusiveness of the other parents-in-law:

My wife and I have always felt accepted. When we are there and all of a sudden something occurs with a family event, my son-in-law's parents are having a dinner or a birthday party, and he encourages us to stay longer so we can partic-ipate in those gatherings. That really makes us feel good because we can solidify our relationship with them.

In the following passage, a third father-in-law shows how families can lead parallel lives socially for years before making a more meaningful connection:

We have a very close relationship with his parents, which just actually started four or five years ago, even though my daughter and son-in-law have been mar-ried almost 25 years. It started through my daughter and my grandson. We started to have Sunday breakfasts together and realized that even though we were socially in different groups years ago, that we are really the same people. We have a lot more in common and only in the last four or five have we really gotten close.

Sometimes the lack of a father in a son's life can lead to the father-in-law being a stand-in. This fourth father-in-law describes the role he plays in his son-in-law's life and the trust that his son-in-law's mother places in him:

I only know my son-in-law's mother. His father has been incarcerated since he was 10 so I never met him. His mother and I get along well. She works for the city and, as far as I can see, wants the best for her son. I think she relies on me to be a role model to him. When he was living with me, she used to tell him that he needed to listen to me and learn how to be a man because he never had a positive role model in his life.

Not all relations between the two sets of parents revolve around the children-in-law, as we heard from this father-in-law who bonded with his counterpart: "His father and I have this love for fishing. He and I will get up real early and head out on the water. Sometimes I will hang out with him and not my son-in-law."

While we have described positive relationships, struggles can occur and may revolve around money or competition for the affection of grandchildren. Those are typical components of grandparenting that all must adjust to regardless of their situation. Some parents can afford to give their children and grandchildren more than others or are more willing to share what they have. One father-in-law told us he was working longer than he wished to in support of this daughter and son-in-law while his son-in-law's parents are not in a position to contribute financially or have taken the philosophical position that the children, now that they were adults, should be taking care of themselves. Another father-in-law reported, without priming, that he does not feel especially close around the other parents: "They live in a different circle than I do and they are financially different as well."

Fathers-in-law can be jealous of the relationship that the other grandparents have, though they may be reluctant to admit it. One father-in-law lamented how much time his grandchildren spend with the other grandparents, who live 1,500 miles away while he lives in the next state.

While a number of fathers-in-law knew the in-laws well as they came from the same community, others started the relationship de novo with the engagement or at the wedding and have not had much contact since. Some are fond of one in-law and not the other; others have to balance dealing with a divorced set of in-laws where the exes may not get along well or may be absent from the family. Decisions then have to be made with the assistance of the son-in-law as to who to invite to family events.

Occasionally, a father-in-law believes his daughter has a better relationship with her in-laws than with him (7% agreed this was the case and 16% were neutral). This is most likely to occur when father and daughter had a less close relationship prior to the marriage, and when they spend less time together.

Our impression from the interviews and surveys is that fathers-in-law do not have the other in-laws on their radar to the extent that mothers-in-law do. The fathers-in-law did not speak expansively about them when interviewed and did not have many nuanced observations about them to share. This would be consistent with women playing a more active role than men when it comes to negotiating interactions in the family.

8. DO FATHERS-IN-LAW GIVE ADVICE TO THEIR SON-IN-LAW? THERE IS A LOT I WANT TO SAY BUT I HOLD MY TONGUE.

Jokes around fathers-in-law nagging or interfering are, as we have pointed out, virtually nonexistent. Fathers-in-law are generally not seen in the same light as mothers-in-law when it comes to advice giving. Depending on the context, advice giving can also be seen as interfering. Whether advice should be given, how it is to be given, and how it is received will depend on that context. The context includes the nature of the father-in-law and son-in-law's relationship, the issue, who is having the issue, and whether advice is being asked for by the daughter or son-in-law. That being said, the most frequently given pieces of advice that fathers-in-law have for other fathers-in-law are "Don't give advice" and "Don't meddle."

Some fathers-in-law will not give advice under any circumstance. This 76-year-old, Davis, is one who takes a "hands off" position: "Don't give advice even when it's asked for—just stay out of it. Don't meddle. It is a no-win situation." He has a lot of contact with his son-in-law, often while his daughter is not around, and still maintains this approach: "We're pals a lot of the time. We both like beer and sports and we sit down and watch games together. When we're free, we'll occasionally go out to dinner together or meet for lunch. We have been known to work on projects at his house together, so, we're pretty good buds."

We asked the mothers-in-law whether the daughter-in-law was receptive to the mother-in-law giving advice about her appearance, her job or career, and her marital relationship. We asked the same questions of the fathers-in-law in relation to their son-in-law. When we asked fathers-in-law about the receptivity of the son-in-law about advice on his appearance, 47% responded they had not offered advice on appearance. Of those who had offered advice, 43% believed the son-in-law was receptive, 48% answered neutral, and 9% believed he was not receptive. Fathers-in-law were more likely to give job or career advice: 60% had offered such advice. The sons-in-law were also more open to work-related advice; 52% believed the son-in-law was receptive to it, 37% were neutral, and 11% believed he was not receptive to it. As to the marital relationship, certainly a situation potentially fraught with familial issues involving his daughter, 54% did not offer any advice. Of those who did, 41% thought the son-in-law was receptive, 50% were neutral, and 9% thought he was not receptive. From these responses, a very small percentage had given advice when the son-in-law was perceived as not receptive to it. In general, and as we discuss in a later chapter on comparisons between in-law groups, fathers-in-law perceive the son-in-law as being more receptive to advice in all three of these areas than do mothers-in-law perceive with their daughter-in-law.

As expected, the perception of receptivity of advice is linked to a closer relationship with the son-in-law. If the father-in-law feels his son-in-law is receptive, the two men are likely to be closer and, of course, if the father-in-law feels closer to his son-in-law, he is more likely to see that son-in-law as being receptive. Fathers-in-law who perceive their son-in-law as receptive are also closer with their daughter.

While keeping quiet may be the best approach, it is not always easy, according to Kurt:

> There have been a few times when we have all been eating together, and my son-in-law [says] to his child kind of like, "You will eat what I tell you to eat, and that's that," and I have to bite my tongue. I would probably handle it a little differently, but it's not my place. I try to be supportive of my daughter and her family, and the best way for me to do that is to let them do their thing, and only give advice if I'm asked for it. It's their family.

This tension about keeping quiet can be especially difficult for some when it comes to the grandchildren, as this next father-in-law also admits: "I'm reluctant to chime in and offer a lot of advice when I see a potential conflict. My attitude is just listen, take it all in. I'm probably more inclined to vocalize my thoughts on things the grandchildren may be involved in."

It is not only concerns about grandchildren that can irk a father-in-law. Lemuel, who does not have a particularly close or distant relationship with his son-in-law, could not keep his mouth shut in relation to support for his wife and daughter. When asked to describe a difficult situation with his son-in-law, Lemuel said:

> I guess it could be when my wife was sick and my daughter was always coming here to help her out. She had just had her second kid so she was really stressed and could have used the help, but my son-in-law was always working or doing things with his buddies, and that really got me mad because I saw it was hard on my daughter. I went over there and gave him a piece of my mind and told him he had to step it up. My daughter wasn't really too pleased with me after I had that conversation, but he ended up doing it, so I guess it worked out for the best.

While one of the themes put forth by many is to not interfere, in some relationships, advice giving, as a father to a son or an elder to a younger, is part and parcel of the relationship and may be consistent with cultural expectations. It can be accepted by both men and is not seen as interference or meddling, as in this next example, where advice is given but with a boundary on it. Stefan may have been primed to offer it by his daughter, who might have valued the fatherly input for her husband or by his own perception that a younger man needs guidance from an older man and his son-in-law was not getting it from his own father:

> He doesn't have a great relationship with his parents. We'll talk and try to work through any problems or questions he has, making it through anything he feels insecure about. He can talk to me freely and I can give him good advice. He does that a lot. I try not to pry into their personal life but I want them to know if they need me I'm there for both of them for emotional and financial support if necessary.

Another theme is the ability to listen without giving advice, as this next father-in-law, Brad, explains happened with his son-in-law who ran into financial difficulties after working in his own father's company. Brad also interprets his son-in-law's behavior through the lens of masculinity that can be used to frame some of the father-in-law/son-in-law expectations:

> I am not so sure he came for advice. I would say more for support. He would talk to me about things he was finding out about how his father ran their company and his frivolous spending, causing the closing of the company and leaving my son-in-law without a job . . . ultimately losing a relationship with his father. He needed to feel comfortable. He needed to talk. At one point, I think he needed to know that I was not upset with him. As a man, I think he needed reassurance that I did not lose respect for him now that he was unemployed . . . He needed to know that I still loved him and was not mad or worried.

9. WHAT PART DOES MY DAUGHTER PLAY IN ALL THIS?

"Our relationship is somewhat connected to how I feel he relates to my daughter." The importance of the daughter's role in the father-in-law and son-in-law relationship cannot be overestimated as her choice of spouse is what made them family. If the father sees his daughter as happy and being well treated, he will work hard to build a good relationship with her spouse. The daughter signals to her father, overtly or covertly, how she feels about her husband and may suggest ways for the two men to get closer. At the same time, she signals, overtly or covertly, to her husband the kind of relationship she would like him to have with her father. Both men pick up the threads and try to weave themselves into the family tapestry. If her marriage is strong and she values her relationship with her father, it can be a strong set of ties. If her marriage is strained or her relationship with her father shaky, the thin thread between the men can be easily broken.

Our first question at the beginning of this chapter describes the nuances of a two-person relationship, or dyad. Here we are exploring a three-person relationship, or triad. In family systems theory, family members are connected to each other and what affects one family member may have a significant effect on other family members. Sometimes a balancing act is needed by family members to keep relationships with different family members working. For these fathers-in-law, those who report being less close with their daughter also report being less close with their son-in-law. In this way, the two younger adults may be supporting each other, consciously or unconsciously, in not wanting to be close with the father-in-law.

During interviews, we asked the fathers-in-law if the son-in-law relationship was important to them. Three-quarters said the relationship with him was very important; when asked why, the reason given most often had to do with the importance of family and, now that the son-in-law was married to his daughter, he was a part of the family. The reason given second most often was that the father-in-law wanted to stay close with his daughter.

How was that expressed? Many fathers used almost the same words about staying close with their daughter. Here are five brief examples:

> "He is married to my daughter and I have to make it work. My son-in-law is the father of my grandchildren and we get together a lot. He is a really nice guy."
> "He's married to my daughter and the father of my granddaughter so it's pretty important that we have some relationship."
> "It is exceedingly important for my child's happiness. It helps make my child's life easier. It also models our values and the importance of family to our grandchildren."
> "To maintain a relationship with my daughter, he's essential."
> "Very important. He started dating my daughter when she was 16. She and I have always been close, so my relationship with him is very important."

The fathers-in-law see the relationship as important and their daughters often assist in its maintenance. Over two-thirds replied that their daughter had a very positive or somewhat positive influence on their relationship with their son-in-law; the remaining fathers-in-law replied she had little or no influence. The fathers-in-law who said her influence was very positive made comments like, "she is central to my relationship with my son-in-law," "she helps with communication," and "her positive relationship with her husband encourages my positive relationship." Only one in 20 said their daughter wished he would work harder on his relationship with the son-in-law.

Some men are accustomed to relying on themselves to handle their relationships, as we heard from this father-in-law: "I have a very strong positive relationship with my son-in-law independent of the influence of anyone else." While this statement can be viewed as having a positive spin to it, a father's having his own relationship with a son-in-law can also mean her potential influence is ignored, as with this next instance: "My daughter tries to maintain a civil relationship with my son-in-law, despite the hardship he has brought on her. I do not feel like I need to bend over to please him. I am and will continue to be indifferent to him."

Eight in 10 fathers-in-law strongly agreed or agreed their daughter was happy with the relationship they had with their son-in-law. We found ample evidence that when the father-in-law believes his daughter is happy with his relationship with her husband, the son-in-law and father-in-law are closer. These positive interactions are mutually reinforcing. The two men are close, so the daughter is happy with the way her husband and father are getting along, which further reinforces the men's positive relationship. On the flip side, if the father-in-law feels uncomfortable with some aspects of his daughter and son-in-law's marriage, as one in nine did, he feels less close to the son-in-law.

Further underscoring the importance of the daughter to the father-in-law and son-in-law relationship, fathers-in-law who sometimes feel caught between the two adult children, as one in nine did, feel less close with their son-in-law. Feeling caught could occur if he inserts himself into the relationship in unwanted ways or if his daughter or son-in-law triangulates him into their relationship. Finally, if the father-in-law feels that he cannot speak directly to his son-in-law about important issues without first speaking with his daughter, as almost one in five felt, he is less close with his son-in-law. In essence, the daughter often functions as the fulcrum in the relationship between the two men: If the marriage troubles the father, if he feels caught in between his daughter and son-in-law, or if he feels he has to communicate first with his daughter before communicating with his son-in-law, he is less close with his son-in-law.

One cautionary note about family communication: It is hard to say that one form of family communication is better than another. In some families, communication flows through blood relatives; in this case, the father communicates with his daughter about all family matters before talking to his son-in-law. That might be consistent with family culture and/or with the idiosyncratic nature of that family. By this, we mean that family members learned a pattern of behavior from their parents and grandparents. Other families may have a history of directly communicating with all family members. They may also have decided that this pattern works for their family and is distinct from their upbringing. When fathers-in-law can speak directly with their sons-in-law, it may be a sign of greater inclusion of the son-in-law. One father-in-law from Pakistan, Ahmed, talked about his closeness with his two sons-in-law, with whom he directly communicates:

> They are both my sons. They take good care of my daughters and, in Islam, as a father, it's my job to find good boys for my daughters. They are very good boys. They are very respectful, well educated. They are part of the family now. They are the same as my [biological] son.

Ahmed's father-in-law treated him the same way.

Occasionally, fathers-in-law find it easier to speak directly to their son-in-law rather than their daughter because he is the more responsive or the more available one, as demonstrated in this next example:

> We frequently call Christopher because Jenny won't answer her phone. They're so busy that a lot of times we are interacting with him, and not her. Last Saturday, we went to two soccer games—one for each grandchild—and Jenny wasn't there, which didn't surprise me, but I only found out later that she was in Los Angeles. A lot of communication goes through Chris. I don't intend it to be that way, but that's what happens frequently. Sometimes she answers emails and sometimes she does not. Sometimes she answers texts and sometimes she doesn't.

Nothing is inherently wrong with either communication pattern. With our sample, though, we did find a clear trend toward not communicating directly with a son-in-law being correlated with less close relationships between the two men.

So, yes, the daughter plays a key role. First, she serves as a linchpin in bringing the two together and then she serves as a central figure in both men working to maintain their relationship.

10. WHAT PART DOES MY SPOUSE/PARTNER PLAY IN MY RELATIONSHIP WITH MY SON-IN-LAW?

We know the daughter plays a key role in the father-in-law and son-in-law relationship. The father-in-law's spouse/partner often does, too. Considering family systems theory again, a father-in-law operates as part of a team with the mother-in-law (more likely if they are married) and may be seen as part of a team by the son-in-law. For example, if the parents-in-law provide childcare, which 30% reported they did, both parents may offer it. If the father-in-law is not engaged in providing direct, hands-on care, the mother-in-law's provision of childcare often means a shift in her availability to do other things that affect the father-in-law and the family. The fathers-in-law and their spouse also help out financially, according to 39% of the fathers-in-law.[17] Just as the provision of childcare requires couple time, financial assistance means less money for the couple. Twenty-two percent of those providing financial assistance described the amount given as very significant. Therefore, to those extents, the father- and mother-in-law are operating as a team.

But there is another consideration for some fathers-in-law. It is not uncommon for wives to try to influence their husband's relationships with family members and friends.[18] Almost two-thirds of the fathers-in-law said their spouse/partner had a somewhat positive or a very positive influence on the relationship with the son-in-law. One in nine reported their spouse wished they worked harder on their relationship with the son-in-law. What does spousal influence look like? According to the fathers-in-law, "she keeps the relationship cordial"; "she encourages time together that I would not have on my own"; "she gets along well with our son-in-law"; "she keeps the family together through family activities"; and "she does not say anything bad about him when I complain about his lack of responsibility as a father/husband." Robert, whose relationship we described earlier, says this about his wife Sherry's influence on his relationship with Mark: "When I am with him, which the majority of the time is at sporting events, Sherry wants to make sure we talk about real things. By real things, I mean family, how he's doing professionally, problems he is having with his parents."

However, wives do not always influence fathers-in-law. This father-in-law remains unconvinced by his wife's behavior: "My spouse treats our son-in-law like a dear old friend, when he has indeed cheated on our daughter, caused her financial hardship and anguish. I find that appalling."

Maybe the greatest assistance a partner can offer the father-in-law, and it may be hard to quantify, is validation for how he is feeling about the son-in-law. This is a primary role of a spouse, to provide support when needed. During many interviews, the father-in-law described how he and his wife talked things out in terms of being a grandparent or in not interfering in the lives of the younger generation. As Chester told us:

> In private my wife and I don't necessarily agree with their parenting style. We've never criticized them or anything like that. We don't really give unsolicited recommendations on how to do anything. We mind our business. I may talk to my wife, but we don't say anything because it's not like our granddaughter is turning out bad; she has great manners and is a wonderful child.

Another talked about the arrangement he came to with his wife: "I guess being on the same page with your wife helps. We both agreed to not get involved in their stuff unless my daughter asked or we felt like we really had to say something or offer our help, so we didn't get wrapped up in their stuff."

So while some fathers-in-law have an independent relationship with their son-in-law and come to their own conclusions, many are still influenced by their spouse/partner and by the general mood and communication between her and their daughter and their son-in-law. Her influence may be most significant in families where the women spend more time together and communicate more than the men.

CONCLUSION

There are no monolithic father-in-law and son-in-law relationships. However, once established, these relationships are usually positive and are often dependent on the daughter's relationship with both men to make them work. We see fathers-in-law who are quite close (Phil and Robert, for example), those who have troubled relationships (such as Harry and Abram), and a wide swath in the middle, who accept the relationship despite its vicissitudes and try to make it work to keep the peace.

By applying family systems theory and understanding the intergenerational relationships maintained between adult children and their parents and in-laws, we see how changes between two or three family members can reverberate positively or negatively through the family sub-systems. The chapters on daughters-in-law and sons-in-law are the next step in digging into the other side of the parent and adult child-in-law processes, thereby furthering our understanding of how families operate.

CHAPTER 6
Sons-in-Law and Their Relationship with Their Father-in-Law

Jokes abound where sons-in-law feel victimized by a mother-in-law, but almost none exist where sons-in-law feel victimized by a father-in-law. Vaudeville is not the only setting where this relationship has gone uncommented on; it has also received scant attention in the social sciences. When research is undertaken on children-in-law, attention is usually paid only to daughters-in-law.[1] If sons-in-law are included in research, their responses are often grouped with those of daughters-in-law.[2]

Where do the sons-in-law fit in family relations? From a family systems perspective, family members influence and are influenced by each other. Understanding sons-in-law's positions in the family is of paramount importance, in part because good in-law relationships and marital happiness often travel together. If sons-in-law are happy with their in-laws, they are more likely to be happy in their marriage. Conversely, if they are happy in their marriage, they are more likely to be happy with their in-laws.[3]

Here we look specifically at sons-in-law and their relationship with their father-in-law—a relationship that is virtually unexplored from either man's perspective. A better understanding of this relationship can lead not only to greater marital happiness but also to better grandparent and grandchild relations as well as better elder care. In the little research that is available, researchers found that sons-in-law were generally very satisfied with their in-law relationships and were more satisfied with their relationship with their father-in-law than with their mother-in-law.[4] Perhaps this is why son-in-law/mother-in-law jokes are dominant. However, researchers have not looked in depth into what contributes to a good relationship between the men, our focus here, nor how the relationship is maintained.

It may be difficult to appreciate fully what a good relationship between a son-in-law and father-in-law even looks like. While closeness may characterize a majority of in-law relationships, ambiguity can pervade and thus would be a typical component of the relationship.[5] Ambiguity arises when people are unsure of how they should act with each other.[6] When people are unsure how to act with each other, their roles may be unclear and they may feel uncomfortable. Simply put, this can lead to men of different generations being unclear as to who should be performing what tasks and what are acceptable interactions in the family.

Ambiguity is often wrapped up with ambivalence (i.e., the holding of mixed or competing feelings toward someone). When the men involved deny their feelings or feel uncomfortable expressing them, trying to work out a relationship where roles are unclear and where feelings are mixed can be even more difficult. Further, if the men have been socialized to not expect much from an in-law relationship, particularly when it is with another man, they may lower their expectations for what the relationship should, or could, look like. For example, a father-in-law who appears brusque or withholding may fulfill a son-in-law's expectations and, potentially, prevent the relationship from evolving, as both men conform to socially gendered expectations. The son-in-law therefore anticipates less from his father-in-law, who is expected to express less. He may still consider the relationship satisfactory. Compared with women, men in the family often are less emotionally and physically expressive and play less of a central role in maintaining communication.[7] Men also tend to be less engaged in the day-to-day caregiving of children or grandchildren,[8] which reduces some of the need for intergenerational communication. Such expectations for and behaviors of men taken together—and *only* if the men subscribe to those expectations (many do not and have relationships with open communication as we show)—affect how men interact with each other. The son-in-law and the father-in-law may unconsciously and mutually contribute to fulfilling their traditionally prescribed roles, leading to low expectations in the relationships.

It is important for us to emphasize here that the majority of the sons-in-law (between two-thirds and three-quarters) strongly agree or agree with statements indicating their father-in-law is kind, warm, and available to them. Those adjectives would be consistent with general expectations of fathers. To the point, our general sense from the interviews with sons-in-law is that most of them have good relationships with their fathers-in-law, had not thought about what they expected their relationship with their father-in-law to be like, and were pleasantly surprised with how it turned out. They also, when asked to talk further about their father-in-law, recounted times when expectations were not always clear and they held mixed feelings toward him. Such feelings between in-laws, as well as between adult children and their parents, are not only common but can be changed when family members make the effort.

As we discuss in Chapter 5, the fathers-in-law bring their own set of expectations to this relationship. These expectations are shaped by their past, their assessment of what their daughter (or son if it is a gay marriage) wants in a husband and how happy she is, as well as their own beliefs about what it means to be a man, husband, and father. The sons-in-law have similar tropes that guide them: What messages were received growing up about roles and marriage? What does it mean to be a man, husband, and father? Ideally, both generations will come with similar expectations and, if not, with the ability to tolerate differences in the other for the greater good of the family.

Some sons-in-law feel they have a nearly perfect relationship with their father-in-law. A 32-year-old lawyer from the Philippines who described his relationship with his father-in-law this way provides a brief example of one such relationship:

> He is a gentleman who hasn't bought a new shirt for himself for years. He still wears the same old tattered polo, but he is willing to donate money to charity willingly. I saw that he is a very giving man. I want to live this simple life just like him. I see his happiness by the simplicity that he lives his life and that's a good model for me to live my own life. It's a very respectful, congenial relationship. We're very open.

We also interviewed men whose relationships fall on the other end of the spectrum where communication has virtually stopped, like this son-in-law:

> My father-in-law and my wife are more or less estranged. I've seen him probably three times since we've been married and I've spoken to him just those three times. He left when she was growing up and he makes no effort to talk to us at all. They haven't talked in five years just because he stopped. He wouldn't call the kids on their birthday or Christmas or anything, so my wife told him to make more of an effort. He said he didn't want to.

These two polar opposites of relationships are easy to document, as we will do. However, between them sit a number of typical relationships where sons-in-law get along fine with their father-in-law, are close enough to keep family relationships cordial, and appreciate the father-in-law's importance to his wife, the father-in-law's daughter. This 25-year-old illustrates this:

> It's important, but it is not the most important thing in my life. It is important enough to maintain a decent relationship. It is beneficial to my wife if I can maintain a relationship with her father. If she is happy, then so am I. The relationship with my father-in-law is comfortable. He doesn't always have a lot to say to me, but it is what it is.

As we delve more deeply into their relationships, we want to reiterate that—in our estimation—some men may provide descriptions that could possibly under-report some of their feelings toward their father-in-law because of how men are socialized to be less emotionally expressive and to expect less emotionally from the other man. They may under-report both some of their warm feelings and some of the discomfort they feel. This does not mean that the relationship is any less important and that men do not feel the need for connection with each other. It is more to point out that the language used to express such closeness just may not be as descriptive.

As we did in the previous in-law chapters, here we provide answers to questions that sons-in-law and other family members may ponder, the answers to which might help to smooth the sometimes difficult transitions families experience leading up to and after a wedding.

1. ARE SONS-IN-LAW CLOSE TO THEIR FATHER-IN-LAW?

To answer this question more completely, we looked at seven key items and created a variable that we believe captures relationship quality. We believed that any one question alone would not capture the range of issues that go into a relationship. The variable is similar to ones we created for other in-law groups. It includes the following five positive statements and asks for levels of agreement from strongly agree to strongly disagree: "My father-in-law and I have a close relationship;" "I admire my father-in-law;" "I can ask my father-in-law for advice;" "I trust my father-in-law;" and "I enjoy spending time with my father-in-law." It also includes two negative statements, "I avoid my father-in-law" and "I have problematic conflicts with my father-in-law." In highly positive relationships, the responses to these statements would be evident just as they would be evident in highly negative ones. However, not all relationships are that cut and dried. Ambivalent feelings can also be held and add nuance to our deeper understanding of how relationships function. In our seven-question assessment, such relationships would be characterized by varied responses across the questions. For example, a son-in-law may enjoy spending time with his father-in-law but not feel he can ask him for advice or feel especially close to him. Caleb, quoted later in this chapter, feels very distant from his father-in-law but admires him. We use this created variable and the term *close* to measure relationship quality as we look at a number of other variables to explain this complex relationship.

Our findings are largely positive. Approximately 60% to 76% agreed or strongly agreed with each positive statement while 11% and 14% agreed or strongly agreed with the negative statements. Specifically, 13% strongly agreed and 48% agreed they had a close relationship with their father-in-law, 19% strongly agreed and 52% agreed they admired their father-in-law, 20% strongly agreed and 45% agreed they could ask him for advice, 20% strongly agreed and 44% agreed they enjoyed spending time with their father-in-law, and 37% strongly agreed and 39% agreed they trusted him. As to the negative statements, 6% strongly agreed and 8% agreed they avoided their father-in-law and 5% strongly agreed and 6% agreed they had problematic conflicts with their father-in-law. To every positive item, the "agrees" were more common than the "strongly agrees," indicating good but not great relationships. Neutral responses were given between 11% and 24% of the time. For the negative relationship questions, 6% strongly agreed and 8% agreed they avoided their father-in-law while 5% strongly agreed and 6% agreed they had problematic conflicts with him, with 14% and 11% responding neutral respectively.

We turn to the interviews to draw a clearer picture of not only those relationships that are very close and those that are not close, but also those in the mid-range where positives and negatives, and ambivalence, may co-exist in the relationship with their father-in-law.

When Relationships Are Highly Satisfying

Will

Will, a security guard, is a 31-year-old African American father of two.[9] His relationship with his father-in-law is important because both his parents-in-law mean a great deal to his wife of five years:[10] "My father-in-law, James, is the older version of myself and my mother-in-law is the older version of my wife. He's a very good person, understanding. The kids improve it and make us a lot closer." Will liked James from the beginning and saw how protective he was of Will's wife, James's daughter:

My wife's sister was dating some guy, kind of a jerk, so James was like, "I lived a full life." He let me know that he has two guns in the house, which meant I wasn't exempt. He was saying to me that if I didn't treat his daughter right, that he'd go to jail for her. So I think I'm going to be that type of father. I have two daughters, too. We clicked immediately because they have two daughters and my wife is the oldest, so I was the first son, so they immediately took a liking to me. I mean so much to her, so I mean something to them.

James provides a needed parenting role model because Will does not have a relationship with his own father: "I don't talk to him . . . he used to abuse my mom . . . We don't have a relationship at all. And my mom, I'm close to her."

When issues do arise between Will and his in-laws, he blames all three of them: "My wife hasn't moved away from the nest and cut the umbilical cord. I think the problem today is that parents hold too tight to their children too long or the kids stay home too long so that sometimes interferes with our relationship. I think she is too close to home and they're too close to her."[11]

Will has become philosophical about the closeness between his wife and her parents. He also has adjusted to the role that he feels he was placed in by her family:

> You need to understand how much your father-in-law means to your wife because what's important to her should be important to you . . . I think when people get married they would like their spouse to be like them. That's not realistic. It's like the men are over here and the women are doing this, so I end up spending more alone time with James hanging out and talking. We're guys and have similar interests. [The men sharing similar interests was highly correlated with a better relationship quality.] This is going to sound like stereotypical man stuff, but we both enjoy watching, playing, and talking sports. But beyond the sports, I think there are a lot of things that we just relate to because we're the same gender. It's more a "buddy-buddy" way. I have a good relationship with both of them, but my relationship with James is more like it's just the guys hanging out.

Horace

Horace, a salesperson, is 46 years old and White. He and his wife are childless. Like Will, Horace brings up issues related to being a man when he talks about his father-in-law: "Our relationship is important because my dad and my father-in-law are both the paternal heads of the family. It was important to me to learn what I could to talk with them about and get their experiences. We do the talking about the man stuff. We also talk about stuff two guys being friends would talk about."

To Horace, "man stuff" means, "We talk about how we feel as men about things. Sometimes it pertains to our wives or about things that we walk through as men, like whether it be relationships or our faith in God or maybe problems we're having at work, as well as how we handle those. What's a good way to handle those as a man?"

While the relationship is very close now, such was not always the case: "There have been misunderstandings at times where we had to . . . things were said and taken in a way that were hurtful and we came back and reconciled. It was about some big things in life. We addressed it after a couple months and talked it out and things went real well."

The good has outweighed the bad, which has allowed them to move on:

> There's been very little that's happened that has been negative. We visit them at their home. It's a good time for us because we don't see them as often as we used to. I think that, over time, as the friendships developed with both of them individually, the interactions grew richer. In the past five years, when they talk to others . . . they'll say, "He's my son-in-law but he's like a son" so we have more of a father–son, mother–son relationship than what you would see as a son-in-law type.

Unlike Will, Horace has a close relationship with both his parents. He views his parents' relationship with their in-laws (his grandparents) as a model for how he should get along with his in-laws: "Because I saw such positive things, it was definitely an encouragement to me."

Mike

A final example of a highly satisfying son-in-law/father-in-law relationship comes from Mike, a 35-year-old African American social worker, married for six years with two children:

> We can be candid and we're able to laugh and joke and not only have formal conversations. Right now, it's occasional and there's distance, like 250 miles. The distance allows us to have deeper conversations when we see each other. [42% of the sons-in-law lived within 20 miles of their in-laws.] He is funny, proud, distant, but caring. He likes privacy, but he cares about my family. I speak to him on

birthdays and Father's Day. We see each other during Thanksgiving and special occasions. My mother in-law visits much more.

Mike describes the impact of children:

My children enhance our relationship. They love their grandchildren dearly. They support them emotionally, financially, and educationally. My father-in-law is a retired postal worker. He now works in an educational setting and provides books to my children and engages them around education when they talk. Also, my kids are silly and he's silly. A silly side of him comes out when he's around kids. He picks up my daughter and chases her around the house, and I think that really enhances the relationship and we can laugh and joke around that.

Mike also provides an example of a long-term relationship:

I've known him since I was 19. We got married at 23, so I've had a long time to know him. I came from a good, strong foundation with my family. I felt like my in-laws believed in who I was as a person, that I came from something special. He's a laid-back guy. There's really no drama to report. He's former military, very predictable. There's no gray area. It is what it is. We've always been close. I'd like to see him more.

Mike, like Horace, also had a role model in his own family about getting along with the older generation:

My mother stopped working and took an early out in her 50s to take care of both mothers under one roof. One had dementia and the other had heart failure. They lived about 20 miles from each other and decided we could all be one household so she could take care of them. I think that she was the ultimate daughter-in-law to do that. We co-habited across family lines . . . My dad was chill, too. That whole in-law drama, that's not related to my situation at all.

Note with all these men how the fathers-in-law (in different ways) provide role models for the sons-in-law and how the two men bond around their masculinity and male roles across generations in the family. Will reports, almost apologetically, that they enjoy watching, playing, and talking sports and relating to each other because they are the same gender. Horace talks about his father-in-law being a role model as a paternal head of the family and that they talk about "man" stuff. Mike sees his father-in-law as chill and former military, no drama. He adds, though, that he can be silly with his grandchildren, which adds another dimension to his view of his father-in-law and helps the two further bond. All three look to their fathers-in-law as role models for how to be a father. There is a sense of inclusivity in these relationships that makes boundaries clear.

These next examples portray relationships that have much less in common. While the sons-in-law were initially willing to have a relationship, the fathers-in-law are either physically or emotionally less available or absent.

When Relationships Are a Struggle

Abner

Abner, a 32-year-old White social worker, has been married for 10 years. He is the father of an eight- and a two-year-old. His parents-in-law are divorced and his own parents are married and had good relationships with their parents-in-law. Abner downplays his relationship with his father-in-law:

> It's not very important. In large part, he has serious mental health issues, and so he's pretty absent and withdrawn most of the time from the family. He's hard to get in touch with, so, on my end I don't even bother. But if he's on the phone with my wife or something then, I'm like, "Hey, tell your dad I said hi." It's not a conflicted relationship; it just doesn't really exist. He's not dependable. so I don't get disappointed because I just don't ever expect or count on him for anything anyways.

Abner's father-in-law was not always ill: "His mental health stuff got worse after we got married. It was kind of on the decline when my wife and I were engaged. I would say it has gotten progressively worse. He started having more physical health problems, too. We're separated by a very large distance—he's in Nevada and we're on the east coast—and he's not the kind of person to come visit."

Abner is keenly aware of the pain his father-in-law's condition causes the family:

> It creates a stress on my family and it causes my wife to be hurt. There will be significant events that happen and he doesn't remember to call or anything like that. My kids don't even really know anything about him because he's been seen so few times in their life, whereas they see my mother-in-law. She's staying with us right now, and they see my parents on a regular basis.

Abner speaks directly with his father-in-law once a year on average, and usually at his wife's behest. He is not even exactly sure where his father-in-law is living. He has visited Abner and his family only twice, after each child was born:

> We don't have a lot in common. When I see him, we get along just fine. He's really into conspiracy theories, which I'm not into at all. He's very anti-government and has very different political beliefs. More the challenge is what he doesn't do, like he doesn't call and my wife is upset because he didn't wish her a happy birthday. Stuff like that. I think it's more distanced now than it was in the beginning. In the beginning, I was more open to trying to hang out and spend time together. Over time, it just became less realistic and it didn't seem like it was worth the energy. I figured if you're marrying into someone's family you expect to be interacting with them the rest of your life. On my end, I wanted to have a positive relationship. I approached him before I proposed to my wife and made sure he was okay with it, and he was.

Abner is much closer with his mother-in-law: "She's very supportive and, in terms of our relationship, we talk trash and it's a lot of jokes. We will go have a beer together. She's very supportive and helpful, and I don't think our parenting styles are that much different. She's maybe slightly stricter, but it's one of those things where my wife and I have never felt compelled to say something."

Abner regrets what the relationship with his father-in-law has become: "I care about him and feel bad for him because I think he's had a pretty cruddy life. He had a terrible childhood and I think that contributed to the development of severe mental illness. I just keep my distance because he won't comply with treatment and he's just kind of all over the place."

Ben

Ben, a 46-year-old African American, married for 16 years, works as a coach. He is the father of three children, ages 16, 14, and six. Both his parents-in-law and his parents are divorced. Similar to Abner, his father-in-law's behavior drives the relationship, which Ben describes as very distant:

> He rarely comes around. If he were to come around I wouldn't mind having a relationship with him, but he lives in Kentucky and doesn't usually come up. If he does come up and come through, he'll call and tell my wife, "Hey, I'm driving by. I'm headed to Philly" or such and such. I think he's been to our house once in

the sixteen years that we've been married. Geography is easy to overcome with phone calls and text messages, whatever, anything. But I say distant because, even when I was dating my wife, he was rarely around.

While Ben's wife has a relationship with her father, Ben feels rejected by him: "She probably doesn't see him often, but she does talk to him more than her brothers and sisters. If he wanted to have a relationship with me, I would gladly have a relationship with him, but he's never made an attempt. I could probably count on both hands how many times we've had a conversation."

Ben's relationship, like Abner's, with his mother-in-law helps to compensate for what he is not getting from his father-in-law. They have grown close over time and he considers her a great source of support:

> I love to talk to her. I feel more close to her because I've gotten to know her and she's spent so much more time with us. She's stayed with us for a couple of months at a time and we go down there and visit her. She comes with us when we go to track and field events for our kids' national championships. She travels with us every summer.

Whereas Ben's mother-in-law is a very involved grandmother, Ben's father-in-law has not made attempts to see Ben's children: "We've actually been to Kentucky, half an hour away from where he lives, kids competing at a track and field event. He won't even come to see them, so . . ."

Caleb

Caleb, a recent first-time father, is a White, 25-year-old who works in real estate. Married for five years, both his parents and parents-in-law are married. While Abner and Ben relate to a father-in-law who is divorced, Caleb interacts with both parents-in-law together. Like Abner and Ben, he feels distance from his father-in-law, although unlike them, he respects his father-in-law, an example of Caleb feeling ambivalent toward his father-in-law:

> We do not have a good relationship, and I do not think that anything will change. I have a relationship with him because, even though my wife understands I do not like my father-in-law, she appreciates that I make an effort to be civil with him during family get-togethers. He is difficult to connect to. We do not have the same priorities, and he is not a very warm or emotionally caring person. I can

only base our relationship on what he talks to me about, which is nothing. He does not say much to me, although I admire him a ton and he has a good work ethic, but we just do not get along.

While Abner and Ben are very happy with their interactions with their mother-in-law, Caleb does not have a close relationship with his: "My mother-in-law is very anxious and passive-aggressive. She is always worried about what people think about her. Nothing bad ever happens to her, but she is neurotic for pretty much no reason."

Caleb's relationship has never been good with either parent-in-law:

> Meeting them for the first time was very difficult. I was just trying to connect to both or either of them, and it was like connecting to a wall. Basically nothing happened, and they haven't tried to reach out to me. That is all I have to say about it. It has not improved much since that event, and each time we go over to their house, it is all surface-level talk and no deep questions are directed at me. My in-laws are emotionless people and that is fine by me, as long as they do not meddle in our relationship.

Caleb's ambivalence is on display when he seems to wish the relationship were better yet seems resigned to how it is and says he does not like his father-in-law.

Caleb's son is still too young for him to have a sense as to whether his son's birth will change the in-law relationship. He is not concerned, though, about a negative impact on his family:

> We live in a different state, so there isn't that much that they can interfere with since we do not see them that often. I like that we are far from them. They act as a team, but it is a very dysfunctional team. If one of them starts acting nasty or passive-aggressive to one of their children, the other will jump in and have the other spouse's back.

For two of these three cases, divorce played a significant part in the emotional and geographic distance—both between the son-in-law and father-in-law, and, to a large extent, between the daughter and the father-in-law. We also heard from other sons-in-law who described situations where their wife's parents had divorced and their father-in-law started a new family. The father-in-law would neglect his prior family and the daughter did not have much of a relationship with him. The son-in-law would, in turn, not have a relationship with him, as demonstrated in the following example provided by Dave, whose in-laws divorced. The father drifted away and remarried a few times:

> Things were okay, and then we began to hit big bumps. Today we are estranged. We are not angry at each other, but my wife has spent many years trying to tolerate this relationship and we have determined it is bad for her. It just makes her unhappy. Things that he has done have not been directed at me, but hurting her hurts me. It makes us feel like we are not as important as his other stepfamilies. I do not need that from him. I am not personally injured by it, but I am baffled by what he does to his daughter. In the past year, my wife has completely cut ties with him.

After parent-in-laws divorced, stepfathers sometimes functioned as the surrogate fathers. The sons-in-law's descriptions of them ranged from very close to very distant. The earlier in the daughter's life the stepfather entered the family, the more favorably he was described and the better the relationship between son-in-law and stepfather-in-law.

When Relationships Are a Mixed Bag or Are Neutral

Sometimes the chemistry is just not there between son-in-law and father-in-law. Opportunities for growing closer may never present themselves because of geographic distance and—aside from mutual affection for the spouse/daughter and grandchildren—few shared interests exist. Relations can be pleasant enough; issues may occasionally arise and may be resolved or simply ignored to keep the peace. Whatever ambiguity or ambivalence that exists can be overlooked for the good of the relationship. Many son-in-law and father-in-law relationships can be described this way and both men are usually comfortable with this dynamic, as things are basically working for them in that there are no problems or conflicts.

Clark

Clark is a 52-year-old African American accountant. He married his wife 22 years ago and they have two teenage children: "It's cordial. My in-laws are not affectionate people. I come from an affectionate family, one that hugs and greets you warmly when you arrive, so it took me a while to figure out that that is not what they need from me. It's respectful."

Clark explains why there may be a little distance between him and his father-in-law:

> My father-in-law is a quiet man. I believe there might be some intimidation on his part because of my success compared to his non-success. When I met them, I was already a college graduate working on my master's and studying for the CPA exam. After we married, we got a modest home. Those who look at it think it is elaborate, but it's modest to me. My home is bigger than his home, so you know . . . Then I'm a city guy and he's a country guy, so not only do we come from two different generations, but we come from different backgrounds. I'm more abrupt and abrasive and he is more subdued, reserved.

Clark goes on to explain what some of the initial struggles were between them, some of which he accepts responsibility for:

> When I met my father-in-law, they were in the process of transitioning back to their hometown, so they had been renting a house and they wanted to save money and they were building a home on their family property, so they moved in with us. At that point, I had been the man in Shaundra's life, and when they came there was a shift in dynamic where, in my mind, I was the man of the house and, in his mind, he's her father so *he's* the man of the house. It was abrasive. I think I was being disrespectful, but it worked out. Now we have a better relationship. We never got into a verbal or physical altercation. I just think it was, with men, someone has to be the "alpha." Men have to establish who's going to be the alpha and two alpha's can coexist, but we have to establish that. So we had to establish who was the alpha male and I'm strong-willed; I like to believe I won.

Clark is clearly describing role conflict, each wanting to occupy the same role in the house.

Clark's father and his father-in-law have no relationship. Clark is not surprised they are not close, and in his description we hear about the expectations that Clark brings to the relationship: "You have to understand: Men of that generation didn't talk a lot, especially in those days. If you were not in that circle of friends, with men, it's hard to gain access. You have your friends and you almost have to be in structured environments and, even then, it's kind of hard to penetrate and become a friend to a man, so they have no relationship."

Clark is still working on the relationship with his father-in-law to leave a legacy for the next generation: "When they come in town they spend time with us. They've been on vacation with us. I figure it's important that my children see that we have a working relationship."

Donald

Staying close with a father-in-law because he is "family" is also a motivating factor for Donald, a 35-year-old African American business consultant. He has been married for 15 years and is the father of a nine-year-old: "It's really important to me that family is something my kids are involved with, and that includes my father-in-law. Family is important as a default, but kids add something more. I want my kids to be around family, to be taken care of by family and stuff. That's kind of how I was raised with family and close friends in and out of the house and spending summers at my grandparents."

Like many of the other sons-in-law whom we quote, Donald is closer with his mother-in-law than his father-in-law:

> She is really loving and treats me like her child. She loves me more than her kids (laughs). She comes over all the time to watch the kids, and I don't know what we would do without her. My relationship with my father-in-law is much more superficial. We talk if we need something from each other, and we'll see each other if he comes over or if we visit them. It's not hostile. It's just not close either.

Donald has worked very hard to get along with his father-in-law as the relationship got off to a rocky start:

> Everything related to the wedding was difficult. Getting our families' approval even though we are both the same religion, especially my father-in-law's, was really hard. Also having our families just meet, figuring out dynamics of the wedding—all of it was difficult. We didn't see eye to eye on things, and it put my wife in a difficult position, and my father-in-law repeatedly disrespected my parents, which was hard.

When Donald spends time with his father-in-law, he carefully navigates: "I just find something he enjoys talking about and steer the conversation in that direction. I let him talk about what he cares about and not have to be invested in it. I avoid controversial topics (laughs). With my father-in-law, we've created a simple, non-confrontational relationship, and it works."

Within some of these relationships, we see the ambivalence or conflicting feelings that can arise. The relationship is maintained, perhaps for the benefit of the wife/spouse or the grandchildren, but it requires effort, as in this next example, where the son-in-law, Ned, views himself as outside of the family despite being married into it for 18 years:

> Sometimes I can be angry at the man and sometimes it can be a pleasure to be around him. Particularly when we play spades because we like to talk junk. That's one thing; we find commonalities when we play cards. It's a pleasure to play cards with him. I would never again confide in him the way that I had once before, considering the fact that the man is incapable of having the ability to have a deep-diving relationship. Mostly everything with him is shallow. Maybe with someone else he might have a deep relationship, but I'm just going based on the relationship he has with his own children. He has four, and their relationships are essentially surface. There isn't any deep relationships because he pretty much gets on his children's nerves and they're like, "I'm not dealing with you." With me it's even shallower because I'm the outsider. It doesn't affect me negatively, so it is what it is.

In thinking about boundary ambiguity, researchers describe the importance of seeking clarity around who is in and who is out.[12] The three sons-in-law who are examples of close relationships with their fathers-in-law, Will, Horace, and Mike, describe connecting and being included around their masculinity and roles as fathers. Will and his father-in-law bond around sports and being "buddy-buddy." Horace and his father-in-law talk about "man stuff." Mike's father-in-law is chill, former military, and with no drama, masculine ideals of the silent man. These three men feel connected to their father-in-law. Yet the sons-in-law who are distant from their fathers-in-law, by definition, feel excluded from their fathers-in-law's lives. Divorce has played a significant part in this for Abner and Ben, who may have absented themselves or may feel excluded by the family. It is both easier and more important to work to establish the relationship with the father-in-law if he is married and engaged in the family. Abner's father-in-law is "pretty absent and withdrawn," Ben's "rarely comes around" and is uninterested in his grandchildren, and Caleb's, who is married to his wife's mother, "is difficult to connect with" and shows little emotion. All three sons-in-law have attempted, to various degrees, to establish relationships but have pulled back in the face of the father-in-law's lack of response to those efforts.

Still, the majority of sons-in-law feel close to their father-in-law, although to varying degrees, with few feeling extremely close. At the same time, it is rare that these relationships are highly conflictual or nonexistent. Many son-in-law and father-in-law relationships are maintained with some degree of intentional effort on the part of the son-in-law and with an emotionally mature perspective that places importance on family togetherness and intergenerational communication.

2. HOW MIGHT MY FAMILY HISTORY AFFECT MY RELATIONSHIP WITH MY FATHER-IN-LAW?

Family history does not always determine the future of the family, though it is an important factor to consider, as we do throughout the book. Family patterns of interaction, positive and negative, are often handed down by example from one generation to the next. Nevertheless, actions in the present can undo the impact of events from the past. For example, in our clinical work, we have seen many men who did not have fathers present in their lives when they were growing up but have taken active roles in their children's lives to "stop the cycle" of father absence. This is one way in which reflecting on the past can help inspire and influence changes in current and future patterns of behavior.

Four-fifths of the sons-in-law came from families where the parents were married to each other.[13] The vast majority were close with their parents. Being close with their mother or father was related to having a good-quality relationship with their father-in-law. Further, if the son-in-law perceived his parents had a good relationship with their in-laws (both sets of the son-in-law's grandparents), he was more likely to have a good relationship with his father-in-law.

Why would having both parents married to each other, who the sons-in-law feel close to, and who got along with their own parents and in-laws be predictors of good son-in-law and father-in-law relationships? We assert that stability and closeness in intergenerational relationships model and teach the son-in-law how to manage getting along with others. He can use his own family history of intergenerational in-law relationships as role models when interacting with his in-laws.

3. MY WIFE IS A DIFFERENT RACE/ETHNICITY/RELIGION FROM ME. SHE COMES FROM A DIFFERENT ECONOMIC BACKGROUND. WHAT CAN I EXPECT FROM MY FATHER-IN-LAW?

Historically, as noted earlier, marrying within one's religious, ethnic, or racial group has been related to better family relations. More recently, interfaith, interethnic, and interracial marriage is on the rise in the United

States.[14] This is likely to mean that intermarriage will not roil families and strain family relations as it has in the past.

In our sample, only one in 10 of the sons-in-law were married to someone of a different religion and only one in 20 were married to someone of a different race or ethnicity, according to the survey responses. Compared to the couples who were from families of the same religion, race, or ethnicity, none of these types of intermarriages were related to the quality of the son-in-law's relationship with his father-in-law.

Initial hesitations about such differences, when any are present, can be overcome, as this 53-year-old college-educated White man, married to an African American woman for 12 years, told us about interactions with his father-in-law:

> He's in his eighties and came from a generation where, and he lived in the South as well, he experienced segregation. He was in the army, so I think that, to some degree, he experienced [racial tension] in the army as well. I know that, at first, he was concerned about his daughter marrying someone who was not African American. I think that was a result of his experiences. I don't understand his life, but I understand why he would feel that way. But that kind of dissolved relatively quickly when he saw how nicely we got along and how I treated his daughter, and how I treated him, that we probably had a lot more in common than maybe he had thought.

Marriages of people from different backgrounds can have benefits, as we heard from another son-in-law, who described how much fun it was for him to celebrate a new tradition:

> I grew up Jewish, and her family is Christian. I have Christmas with their family and, just this past year, my parents were invited down to do Christmas, and they'd never done Christmas before, with my wife's family. My parents and my wife's parents generally get along very well. Jewish holidays are less fun. Christmas morning? That's fun! I wasn't accustomed to that, and once I got to Christmas I was like, "this is awesome."

Levels of religiosity—even within the same religion—can cause strain, as it did between the following son-in-law, who is a Conservative Jew, and his father-in-law, who is an Orthodox Jew:

> Around the time that my wife and I were first married, I avoided him a little bit more because I wasn't sure what his deal was fully. I didn't want him to judge or say I was coming over too little or too much. It had to do with religion, too. For

example, if I ate a meal at his house and I didn't say something that he liked religiously or if he asked a question about that week's reading in the Torah and if I didn't have the answer, I was more nervous. So I felt like I didn't want to go to his house as much, probably for the first six months of my marriage.

While growing up in a different economic background was not a clear predictor of a strained current son-in-law and father-in-law relationship, it definitely was a barrier for Dick, a 52-year-old White man, at the beginning of his relationship with his father-in-law. Dick perceived that being able to provide for a wife was a key characteristic of what it means to be a man:

When my wife and I first married, my father-in-law had to help us buy our first house and pay for our mortgage. I think he really looked down on me that I couldn't provide for his daughter. Then, when our daughter was born, I realized that I needed to be able to make enough to provide for her and my wife, so I got a new job and we didn't ask him for money and I was able to start paying him back. It was like he started to see me as a man once I proved to him that I could be a provider.

Married for 30 years now and with two children, Dick has made peace with the relationship, though the memory still stings:

When I asked him for his permission to marry his daughter, he did not react how I wanted. He told me he didn't think I was good enough for her, but knew he didn't really have a choice. I was raised in poverty. When I asked him, I was working minimum wage in a factory with my father and brothers. I had no college education and no money to get one. He thought I was a loser. My wife came from a nice suburban town and her father made a lot of money, so he looked down on me and my family. He didn't think that I would be able to give her the life she was accustomed to, so he didn't approve of our marriage at first.

As stated, we did not find significant differences in the relationship quality between those sons-in-law and their fathers-in-law when they married outside of their race, faith, or socio-economic class. It may be that these differences are not as important in our society as they once were and that other issues, like character and values, have become more important. This does not mean, though, that there will not be bumps in the road for some of the family relationships when such differences exist. Such bumps seem especially likely in the early stages of these relationships before the in-laws get to know each other.

4. HOW WILL MY RELATIONSHIP WITH MY FATHER-IN-LAW CHANGE WHEN I BECOME A FATHER?

Parenthood adds a cascade of new interactions to in-law relations—sometimes welcome and sometimes not. The son-in-law interacts with his father-in-law and mother-in-law in his new role as parent while he sees his in-laws interacting with his child, perhaps in their new roles as grandparents. If this is their first grandchild (or their tenth), it may be a particularly happy time for them and they may increase their engagement with their daughter and her family around the new baby. Parents-in-law who have sat back while the couple establishes their own identity may invite themselves in more with the birth of a grandchild or be invited in to assist in a variety of ways. This can be a wonderful shift for sons-in-law who value their in-laws' engagement, yet it can also be a difficult time for sons-in-law who have a more ambivalent or even a problematic relationship with their parents-in-law. If the son-in-law felt he could accommodate to his in-laws' difficult or troubling behavior before the birth, as it only affected him, with a baby present, unpleasant behavior may be harder to ignore or to accommodate.

For the sons-in-law in our survey, almost 75% had children who were the product of their current marriage.[15] Forty percent were the first to bring a child into the extended family, producing the in-laws' first grandchild. We asked about any changes in the son-in-law's relationship with the father-in-law since the birth of the first child: 47% believed there had been no change in the relationship; 37% believed there had been a change for the better; 13% believed it had changed in some ways for the better and in some ways for the worse; only 2% reported it changed for the worse. It is easy to understand how the birth could bring the son-in-law and father-in-law closer—they experience each other in a new and positive way and bond over fatherhood. When the birth had no effect on the relationship with the father-in-law (almost half of those with children), the two men could have been close already and were not brought closer or they could have not been particularly close to begin with and the birth had no impact.[16]

What might be a barrier to greater closeness between the two men after the birth? Differing parenting philosophies. Only 34% strongly agreed or agreed that they had the same parenting philosophy as their father-in-law, with 40% disagreeing or strongly disagreeing; 26% responded "neutral." Having children, then, could add distance to the son-in-law and father-in-law relationship if their parenting philosophies differ. In fact, not only is having a different parenting philosophy related to the son-in-law having less of a quality relationship with his father-in-law, it is also related to the son-in-law reporting becoming less close or having no change occur in the relationship following the birth of the first child. The son-in-law's having a different parenting philosophy than the father-in-law is also related to having a less close relationship with the mother-in-law. From this, we assume that the father-in-law and mother-in-law are likely to share similar parenting philosophies or be perceived to share similar parenting philosophies.

We also asked if the father-in-law and/or mother-in-law provided childcare. Twenty-eight percent had provided some childcare; 75% of those reported it was somewhat or very significant childcare, with 31% reporting their relationship with their father-in-law got better after providing childcare. A number of these variables coalesce to paint a picture. The son-in-law and daughter may be more willing to receive childcare from the grandparents if they share parenting philosophies and felt close to them before the child was born.

The circumstances around the son-in-law becoming a parent need examination. For a couple, the decision whether and when to have children will affect the marriage. Some parents-in-law may actively encourage it, which can feel inappropriate, as it did to this son-in-law: "There is pressure from her parents for grandbabies. I get that my wife wants kids sooner than I do, but I would say that affects our marriage. Like strains it, kind of."

When the child arrives, some fathers-in-law become more engaged, as exemplified in the following description of a father-in-law, who had initially maintained distance from his daughter and son-in-law when they first married: "He has been more active in reaching out to my wife communication-wise, and he has been very keen on when he would come down to meet the baby. That kind of stuff is a newer thing, and he has been much more proactive; we didn't have to initiate contact anymore."

The birth can also be a reason for families to not only communicate more, but also to see each other more often and work to put past difficulties aside: "I think we've all grown closer since the kids have shown up. Well, for one, we see them a lot more often. We need their help and I think kids provide a good buffer so things that were issues when we first got married are no longer at the forefront."

A birth sometimes comes before a marriage. Both events brought this son-in-law closer to his father-in-law:

My son's birth was the first step. If we were writing a paper, my son being born was the rough draft and getting married was the final paper that you would turn in. It was awkward because we were not married and I knocked up his daughter.

He was feeling ambivalent. Then he saw that I was around and I stuck around. We had a man-to-man talk and it allowed for him to trust me more. I was really in the family then.

While the last three examples were of fathers-in-law becoming closer after being distant, having a child can also strengthen an already strong relationship, as happened for Tony, this next son-in-law who saw his father-in-law in a new light:

He loves seeing the kids, so I'm sure that, even though our relationship was already on good terms, it only helped make something for him to look forward to when June and I take the kids down to see him. I saw a side of him I hadn't seen before. Even though I don't see him that often. He's a big . . . this is a guy who has worked on the water his whole life, baking in the sun, not taking good care of himself, just working to the bone. Probably since he was 15 years old . . . Bought a house at 17 or 18 . . . So, a big, tough, hard-working guy who it was neat to see soften up with babies in his hands. Pretty cool.

Albert echoes a similar sentiment about his newfound appreciation for his father-in-law:

I can honestly tell you, my father-in-law is awesome to my children. Flat out. We were over there yesterday for dinner and he got up off the sofa, put his jacket on, and took Jimmy outside and was playing with him. It was cold. I didn't want to be out there, but he was like, "that's my grandson, that's what I'm going to do." He takes them on bike rides. He picks them up to play with them. He's an awesome grandfather. At one point in time, I would never have thought that he would be as involved with them as he is. For that man to go through everything he's gone through and to be where he is and to do what he does with his grandkids, my hat's off to him.

For families who live far from each other, grandchildren can often function as a reason to see each other. Terry told us,

They strengthen it. Like many grandparents, my in-laws are extremely fond of the kids. They would do anything for them. They spoil them when they get the chance. We have always lived in separate cities, so it's a treat for both parties when they get to see one another. They are always there for the main events in their lives. It really strengthens the relationship. I think my in-laws are very pleased that we have kids. It makes the bond stronger between all of us.

However, the above statement does not mean that things are always great between Terry and his in-laws. The children did bring them closer, but these relationships can contain both affection and ambivalence, as we see when Terry was asked about differences in parenting philosophy:

> I think sometimes it is on display. It's not outright like, "you should do this, or you should do that," but I think there are some suggestions in subtle ways occasionally. It has never been a huge issue creating a rift between us. But there have been moments—our kids are pretty active, young, and high energy, so if grandpa is not in the best mood or feeling so great, his tolerance for that may be lower, his voice might get raised, and there may be a suggestion of "why don't you do something with your kids? Why are you letting them roam free?"

Another son-in-law remarked that differing parenting philosophies strained his relationship with his father-in-law. Parents and grandparents may agree about how to care for newborns but not how to deal with obstreperous teenagers. Here the difficulties arise around older children:

> When there is any conflict, it's over children. They were once parents, too. They feel like they have done it before, so they are trying to tell us, which I understand but, at the same time, it is a different era, and different things going on. That's where the conflict comes in. They're not going through it as we're going through it, and when they get the children it's only for short periods of time and don't actually live with them and don't see how they really are.

Sons-in-law not only interact with their fathers-in-law; the mother-in-law often plays a significant role. In fact, her role may be more significant in terms of dictating childcare and parenting philosophy, as she is often the more involved parent and grandparent. Roderick speaks to the different paths that his parents-in-law have followed and how he became closer with his mother-in-law than his father-in-law:

> My mother-in-law is very supportive and she's helpful and I don't think our parenting styles are that much different. She's maybe slightly more strict, but it's one of those things where my wife and I have never felt compelled to say something. She's pretty good when she comes and stays with us. She has a good idea about what our rules and boundaries are and is good at reinforcing those whether she agrees with them or not. My father-in-law came after my son was born at some point and said hi, and he came at some point after my daughter was born, but that was when we were still living in Texas so it was easier for him then, but that would have been almost five years ago. I haven't seen him in five years.

A mother-in-law is not always the key to the parents-in-law's relationship with the children. This example describes the admiration that Paul feels toward his father-in-law during the emotional absence of his mother-in-law and how fatherhood forged the men's connection. Their relationship shifted favorably before Paul and Meredith married. Paul felt his father-in-law was initially hesitant about the young couple's relationship and came around when he saw how the son-in-law handled fatherhood:

> Meredith got pregnant prior to us being married, so it went from a boyfriend–girlfriend relationship to, this is going to be my son-in-law or whatever. I think there was a different respect level on both accounts after that. He respected me more because when Meredith got pregnant, it was, "Okay, we are buying a house, we are moving out, and I will take care of your daughter and your grandchild." So I would say things changed, absolutely. I think we have a very good relationship because we are both Christians so that in itself brought us on common ground. Our values and things with the children are the same. We never really had an issue with that. My mother-in-law has a couple of issues. She's been standoffish ever since I remember, 10 years ago. Very non-confrontational. We'll all be in a room together and she'll be off reading a book somewhere by herself . . . At first, I really didn't understand my father-in-law because the way he ran his house was different than what I saw growing up. My mother-in-law had some alcohol and drug abuse issues so he was the mother and father of the household. He did the best he could, but he struggled trying to keep all the kids in order, the finances, so forth.

New parenthood provides the opportunity for both the son-in-law and father-in-law to construct a different and potentially more appreciative relationship. Each man may see something new in the other that, hopefully, brings them closer—although, as we have found, the birth can have mixed effects on the relationship.

5. HOW MIGHT MY PARENTS AFFECT MY RELATIONSHIP WITH MY FATHER-IN-LAW?

When we consider family systems, any investigation of how a son-in-law interacts with his father-in-law has to take into consideration how his own parents fit into the picture. The son-in-law and his spouse balance two sets of in-laws simultaneously, and no two sets bring the same relationship patterns, nor can they provide the same amount of love, time, and resources to the couple. One set will live closer, have more time, have greater financial resources, and be more emotionally available. One set will be give "better" gifts and offer more exciting vacations with the family. Each set will also have its own family tree and history of togetherness that might exert a stronger or weaker pull on the couple. One or both sets of parents-in-law may have divorced, which could mean complicated arrangements might need to be made to accommodate multiple households, problematic relationships, and stepfamily members. Finally, as discussed, the arrival of grandchildren will bring different levels of significance to each set of in-laws.

As discussed earlier, in our data the son-in-law being close with his own parents is related to a better-quality relationship with his father-in-law. Strong relationships usually build on other strong relationships. The son-in-law's parents may have modeled and can encourage or give advice about how to deal with in-laws. If parents are not interfering or requiring an unrealistic amount of time from their son, the son-in-law will have more emotional energy for his in-laws. And if his wife/spouse gets along with his parents, all the better.

We saw a wide range of relationships *between* the sets of in-laws. Some in-laws have longstanding friendships that preceded their children knowing each other; this happens when people from the same community marry. Other times there may be little or no contact between the two sets of in-laws before the planning of or even the wedding itself. The reason may be either geographic distance or the basic chemistry between the parents; it could even be a combination of factors, as in this next example:

> I think because my mother is a widow, she was hoping that she would become close with my in-laws, that she would have new friends that she would spend time with. They were less interested in that because they already had other friends. They differ a lot in their politics and religion, so they do not naturally get along with each other. They both love our kids. They have that in common, but they see things differently.

Fathers-in-law who get along with each other can make family events easier. As Elijah told us:

> I don't believe they have a lot in common apart from hanging out in the kitchen eating and socializing and just having a good time. My father-in-law watches sports a lot. My dad watches the news a lot. But they like watching TV together. It's just different upbringings, but when you bring them together, they find some sort of commonality.

Elijah clearly understands the roles that two older males can play in his life. When speaking about his father-in-law and contrasting him with his father, he said, "Feelings, positive feelings like his open-mindedness, his wisdom, really lots of wisdom. I rely on him for advice. He's easier to access than my father. I love my father equally, but he is in a different country. He doesn't really see everyday things on the ground."

Sometimes the son-in-law's parents have negative feelings about his parents-in-law and express them, as in Mike's family. This can place the son-in-law in an awkward, triangulated position unless he puts a stop to it:

> My mother and my father think my mother-in-law is crazy. My mother feels my mother-in-law hasn't taught her daughter, my wife, how to take care of stuff. She taught her about having a strong work ethic in the job but not at home. For my wife and me it works okay because I'm that person, I'm the one that's regimented and disciplined. I'll work until midnight at home to make sure everyone else is ready to go when the alarm clock goes off. But for my mother, me being her son, and me marrying this woman and this woman, in her eyes, taking care of me, so to speak, creates issues and then I am stuck in the middle. After a while, I said to my mom, "Okay, I've heard enough. She is what she is."

When there is jealousy in the relationship between the in-law sets, it can affect the son-in-law's relationship with the father-in-law. A small percentage of sons-in-law believed that their father-in-law was jealous of the son-in-law's relationship with his own parents. While this could be interpreted to mean that the father-in-law appreciated, in a positive sense, the good relationship between his son-in-law and his parents, we think it has more of an unhappy connotation because the presence of jealousy was related to those sons-in-law also having a poorer-quality relationship with the father-in-law. A slightly larger percentage of sons-in-law believed their father-in-law was jealous of their wife's (the father-in-law's daughter) relationship with the son-in-law's parents. This significant, and potentially problematic, feeling could arise in instances where the father-in-law feels replaced by the son-in-law's parents. Those sons-in-law (about two-thirds being the same ones who agreed with the previous statement) were much more likely to report a lower-quality relationship with their father-in-law. It may be that when a son-in-law believes his father-in-law is vulnerable to these feelings of jealousy, other issues are going on that add emotional distance in the two men's relationship.

While we have noted some of the potential signs of relationship struggle, it is important to emphasize that over 50% of the sons-in-law believed that their father-in-law was supportive of the son-in-law's relationship with his own parents.

Finally, a son-in-law's father, by his absence, can impact the son-in-law's relationship with his father-in-law as the father-in-law can serve as a father substitute, as in John's case:

> My father passed away before he even had a chance to see my girls really grow up, so to have my father-in-law say that he was proud of the way I raised my children meant a lot to me because my own father wasn't able to say that. I always looked up to my father-in-law because he came from nothing and was able to create this amazing life for his wife and children, so I always hoped that I would be able to do that too, so by him acknowledging me like that meant a lot.

6. WHAT PART MIGHT MY WIFE PLAY IN MY RELATIONSHIP WITH MY FATHER-IN-LAW?

As we have stated throughout, it is the child of the parent-in-law, also considered the linchpin, who creates and then often drives many of these relationships. We began this chapter by describing the dyadic or two-person relationship between the father-in-law and son-in-law. Now we look at the role that the daughter/wife plays in the men's relationship. It is considerable.

To understand the role she plays, we asked: "To what extent does your wife influence your relationship with your father-in-law?" Two-thirds said the influence was very or somewhat positive, a little less than one-third said there was little or no influence, and a fraction said she was a negative influence. The wife of the son-in-law may encourage contact between the two men by directly asking them to spend time together, arranging for them to be together, keeping close contact with her father and, by that association, keeping the two men in contact, and complimenting or speaking highly of one to the other. As an example of a positive influence that she can play, this son-in-law told us, "My wife has a small, tight-knit family, and maintains a very close relationship with her father. That brings me into contact with her father and family in general much more frequently than I have contact with my side of the family." That type of response from a son-in-law speaks to the warmth felt in his wife's family.

A quite different response, given the implicit connotation about a spouse's positive influence, was this son-in-law's: "She defends me when we are together." Here we see an indication of the wife as a mediator between the two men. Another son-in-law gave a similar response: "She keeps the peace." We also received the response "She makes us hang out together," indicating that the interaction would not happen without her pushing for it.

And, as we suspected, when she is identified as a negative influence in the relationship between the son-in-law and his father-in-law, it is because of the nature of the wife/daughter's relationship with her father, as we learned from this son-in-law: "She does not get along very well with her father. There is a strain between them, which distances me from him." Having a good relationship with the father-in-law may feel like a betrayal in relation to his wife.

We also explored how close the sons-in-law believed their wife was to her parents: 73% strongly agreed or agreed she was close with her father and 84% strongly agreed or agreed she was close with her mother. This level of closeness is consistent with our research throughout this book—adult children feel closer with their mother than their father and they perceive their spouse to be closer with their own mother than their own father. (We return to these findings about closeness to a father relative to closeness to a mother in Chapter 8.) Given how close she feels, the stage is set for the wife to want her husband to be close with her parents. And because this is a generally happily married group of sons-in-law (86% strongly agreed or agreed they are happy in their marital relationship), their wife's closeness with her parents does not seem to be a major issue. Further, the sons-in-law—to a large degree—believe their wife is happy with the relationship the husband/son-in-law has with her father.

So, when each of these three items (the wife is close with father and mother, the marriage is happy, and the wife is happy with the son-in-law/father-in-law relationship) is positive, the two men's relationship quality is stronger. Sons-in-law with happy marriages would naturally work to keep their wife happy, particularly when she is close with her parents. If a son-in-law's wife tells him that she feels good about his relationship with her father (with whom she is close), there is further reinforcement for the two men's relationship.

To understand the wife's influence further, when we asked during the interviews with the sons-in-law why his relationship with his father-in-law was important, keeping his wife happy was mentioned frequently. It is his impression of her need to have good relationships with her parents that can spur the son-in-law to work on the relationship with his father-in-law.

While the majority of sons-in-law feel good about their wife's role with her father and in the son-in-law's relationship with his father-in-law, the picture is not always roses. More than one in five of the sons-in-law feel caught at times between their wife and their father-in-law. Almost one in five feel uneasy about their wife's relationship with her father. One in 10 feel that their father-in-law hinders their marriage. One in six felt his wife was more loyal to her parents than to him. Sons-in-law who give these responses are, as would be expected, less comfortable with their own relationship with their father-in-law.

Feelings of discomfort about the relationship can derive from the son-in-law feeling his wife is too close with both her parents. Will, who was introduced at the beginning of the chapter, is very close with his father-in-law yet is also irked by the closeness of his wife with her parents, as evidenced by his umbilical cor remark. He has to work hard to not let those feelings interfere too much.

In this next example, the son-in-law feels caught between his wife and father-in-law. The father-in-law was a widower and has a very close relationship with his daughter, perhaps due to the early death of her mother. The daughter was unhappy with how the son-in-law and father-in-law were spending their time when together:

> My father-in-law seemed to be more interfering in our marriage when it was new, but he knows that I am going to take care of his daughter. He struggles with alcoholism.[17] He contracted a chronic illness because of his addiction and it really took my wife for a loop. He continues to drink and I don't drink that often because I am not a big drinker except when I go to his house and have a beer. Every week that I go, my wife gets angry because she feels that it's wrong for me to drink with him because he is a problem drinker.

One of the best examples of how complicated these son-in-law/father-in-law relationships can be and the role that the daughter plays comes from Carlos, a 28-year-old who has been married for three years:

> There's somewhere in my head an idea of a son-in-law and father-in-law being really buddy-buddy and going to do activities, just the two of them. That really didn't fit for me. I definitely have a relationship with my father-in-law. Independent of my wife, my father-in-law and I have some connections, but they are dwarfed by my wife's presence in our relationship. Our concern for my wife trumps so much our concern for one another as individuals. If she were removed, we could have a relationship but I don't know if I would want that. In any event, my wife's really important to me, and my father-in-law's daughter is really important to him. That's our connection, and so pretty much all of our interactions are based around that relationship. Except for that one dinner to ask for his daughter's hand, I don't see my father-in-law one on one ever. It's always me and my wife that see him, or she's interacting with him. They have

a pretty challenging relationship in a lot of ways, and often I'm an observer or sometimes like her therapist, but I try not to be that too much. I have to support her in her dealing with some challenging things in their relationship. There have been times where she has explicitly expressed that she does not like me taking his side or being too understanding towards him when they're having conflict. My loyalties are to her. So that trumps any affection or any friendship or any other kind of relationship that I would have with my father-in-law.

We cannot emphasize enough the important role that the daughter plays in the men's relationship. While some relationships between the men are very close and involve friendships, as we heard from Mike, Will, and Horace, it is the daughter/wife who brings and keeps the two men together and, as in the last example, may keep them apart.

7. WHAT PART MIGHT MY MOTHER-IN-LAW PLAY IN MY RELATIONSHIP WITH MY FATHER-IN-LAW?

For obvious reasons, we need to consider the role that the father-in-law's wife, the mother-in-law, plays with both her husband and her son-in-law. Mothers-in-law are not always immediately accepting of a son-in-law, as was the experience with Sigmund Freud. Freud's future mother-in-law, a widow, expressed doubts about his suitability for her daughter, Martha, as he had neither social prestige nor money. It took three years to disarm her. The Freuds were married for more than 50 years.[18]

Mothers-in-law loom large for the sons-in-law. How large? When asked which parent-in-law they were closer to, 27% of the sons-in-law indicated they were closer with their father-in-law while a greater percentage, 42%, indicated they were closer to their mother-in-law; the rest indicated they were equally close with them both. To solidify further the mother-in-law's position in the family, and as stated already, the sons-in-law believed their wife to be closer with her mother than her father. It is likely then that the mother-in-law, to whom both adult children are closer, could be highly influential on all the relationships in the family. Her role may be further cemented if there are grandchildren, as the daughter is more likely to engage with her mother around childcare after she has a child than to engage with her father.

While not universally true—and we offer other scenarios throughout this book—mothers, women, and thus mothers-in-law are often more engaged in the interior of the family, as these responses reveal, as the emotional linkages. Sometimes because of this engagement and because men are often engaged as the primary provider, mothers-in-law can be seen as interfering. Other times they can be seen as nurturing. This can occur even for the same types of behaviors! Still other times they can be the axis around which the family revolves and thus fulfill many roles. They might push for contact with children and grandchildren and, in so doing, bring their husbands along. This could increase interaction between fathers-in-law and sons-in-law in ways that might not occur if they were not as actively engaged.

John, whom we quoted about the loss of his father and how his father-in-law stepped up, struggled at times with his mother-in-law and saw her as interfering. She may have been a stand-in for anger he was feeling toward his wife:

> I think the most difficult time for me with my mother-in-law was when I was traveling a lot for work. My wife and I were having many problems in our marriage because I was leaving her alone to take care of two babies at home. We had many arguments for a while, and she would tell her mom everything. She only had her mom for support, so her mom would get really upset around her. Then her mom started to go at it with me when I would leave. We would argue because she would try to intervene in our relationship and I would get really frustrated. It was just a very difficult time with my wife, and I didn't need her mom getting involved, too. My wife and I decided to go to couples counseling to work out our issues, so she stopped going to her mom with our problems. After my wife stopped telling my mother-in-law, then she stopped getting at me. I think my mother-in-law also realized that I needed to travel for work so I could provide for my family.

As John's account of his relationship with his mother-in-law continued, he revealed another role that his mother-in-law played—a nurturing role. She offered comfort when a crisis arose:

> The most significant interaction with my mother-in-law was when my brother died. I was a mess. My parents had died within a year of each other about three years before that. I had a terrible relationship with my brother and I felt like an orphan. My wife talked to her mom about how I was feeling and went to her for advice because I was really down and my wife didn't know what to do. After the funeral was over, my mother-in-law came to me and told me that, even though my family was gone, I always had a family with her. She told me that I wasn't alone and that she would be there for me and my girls for as long as she lives. It was huge to me. It was the comfort I needed. It was really awesome.

John was open to receiving that support, whereas a different son-in-law might see that as interference even when it was offered in such a loving way.

Another son-in-law whose in-laws were never married echoes the dual perspective of both interference and nurturance that John offered about his mother-in-law's role. He also offers a traditional view of both parents-in-law's role in the family:

> My mother-in-law is more invasive, but actually helpful. My father-in-law is a lot less invasive but still helpful. So, she is more in the day to day, and knows what is going on with the kids. Sometimes she may speak her opinion on certain things dealing with the kids, and what you should or shouldn't do, where my father-in-law doesn't really get into it as much or just follows along with what we say. So he's not . . . he doesn't debunk whatever we are saying at all, ever, whereas she does sometimes.

Oliver, who lives on the east coast, felt his mother-in-law's presence much more than his father-in-law's presence when it came to looking at colleges for his daughter:

> My mother-in-law tried to influence where she would like to see my daughter go to college, and that's out west. It's easy for them to just pull people out of the equation and plop them down somewhere else because that's what they did with their own lives, whereas I knew everybody in the family, we lived close, and I saw my grandparents every weekend. So her suggestion about the west coast bothered me. The "Oh, just send them out there" in my mind possibly leads to other things, establishing themselves out there, and then we would have very limited contact.

We wondered what the father-in-law's role was in Oliver's family: "He's not the man in charge. I have never had a negative interaction with him, only her. He deals with stuff, just amongst those two, from what I can tell. He won't do it in front of his family and grandkids. The men kind of go off to the side and sit."

In many families, the mother-in-law may serve as a conduit between the son-in-law and father-in-law. One son-in-law—an immigrant from Chad whose wife and children are now back home with his in-laws while he works in the United States—has a mother-in-law who served as a mediator with the father-in-law. She was in the United States a few years ago and has reassured her husband, the father-in-law, about the trustworthiness of the son-in-law. According to the son-in-law:

My father-in-law and I so far have no kind of conflict. We live happily. I have lived here for two years, but I have only called him personally maybe three times. He might consider that a bad thing, so it's not perfect. But I talk to my wife and kids often, and my mother-in-law was here and could go back and share experiences, so I think that helped him to understand me.

Sometimes there is a stronger connection with the mother-in-law than the father-in-law because of her nature. In this next example, illness has also intruded: "I definitely feel that I have a closer, stronger relationship with my mother-in-law because I interact with her a lot more. My father-in-law is a serious stroke victim, and his communication is somewhat limited. He is also not as social as my mother-in-law, so I definitely feel closer to her."

In another example, we see how the warmth of one parent can spark greater connection. Again, typical gender roles in the older generation seem to be playing out here:

I am not really close with my father-in-law. He's not a warm person, so it's hard to get close to him. He's kind of more of an authority figure than an actual parent you can have a relationship with. We don't agree on a lot of religious things, but I don't argue with him. We can have a long conversation, but I'll usually listen to him and just nod and not necessarily interact any more than that. I'm as close as I could be with my mother-in-law in a sense that she is very sweet, very caring, and very kind. She is non-judgmental and we have a great relationship. She wants us to come over more to see her granddaughter, so we've been spending a little more time there, especially over the summer. Things are chiller. When all the family is there, my father-in-law is in a good mood.

While we have given examples of the more social and engaged mother-in-law, in some families, the father-in-law is the dominant force and the more extroverted and the mother-in-law does not play as significant a role. Couples may form complementary relationships where the loquaciousness of one makes the other, by comparison, seem quiet or the warmth of one parent-in-law makes the other appear, or even be, more withholding. In this next and last example, the father-in-law is American born and his wife is Vietnamese, so some of the differences could be cultural:

There are two different personalities between them. My mother-in-law is quiet, I almost want to say shy. I definitely spend a lot more time talking to my father-in-law. He has told me a lot about his past about before he got married. So I'm closer to him. He tries more to connect with me. He's a very outspoken individual who likes to connect with people. My mother-in-law cares a lot about people and we can have conversations. Sometimes we talk about nothing at all or something very serious. But I spend a lot less time with her than him just because he's more talkative and more charismatic.

While the omnipresent depictions of interfering mothers-in-law in the lives of sons-in-law have some basis from what we heard from a handful of sons-in-law, we found other characteristics described and more prevalent. The mother-in-law is nurturing, engaged, warm, caring, and sweet. Her desire for contact with her daughter and son-in-law, as well as her grandchildren, may result in the son-in-law and father-in-law having more contact. If the family's relationships with the mother-in-law are closer, the children and grandchildren may reach out to her, and this will, in turn, bring the two men into more frequent, and potentially closer, contact.

8. WHAT HAPPENS WHEN MY FATHER-IN-LAW IS CLOSER TO ANOTHER CHILD-IN-LAW THAN TO ME?

A son-in-law may not be the only child-in-law in the family and may believe that his father-in-law likes another son-in-law or daughter-in-law more. Feeling less close to or, at times, less accepted by a parent-in-law can be difficult to handle. If the son-in-law believes that the father-in-law is closer to another son-in-law (as opposed to a daughter-in-law), that dynamic in particular could set up competition or feeling excluded, depending on how it manifests itself.

Feeling less close to a father-in-law can happen for many reasons: (1) the son-in-law has not helped produce grandchildren while the child and more favored child-in-law have; (2) the son-in-law was of a different religion, race, or economic background than his wife (the father-in-law's daughter) while another child-in-law matched the father-in-law's family more closely; (3) the father-in-law is less close with his own child and that emotional distance extends to the son-in-law; or (4) the father-in-law is particularly close to another child-in-law because they work together, knew each other before, have similar interests, etc. In fact, the son-in-law might feel close to the father-in-law while realizing that the father-in-law is just closer to the other child-in-law.

Many sons-in-law are comfortable with their relationship with the father-in-law and may not care that they are not quite as close. They may prefer a little distance, in fact, if they do not want a closer relationship. They may, for example, have fewer interests in common and be happy to attend the antique show on Sunday rather than watch the football game with their father-in-law. We did find, however, that sons-in-law who endorsed this feeling (about one in four of those with another child-in-law in their family either strongly agreed or agreed that their father-in-law was closer with another child-in-law) felt less good about the quality of their relationship with their father-in-law. Feeling that the father-in-law is closer to another child-in-law may have been spawned by earlier interactions in their relationship, as these sons-in-law are also more likely to feel their father-in-law was less approving of their marrying his daughter in the first place. Feeling less close could also sprout up years into the relationship when events cause a rift.

To add a complicated layer, we dug further into this group of sons-in-law and found that this feeling that the father-in-law was closer to another child-in-law occurs more often in marriages where the sons-in-law do not share their true feelings about their father-in-law with their wife. We sense that a dynamic is set up where the son-in-law does not initially feel accepted, continues to feel less accepted by comparison, and may keep those feelings from his wife. His wife may sense there are issues between her husband and father, as these tend to also be marriages where the wife wants her husband to work harder on his relationship with her father than marriages where the son-in-law does not feel less favored.

Income and distance matter here. When we looked at sons-in-law who felt the father-in-law was closer to another child-in-law, we found that the higher the son-in-law's combined family income was, the less likely the son-in-law felt that way. In terms of distance between them, the farther the son-in-law and father-in-law lived apart, the more likely he was to feel that the father-in-law was closer to another child-in-law.

9. I HAVE DIFFICULTY BALANCING TIME BETWEEN BOTH SIDES OF THE FAMILY. IS THAT TYPICAL?

One of the hardest things for couples to do is to find the right amount of time to spend with their respective families. Many want their own separate family life and also want to be loyal and connected to their families of origin. The challenge for couples is to balance time for the couple, time for individual and couple friends, time for immediate family, time with extended families, and time to be alone or to pursue hobbies or other interests, like sports or going to the gym. Some couples may be successful at this balancing act during one stage of their life and then might find that they have to renegotiate as new challenges (e.g., monitoring teenagers, new jobs, taking care of aging parents) arise.

One in five sons-in-law strongly agreed or agreed that they and their wife have difficulty balancing time with both sides of the family. If the son-in-law reports that the father-in-law did not approve of the marriage, he is more likely to report they have trouble balancing time with the two sets of in-laws. The newer the son-in-law's marriage, the more likely he and his wife have trouble balancing both families. Given what we know about the formation of new families, this makes sense. When younger and first married, a son-in-law may be more tied to his parents and his wife to hers while the in-law relationships are still forming. Those ties can be strong, as we did find that sons-in-law who were close to their mother,[19] though not to their father (!), had a greater difficulty in balancing both sides of the families. With age, people separate more and competing pulls become easier to manage with experience.

Jealousy also appears as a factor in balancing time with both sides of the family. If the son-in-law believed his own parents were jealous of the relationship he had with his father-in-law, he had a harder time with balancing. Likewise, if the son-in-law views his parents as interfering in his marriage, balancing is more difficult. This sense of their jealousy and of their interfering could be signs to the son that his parents are unhappy with the way their relationship is evolving.

Further, balancing is more difficult if a son-in-law is receiving childcare and financial assistance from his in-laws. This is not to suggest that aid be avoided. It could suggest that when in-laws are giving such assistance, a son-in-law should be aware of the potential impact on his time with his own parents, who may feel they are not helping out as much and could be feeling jealous of the other parents' level of input.

These characteristics give us a picture for sons-in-law to consider. Early on in his marriage, balancing two families of origin is more difficult. It may be made harder if the son-in-law is close with his mother; if he feels his in-laws did not approve of the marriage; if his parents are jealous and if they interfere in his marriage; or if childcare and financial assistance are provided. The good news is that balancing both families becomes easier with time.

CONCLUSION

While this discussion has focused on the sons-in-law's views and experiences of their father-in-law, it is also important to highlight that the father-in-law often wants the relationship to work for his daughter's (and grandchildren's) well-being and for the good of his own relationship with his daughter. In the best of worlds, both men work hard to have a quality relationship with each other that benefits all family members. It is also clear in our data that many relationships work because the sons-in-law genuinely like and admire their fathers-in-law as people.

CHAPTER 7

Gay and Lesbian In-Law Relationships

My father asked, "Why don't you just adopt?" and I said, "Dad, if I was married to a man, would you ask me that question?" There aren't exceptions because we are from the same gender. We want to have the house and the yard and the cars and the kids and everything that suburban America is about, with a social conscience. I think the fact that we are two women together changes in-law perspectives about what that is about.

Lana

In this chapter, we discuss the hurdles that same sex-couples and their in-laws overcome in forging their relationships while striving for the same marriage and family opportunities and love and support as other married couples. As detailed in previous chapters, in-law relationships are complex and, even when they are going smoothly, can be ambivalent and ambiguous. That complexity is extended in same-sex couples, and from the cases we present, it is clear that when two gays or two lesbians marry, someone in the immediate or extended family is likely to be uncomfortable with the union in a way that does not occur with heterosexual marriages. The discomfort poses challenges for the relationships between same-sex couples and their parents and in-laws that do not exist for heterosexual couples.

Same-sex marriage has been legal across the United States since the Supreme Court decision in *Obergefell v. Hodges* in 2015. Prior to 2015, same-sex marriage was legal in some states; there were an estimated 390,000 same-sex marriages by the time the Supreme Court made its ruling.[1] As part of our research, a small cohort of children-in-law who were in same-sex marriages and parents-in-law who had a child married to someone of the same sex were interviewed. Here we offer a look at some of them in the hope of providing a beginning understanding of in-law relationships in gay and lesbian families. We recognize that these classifications are binary, which is consistent with how the interviewees defined themselves, and that there are other definitions of self in addition to gay, lesbian, and straight.[2]

Like all in-law relationships, these are complex and become more complex when viewed through the lens of being a sexual minority. In many ways, these children-in-law and parents-in-law struggle with the same issues as heterosexual marriages—being accepted into a new family and dealing with how parents-in-law think their grandchild is being raised. Still, for some of those interviewed, being a sexual minority causes additional struggles within the immediate and the extended families, as well as within their wider social networks. Daniel Alonzo and Deborah Buttitta from California State University Northridge, in a review of the literature specific to lesbian, gay, and bi-sexual well-being, found that well-being is greatly affected by the internalization of sexual stigma and the stress of being a minority in a heterosexual world.[3] A Pew Research Center report found that while acceptance of LGBT peoples has increased—63% of the population in 2016 said homosexuality should be accepted by society, a 25% increase over 2006—the LGBT population still feel they have been stigmatized.[4] Where one lives geographically, as well as the ethnic and religious group with which one affiliates (intersectionality), can affect attitudes toward being LGBT,[5] as we hear from families with members who live in rural states, in a Latin American country, or as part of a conservative religious community.

Research on gay and lesbian families is not new, nor is the discussion about being accepted by a spouse's family as an in-law. The process of coming out to one's own family can be one of the most difficult events in a gay or lesbian person's life, particularly if the family is perceived as non-accepting. Acceptance of one's own sexuality often happens in stages, just as acceptance by one's family often unfurls over time. The recent hit TV series *This Is Us* aired a touching scene of acceptance when Randall and Beth's teenage daughter, Tess, comes out to them and they offer her loving support. The context of the family and the context of the community can make such acceptance more or less likely. Mothers and sisters tend to be told before fathers and brothers[6] and are often more accepting. Someone may be out in a new city to which they have moved but not be out in their home community, which is less accepting. For some parents-in-law we interviewed, acceptance meant having to first accept their child being lesbian or gay. Part of accepting their child being lesbian or gay could include parents mourning the loss of the idealized child, the one they always dreamed would grow up, have children (note the quote from Lana at the beginning of the chapter), and live a heteronormative life. This can be considered an ambiguous loss for some parents—the child is present in their life but is not living the life the parents had imagined, hence the ambiguity of the loss. The parents, when their gay or lesbian child marries, particularly in a public ceremony, are reminded of their child's sexual orientation. They may struggle to adjust to both the public nature of the ceremony, as in Lana's case, and to a new in-law entering their family. While 63% of those in the Pew poll said homosexuality should be accepted in society, the questions behind the poll do not ask about acceptance in one's *own* family. Further, many parents fear, for good reasons, their child will not be safe if they announce to the public through the act of marriage that they are lesbian or gay. Hate crimes in general have been on the rise, according to 2018 Hate Crime Statistics gathered by the Department of Justice, with 17% of those being classified as motivated by sexual orientation and gender-identity bias, including against gays, lesbians, transgender and gender non-conforming people. Gay men, in particular, tend to be victimized more than lesbians, and people of color are victimized more than Whites.[7]

Corinne Reczek, an associate professor in the Department of Sociology at Ohio State University, has written about the ambivalence that family members feel about gay and lesbian family relationships.[8] Reczek, in explaining the mixed feelings experienced between generations, details ambivalence on the psychological level, such as when parents are unhappy with their adult children's career path, and ambivalence on the sociological level, wherein the values of society (one *should* be heterosexual and marry someone of the opposite sex) cause contradictory expectations between family members. Parents may experience a loss of the idealized adult child while also wanting to provide support. Family members can provide love and support for each other while also acting negatively or disapprovingly. Ambivalence can be felt by a family member toward someone else or may be perceived as occurring in someone. Eighty-five percent of the 60 gay- and lesbian-identified adults Reczek interviewed described at least one family member whose actions were perceived as ambivalent toward them. Those defined as ambivalent manifested it either overtly (showing both outward support and outward disapproval) or covertly (having positive interactions while telegraphing negative hidden feelings). Ambivalence was seen in interactions between parent and child as well as in interactions between parent and child-in-law.

Here we delve into what the specific relationships are like between the parents and their gay or lesbian son- or daughter-in-law. We show the hurdles that may exist for these parents and children-in-law in forging their relationship. We first provide the stories of three parents-in-law who describe their relationships with their child-in-law who is married to their own son or daughter. The parents-in-law are in communication with their children—a requirement for being in the research. Thus, they already have relationships with their children that are more accepting than some parents who have disowned or cut themselves off emotionally from children who have come out as lesbian or gay. We will use a lens of intergenerational ambivalence to understand what has transpired in these families.

THREE PARENTS-IN-LAW

Ariel: "We love Ella and she is the perfect mate for my daughter."

Ariel's experiences with her daughter's wife, Ella, 38, provide what may be a fairly typical scenario for many families with a gay or lesbian marriage. Ariel is 70, White, and married to Jim. She is a retired librarian with a middle-class income. Ariel's daughter, Tina, is 42 and has been married for 10 years following 10 years of living with Ella. Tina and Ella have one child. Tina has a married older brother with one child. Ariel was reasonably close with her parents and her parents-in-law when they were alive.

When asked how important her relationship is with her daughter-in-law, Ariel said:

> Very. We love Ella and she is the perfect mate for my daughter. Tina is exactly like her father, very driven, very opinionated. If she says she will do something, even if it's going to kill her, she's going to stay by it. Ella is the calming spirit in that relationship and she's very agreeable with Tina. I've never seen them have a cross word, not that I'm with them all the time, but they complement each other.

Tina and Ella met in college. Ariel said:

> I can't quite remember how long it was before we met Ella. I think it was when I went to visit Tina in Denver when she had an apartment. I can't remember if Ella lived with her then. Once they became an item, they always came together to our house, mostly for holidays, or they went to Ella's family, who were very accepting of them. I loved Ella right away. But there were people saying things about the relationship [implying that being lesbian was something of which to be ashamed] and my comment always was, "I pray as much for Ella as I do for my daughter." And I do. They're a unit. She helps Tina immensely. We don't talk a lot with them being so far away, but she always makes me feel comfortable when I'm there. She just fits in so well with the whole family.

While Ariel gets along well with Ella, she had a more strained relationship with her son, Stan's, first wife (Ariel's other daughter-in-law). Both Stan and that daughter-in-law were uncomfortable with Tina's sexuality:

Stan divorced her and he remarried two years later. He had one child with his first marriage and one with his second. His first wife is bipolar and was very, very difficult. I would go for months without even seeing my grandchild because there were times when she just didn't want to be any part of the family. I begged Stan to bring the grandchild over, but he said that wouldn't work and would cause friction between him and his wife. That, and because they didn't accept Tina, made our relationship very difficult.

Stan's second wife, Hannah, appeared as a savior to the family and caused a shift in the dynamics that helped to bring Stan and Tina closer:

Hannah thinks the world of both Tina and Ella. She helped Stan adjust to their relationship because he had a really hard time with Tina being a lesbian. Hannah somehow helped him see it was more important to have a relationship with her. In the last 10 years, you see brother and sister with their heads together in the corner talking at family events. Tina worshiped her brother at one point, but they're so different. Stan is a Republican and Tina is a Democrat.

Some parents, like Ariel, become fearful for their children when they do not follow a heteronormative life: "I worried so much if something happened to me or if Tina's relationship doesn't work, she's got to have somebody."

Ariel especially appreciates how Ella and Tina work together to raise their son:

Tina doesn't do well with babies. She loves when they get older, but when they are younger she kind of holds them at a distance. I was concerned how she would do with her son. Tina takes on the role of what a father would do, while Ella is very nurturing. [When we introduce Lana later in this chapter, questions about gender roles in parenting emerge again; while gender differences in parenting exist, they may not be as fixed as many believe.[9] Here we are reporting on Ariel's views of these roles.] Eventually Tina did great and I would just laugh at her because I knew it was just the way she is. Ella would pick up where they needed. And if Ella has something going on, Tina immediately takes over. They are so in sync. I wish I had that in my marriage!

We wondered after Ariel learned that Tina was a lesbian if she had pre-conceived notions about what a relationship with a daughter-in-law would be like. But given who Tina had dated before, Ariel is thrilled with the choice of Ella:

> Tina had another relationship before Ella and I wasn't comfortable with her. I don't like to see anybody being very physically demonstrative in front of someone, no matter what the sex. Things like that bother me. But with Ella and Tina, I've never felt awkward or uncomfortable. It was a good fit from the beginning. As for our in-law relationship, it was really a whole new venue. I guess I just always treated her as a daughter-in-law and as a friend and part of the family.

One's own history with feeling excluded can affect one's own attempts to combat it. Ariel worked very hard to be inclusive of Ella because she struggled with her relationship with her own in-laws:

> Jim's family is a very proud family. I'm just Ariel. Everything in his family had to be just so. I didn't know how to cook or iron, and they were all just so prim and proper. My father-in-law was a wonderful calm man, always nice to me, but I never felt close to him. He taught high school, and had 20 acres and he was working on them all the time. My mother-in-law has been a challenge. I'm from New York City and I think they would have preferred him marrying a local girl who knew how to do all the things they'd been doing all their lives. I've always felt like I was beneath her. I didn't feel welcomed in the family. My mother-in-law has made me cry many, many times. Maybe it's why I try so hard with my children-in-law.

We asked Ariel how Jim was affected by Tina and Ella's relationship:

> Jim is not real close with Tina and I used to really try to push it. I can't . . . usually before they leave, they've had words. They do not get along at all. Jim is very domineering. I used to try to make it better, but I've decided that's between the two of them. He knows how I feel and I know how he feels and I just leave it be now. I pray that they will be okay one day.

Jim and his family came up again as an issue when Ariel was asked what it was like having a lesbian daughter married to a woman:

> Jim's side of the family had a very difficult time, especially his mother. She didn't want anyone to know. I actually left the church because the minister

was preaching negatively about it. I loved that church. I went a couple different places, but didn't feel comfortable. And then one day the Lord told me, "Ariel, be yourself and go back." I did and I shared with people and I wasn't ashamed. This is the path Tina chose. It was fine with my side of the family. There was no issue and my friends were very supportive. I think if anything, Tina being lesbian made my relationship with Tina stronger because I was determined to be very supportive.

While Ariel has always been clearly in Tina and Ella's corner, she had to navigate multiple relationships with family members. We see here that Ariel was part of a triangle with Tina and Jim but stepped away from that position more recently. For many of those we interviewed, this seems to be a pattern: Married children receive support from some family members but are emotionally distant from others. Stan, Jim, Jim's family, and Ariel's church family were not accepting of Tina initially. It may have been Ariel's struggles with her own in-laws that have caused her to work so hard to build a relationship with Ella, it may have been her innate belief in acceptance, or it could have been both.

Andy: "I liked being part of a family, so yes, it hurts."

While Ariel has a wonderful relationship with Ella, Andy's relationship with his son-in-law provides a stark contrast. In this relationship, it is unclear how being gay has shaped the father-in-law/son-in-law relationship or if it has shaped it at all. Andy is a married, White, 65-year-old rabbi who describes his income as upper-middle. His son, David, 32, has been married to Rex, 31, for two years.[10] Andy and his wife live 1,000 miles away from David and Rex. Andy reports having a close relationship with his in-laws and with his own parents. In addition, he describes his parents as being close with their in-laws (Andy's grandparents). He brings a history of familial closeness to his relationship with his own children and their spouses. Here we see that such a positive history may not redound to the next generation.

While Andy's relationship with Rex is important to him, he laments that it has been highly problematic:

Rex has a number of serious issues of which David is quite aware. We are open about discussing them. Rex is an addict, drugs and alcohol, and he won't go into treatment. He's been in therapy for probably the past 20 years as he has significant issues with his mom. When his parents divorced, he was 10. His father stayed in the house for another three years with his mother. With the parents not talking to each other but living side by side, you can imagine the type of dysfunction that there was. Rex came out when he was 15 and his father beat him remorselessly. Rex is very funny and smart; he can be very witty—I can see the attraction that David has to him, but he's got a number of issues.

In a parallel process, just as Andy struggles with Rex, David struggles with Rex's mother:

She is so controlling. Her second husband was very well to do and died, which left them with a lot of money. So, David's relationship with his mother-in-law has been troubled because she accused him of being a gold-digger, of marrying Rex for his money. Believe me, that's not why he married Rex. It's not worth the money, and his mother has not been terribly generous. She has a problem with alcohol. We got along with her and her current husband very well until Rex had a terrible breakdown last year . . . drugs, alcohol. His relationship with his mother was terrible, and she said some terrible things about David. She hated David and she was sorry Rex and David ever got married. David was very hurt, which he shared with us. It takes David a lot to open up, but he does share with us. We won't have anything to do with his mother-in-law unless she makes atonement to David, which she hasn't done. She was under the influence when she said those things so I'm not even sure she remembers.

Besides dealing with Rex's mother from a distance, Andy has his hands full with Rex:

He can be highly critical and has a mean side to him. He's not been critical of me because he has his own issues with fathers and men, but he's been very critical of my wife's cooking and her intelligence. Once he called her stupid. For David, it's been very hard. On a recent phone call, he just broke down and cried and said that it was just too hard.

Some parents-in-law deal directly with their children-in-law. Andy does not:

Our relationship is mediated through David. We haven't seen or spoken to Rex since May when there was a big blow-up at a family wedding at the rehearsal dinner. So, as of now, we have no relationship. He wished us a happy new year on Rosh Hashanah, but that's about it. We talked to David about leaving Rex, but he loves him. Rex is his husband and he's really committed and that's the last time we've discussed that.

Andy and his wife learned that David was gay when he came out to them his senior year of college. Andy says being gay has nothing to do with the problems they have in their relationship with Rex:

> We've always thought that David was gay, from the time he was three years old. We needed him to figure it out and, obviously, we couldn't be certain. He had lots of relationships with girls, even in college. So when he came out to us we weren't shocked. We simply said to him, "We're not surprised, and we love you." Would I prefer he be heterosexual? Yes, because it would be easier for him in life and, for my own selfish reasons, I'd always imagined that he'd bring home a young, beautiful woman and they'd have children one day. But that's my problem, not his. I can't let my issues affect his life. So once I realized that and was able to deal with it, it was a non-issue for me.

David is not Andy's only child. His relationships with his other two children-in-law are mixed, with one being strained and the other going smoothly. Andy has regrets about the message his children received growing up and offers an illustration of what society (in this case Jewish society) tells its members:

> Being rabbi's kids, we told them they had to marry Jewish people. We forgot to tell them that their spouses had to be smart and kind and productive people, mostly kind; we forgot that part. So my daughter-in-law (who is Jewish) is pretty much a bitch. She doesn't do anything at home and our son does everything. She doesn't share her income with him, so they live very modestly. He's a nurse. My relationship with her is quite strained. We actually urged them [just as David was urged] to break up because we knew this was a disaster. She did break up with him and then, because my son doesn't have any courage, he took her back when she asked him to. Ever since that breakup, his mother-in-law hasn't spoken to us. My daughter's husband, Jake, we love. He's a really good person. He's kind and sweet and funny. Obviously, everybody has their own issues, but he's really good for her and good to her.

Clearly it has not been easy for Andy, and being a rabbi, a spiritual leader who is supposed to bring people together, it may be especially difficult. When asked to describe his feelings he said, "I'm sad. I like being inclusive, not exclusive. I liked being part of a family, so yes, it hurts [to have this separation from a son-in-law]. I wanted to be close with them. I love my mother-in-law and I wanted my children-in-law to love me. I wanted to be a father to them."

We asked Andy if the relationship was what he thought it would be when David and Rex first got married. As we have discussed, David is the linchpin here for Andy: "A lot of our relationships with our in-law children are mediated through our children. If our children are happy, then we should generally be happy. We can't control them. We can't control people. Once they are 11 or 12 years old, forget it. You have to give up control."

Andy is very accepting of David's being gay, and his statement about not being able to control people after the age of 12 could be seen as a confirmation of this. But there is also a hint of his ambivalence about not interfering in family members' relationships in general. On the one hand, people cannot be controlled but, on the other hand, Andy suggests David should leave Rex and that his other son leave the daughter-in-law he does not like. Despite the mixed messages Andy may have sent to his children, Andy places great value on staying close. By being supportive of David, he is keeping his son close even though his marriage to Rex, which could have separated Andy and David, causes him great pain.

Sara: "Any person my child would marry would be very important to me."

Sara is a White, married, 57-year-old computer analyst with a 29-year-old daughter, Sylvia, married to Flora. Sara has another, younger daughter who is married to a man. Sara's parents are divorced and she is close with her mother but not her father. In interviewing Sara, we see the impact that being a lesbian can have on in-law relationships when the daughter-in-law's parents are not accepting of their own daughter, in this case Flora.

During the interview with Sara, when asked about the importance of her relationship with Flora, Sara described the void she felt she was filling for Flora:

> I think any person my child would marry would be very important to me because my daughters are very important to me and the person they choose to be in a life-long relationship with is definitely someone I want to embrace as family. We love Flora and we like her. But she has real struggles with her own parents and she has told us that we very much play that role of mom and dad. Her parents can't totally accept her being gay. I think they're working on it, but she feels a real loss.

Similar to Andy, Sara was not surprised to find Sylvia in a lesbian relationship:

As far as Sylvia's coming out, I think we kind of always knew she was lesbian. I mean, she had non-conforming gender characteristics, but actually we tried really hard not to put her in any specific sexual orientation box because she had lots of girlfriends and boyfriends. From age four, she wanted all the boy stuff, from clothes to games to toys and activities. We saw that early, so we weren't surprised when she had her first girlfriend in high school. I think she was 15 when she said to me, "Mom, I think I'm gay" and I remember saying, "Okay, great; what do you want for dinner?" I actually used to feel really good about that and then, more recently, I've thought maybe I was a little too casual about that. I'm sure I said more, but that's mostly what I remember. If someone were to tell me that today, I think I'd be a little more like, "Well, what do you want to talk about with regards to this? I love you and accept you." I think I could do better now, so I criticize myself for not being perfect. I also remember when she was in high school she got called into the principal's office because she and her girlfriend were holding hands in public. So Arnold and I went to talk to the principal, and I think the principal brought us in thinking, "Oh, my gosh! I have to tell these parents that their daughter was holding hands with another girl." But we were like, "Wait a minute. If they were a boy and a girl would you have called them out in the way you did?" We were really pissed that he was discriminating against them. We had a big conversation with her first girlfriend's mom. Her parents called Arnold and me over to have a talk and wanted to know what we were going to do about it; we had to stop this! They were so anti their relationship. Fortunately, Arnold holds it all together; he's really good in crisis while I just freak out and get emotional. I was so angry, but I just sat there during this conversation and Arnold handled things very well.

The mother-in-law/daughter-in-law relationship was not easy at the beginning. Flora was Sylvia's lacrosse teammate in college. It dawned on Sara over time as Sylvia and Flora began spending more time together outside of the player relationship that something was developing between them:

It wasn't really until they came back from a vacation that it sunk in for me and I was like, "Oh! Okay, this is more than a friend relationship." Flora was hesitant with us at first, but Sylvia told us, "I really love this person." Flora didn't know quite what to make of us at first. She grew up in a very conservative household. We're very casual. We call one another by our first names and we're not part of an organized religion. Flora grew up in a Methodist household, went to church every Sunday, and had different expectations for how elders and children interact and behave, more conventional than we've ever seen ourselves. Sylvia was like, "My parents are cool. You can call them by their first names." And Flora was definitely like, "Uhhh, I don't know about that. That seems awkward or disrespectful." So it was kind of a gradual process of getting to know each other. We're so open and nurturing and sexual orientation makes no difference to us, which was very different for Flora. She had just recently accepted herself as being gay. So in the first several years of their relationship she was coming to terms with "this is the person I love and it's okay to be this way," because that just wasn't the environment she grew up in. I think she was wary of us in the beginning. Maybe we were going to pretend we were okay with it all, but weren't really because her parents were tough on her. Some really mean things were said to her by her parents, mostly her mother. Her dad doesn't say much in general, which is hurtful in and of itself. I think slowly, over time, she grew to accept our love and support and to believe it was real. She has become very dear to us and we count her as our daughter and refer to her as daughter instead of daughter-in-law, although sometimes we say daughter-in-law so that people will understand they are in a same-sex marriage.

Sara, in a manner similar to Ariel and Ella's relationship, feels she has crafted a relationship with Flora separate from Sylvia. They share interests, like walking dogs together and consulting about makeup. When asked, Sara could not think of a difficult situation that had arisen between them. She works hard to restrain herself from feeling angry at Flora's parents, not wanting to add any fuel to that fire, and hopes they reconcile with Flora someday.

Sara is especially impressed by the teamwork she sees: "They are great partners. They have built a home together, raised a garden and chicks and bought a house. They have two dogs they adore and take care of. They travel and coach lacrosse together. They're very different personalities that fit together well."

Sara was not especially close with her in-laws, and some of what drives her behavior with Flora echoes what we learned from Ariel in terms of wanting a different relationship with the next generation:

I felt a little bit like Flora probably did when she first met us. My in-laws were very nonconventional and would call one another by their first names, which was not the environment I grew up in. We've had regular contact over the years, friendly but not particularly close. We don't talk about anything terribly deep or emotional, but it's certainly pleasant. They're passive, non-communicative people. They don't talk a lot about feelings, which can be challenging. Because of my experiences with them I wanted to do better with my own kids and family.

In other chapters we have looked at the role the father-in-law/husband plays in the mother-in-law and daughter-in-law relationship. Does having a lesbian daughter and daughter-in-law affect Sara's relationship with her husband as it does for Ariel? "For the most part Arnold and I are on the same page. I would say it's probably brought us closer together, because it's like we have another daughter."

Sara had many reflections on what *Obergefell* means for her family:

It's a huge impact that the marriage is considered legal because it impacts their daily lives, like when they try to open a bank account or buy a house together or a car or do their taxes. When you can't do those things and you constantly get this message that you're the "other" and you're different, it's hurtful. It's really hard. They recently changed their name. They created a new last name so they could be more one and hopefully get fewer questions. They wanted to do that to feel more bonded in the eyes of the world. I'm really concerned with our current political climate that someone's going to try to take that away. And I worry about their safety; they worry about their safety. They know there are certain places that they just won't hold hands. They have to constantly be aware of that. It's definitely much easier for two women than for two men, but it's still hard.

It is not only society that may put pressure on a relationship. Flora's parents, Sylvia's in-laws, are also making their life difficult, too:

At first, they didn't understand their relationship, but then Flora told them, "I'm gay, I love Sylvia; we're together," and they were flat out in denial, angry about it. They even referred to our family as "the cult" at one point. We've met them a number of times and tried to be pleasant. Flora's mom has a number of mental health issues. At a certain point, Flora just had to cut them off because they were causing a lot of anxiety for her. They were questioning her entire self-worth. It was just negative. They don't really have any relationship right now. Before, there was a period of about three years where they sort of got along. Her mom and her sister came to the wedding; her dad and her brother did not. Her dad's brother never responded, completely ignored it. Her mom tried, to her credit, to help Flora with her wedding dress and do all the stereotypical things a mom of the bride does, except this time there were two brides. But I think she just can't quite come to terms with it. For a while, the girls would spend holidays, Christmas, Thanksgiving with Flora's family. They were trying so hard to forge a relationship and the dad was embracing Sylvia like he would a son and was treating her like he would one of the guys. I think that's the only way he could get his head around it. He gave her tools for Christmas and they would do projects together. They did spend some time together, but now it's nonexistent. It's very strange and sad. I think Sylvia felt they were trying to be welcoming at one point, but they weren't ever being genuine with one another. It was very surface-y. When Caitlyn Jenner came out as transgender, that sparked a family debate. It started through Facebook with her mother or brother saying something really disparaging about Caitlyn and how horrible and disgusting it was. Flora couldn't take it anymore. She said, "If you can say that or feel this about this person, then you can't love and accept me." Sylvia just wants to protect Flora. She's tried to be the go-between, but mostly her role is to support Flora in whatever she needs to do. She's really encouraged Flora to speak her mind and to let them know how she feels. We all hope that it evolves, but I think it's very hard for people when they perceive this goes against their religious viewpoint, and that's where they get really hung up. I do believe that Flora's parents love their daughter. I think they're terrible at showing it and expressing it, and I think they are selfish. I do remember Flora's mom saying, "I just don't know what to call Sylvia. Do I call her my daughter-in-law?" She didn't know what words, and that was a big problem. "How do I explain to my friends who she is?" and that was the manifestation of her discomfort with the relationship. I think she did surprise herself. She met another couple of women through the church who also have gay children and I think it did open the door for her a little bit. She started feeling like, "Oh, other people have done this, maybe I can do it." I have no hope for Flora's dad. They have not talked in two years. He does not reach out. He's silent. He's sullen. He is just nonexistent in that way. It's very sad.

Themes

Sara and Arnold offer a different perspective than Ariel and Jim and Andy and his wife of parents accepting their own child and then, by extension, their child-in-law. For Sara and Arnold there is no ambivalence. For the other men, levels of acceptance came more slowly, and this remains an issue for Jim. Most starkly, we see the roles that other family members, including the other parents-in-law, play in the broader family system and how systems of support, including the church, can add to or ameliorate the struggles that in-laws experience. Clearly, their daughter being lesbian has added to the hurdles for these mothers-in-law and has pushed them to take on other battles and provide additional support to their daughters-in-law. For Andy, he has worked through many of the issues, though he still has slight residual feelings of disappointment with having a gay son and may be sending his son and son-in-law mixed messages.

In short, managing in-law relationships can be quite difficult for parents of gays and lesbians (and we suspect for other sexual- or gender-minority relationships, too). Marriage is a very public event requiring public definitions of one's own child as well as the person she or he or they is

marrying. Not only must parents accept their own child's sexual orientation, they must accept a child-in-law's sexual orientation, and navigate
through the thicket of family members, friends, and communities that may
or may not be supportive.

SIX CHILDREN-IN-LAW

As stated, it is only since 2015 that marriage has been possible nationally in
the United States for gays and lesbians. Sociologist Abigail Ocobock at the
University of Notre Dame notes the previous denial of marriage to lesbian
and gay couples made them feel like second-class citizens and had a negative impact on their health.[11] Marriage provides the social legitimacy to
couples that Flora and Sylvia sought and concretized by creating a new last
name. Ocobock also notes that same-sex marriages tend to be more egal-
itarian than heterosexual marriages; for instance, we learned from Ariel
about how Ella and Tina worked as a team to share childcare duties. As
we hear from children in gay and lesbian marriages, a younger generation
than the parents-in-law, we gain a sense of the tenuous nature of some of
their relationships, some of which were formed well before 2015. While
we specifically focus on how these six couples deal with their in-laws, the
social context of their lives and their personal histories also need to be
considered when looking at how they help define the relationships.

Michelle: "She came to terms with it and finally was willing to tell her friends."

Some relationships, as we have seen throughout, are neither particularly
close nor especially distant; they are pleasant and work for both the parent
and the child-in-law. Michelle's relationship with her mother-in-law, Gina,
is one such relationship. Michelle is 28 and White, works as a nurse, and
has been married to Lilly, also a nurse, for two years. They have no children
but hope to have them in the future.

When we asked Michelle how important the relationship with Gina was,
she replied:

> At this point, it's not unimportant, but I wouldn't say it is important. I feel if
> we lived closer we would have a lot more interaction. It's not a close relation-
> ship, but it's not a not close relationship and it's not strained. I would say it's
> supportive. I think it's genuine. Relaxed. It's gotten better since we've married,

and since her relationship with her other daughter has become more strained. I think she's realizing maybe I'm not so bad after all.

As we saw with Ariel and Jim and in other chapters, some spouses might try to engineer family relations between their spouse and the younger generation. In the younger generation, a daughter, for example, may try to make things better between her spouse and her mother or father. Lilly does not interfere in the relationship between Michelle and Gina. She lets it play out and knows they are not going to be especially close, in part because she believes that Gina cannot be "managed" even if Lilly tried. As Michelle describes Gina:

> She's very opinionated. She's boisterous, very curious, and loves learning. She definitely thinks that her answers and opinions are the end-all, be-all. She's generous, funny, and down to earth. She's very practical and not highly emotional. That's where her relationship with her husband deteriorated when they lost their third child during birth. Her response was, "Shit happens. We've got to pick ourselves up. We can grieve him, but let's move on." And he practically crumbled.

Lilly's parents divorced after the death of that child. The father then faded away in his grieving. Michelle's current relationship with him "is pretty nonexistent." She says:

> I saw him when we were in Philadelphia. He has come down here once and not since our wedding. He has gone through here to visit friends but has never come here, which I know is a point of sadness for Lilly. I don't really care because, frankly, I don't particularly like him. I don't think I interacted with him much even at our wedding. He showed up for the rehearsal dinner and was here for the wedding, but he wasn't an integral part of it. I don't think his support for our relationship now is genuine. For someone who left his family and didn't really have a great relationship thereafter, he's very emotional now. Lilly will get these strange, very mushy-gushy texts from him, "I love you. I'm so proud of you. You're the apple of my eye. Hug hug, kiss kiss." And we're like, "What the hell?" It doesn't match his actions and is just very peculiar. I think Lilly wants to maintain a relationship with him, and I am totally supportive of that. I would do whatever Lilly thought was best.

Still, Michelle's relationship with Gina can be viewed in the context of Gina having to adjust to having a lesbian daughter. As we heard from other parents-in-law, coming to terms with her friends' reactions helped to ease Gina's discomfort:

> At first Gina wasn't happy that Lilly had a relationship with a woman [Gina had them sleep in separate bedrooms when they would visit], so my relationship with her was impacted by that, regardless of who I was or what I was like. Gina thought it was a phase Lilly would grow out of. Then she came to terms with it and finally was willing to tell her friends. It was all hush-hush. Once we bought a house, she became more comfortable telling her friends and it seemed everyone else was like, "Oh okay, whatever." She got acceptance from other people so it started to be okay with her as well. When we got engaged and showed her the ring, she really came around and got excited about planning a wedding.

Not all of the friends in Gina's network were on board with Lilly being a lesbian, according to Michelle. Part of accepting Lilly as a lesbian was Gina having to let go of some friends:

> Susan and Ian are incredibly religious and incredibly conservative and, since our relationship, Gina no longer talks to them. I think in the beginning it was like, "We can't tell Susan and Ian about Lilly." But now she's come to the point where she's like, "Yeah, Susan and Ian know and they don't want to talk to me anymore, so ehh." But that was really hard for Gina because she felt some sort of guilt, that she was to blame for there being something "wrong" with her daughter that is now going to impact her life. But I think she's moved past that.

Gina now keeps a picture of Michelle and Lilly on display in her office. It was not only most of her friends who helped Gina accept Lilly and Michelle: Gina feels her other daughter is using her for childcare and is otherwise not interested in being with her. This has put emotional distance between mother and daughter. Michelle thinks that if she and Lilly have children, Gina will be as involved as she can be living hundreds of miles away: "Lilly's her baby and Lilly's her best friend, and after her dad left and her sister went to college it was just the two of them, so they were best friends. I expect her to be fully involved."

Michelle and Gina's relationship was initially slow to develop because of Gina's reluctance to accept Lilly as a lesbian. Once Gina moved past that and some of her friends were on board, Michelle felt accepted by Gina. With the strain in Gina's relationship with her other daughter, Lilly and Michelle seem to have moved even closer. As with some of the other examples, after overcoming initial shock, sadness, anger, or unhappiness about a child's sexual orientation, their relationship moved forward. Now it is satisfactory for both daughter-in-law and mother-in-law.

Rachel: "Within the past few years my spouse has finally realized and accepted her mom's faults."

An account executive for a west coast firm, Rachel is 38, White, and Jewish. She has been married to her wife, Ynez, for eight years, well before *Obergefell*. Not only was coming out difficult for Rachel's relationship with her own mother, but it was also difficult for Ynez and her mother, Karun. Ynez is Muslim and her mother, who lives in India, once asked Rachel to convert. Rachel's mother felt hit doubly hard when she learned her daughter was lesbian and was dating a Muslim. They did not speak for a number of years. Finally, after seeing how happy Rachel and Ynez were at family events, they re-established a relationship.

Rachel's relationship with Karun was initially wonderful. [Ynez's father lives in Singapore and is not in contact.] Karun would visit them for a few weeks at a time and was charming: "She has always been there for important events and has been consistent with her overall behavior." But over time, Rachel began to see how controlling Karun was. In a family dynamic that we have seen in other in-law relationships, heterosexual, lesbian, and gay, Rachel began to get to know her mother-in-law better and was less enamored with her. While she was willing to accommodate to her at first, with time Rachel became tired of that pattern of accommodating behavior in herself and began to resent Karun's behavior. To complicate matters, she felt Ynez was siding with Karun. Rachel and Ynez's biggest fights were around Karun and were exacerbated by Karun being in the house for six to eight weeks at a time when she would visit:

> Karun would be home with me while I was working and would interrupt what I was doing to talk about nothing. I would bend over backwards to help her by doing more for her than I do with my own mother. I would drive her to the doctor's and make her appointments for her. Sometimes she would treat me like a wife to Ynez and expect me to do everything for them both. She is so high maintenance yet she thinks she is easy to get along with.

Rachel believes Karun has great ambivalence about her daughter being a lesbian: "It should have been clear to her for years but she will not talk about it. Yet she did attend our wedding. She consistently ensures she is there for important events, while my parents did not attend."

Finally, the relationship, the triangulation, between the three women began to shift because of Ynez:

> Within the past few years my spouse has finally realized and accepted her mom's faults. This has helped our marital relationship considerably. I feel that it is not all in my head. I also learned to stop being a buffer between the two of them. She has raised such conflicting feelings in me. On the one hand, I love her because she has done very nice, kind, and thoughtful things for me. On the other hand, I detest her because of how needy, self-centered, and overly controlling she is and how she sets too high expectations for Ynez and me.

Lana: "I think Betty does a very good job in terms of balancing her relationship with them and balancing her relationship with me."

Lana, a 44-year-old White psychologist, has been married for seven years to her wife, Betty, after they dated for three years. They have one son. Like many others, Lana highlights that her relationship with her parents-in-law is governed by her spouse's relationship with them: "Betty is very close to her parents, so my ability to get along with her parents is very important to her and to me in support of her as well as just for myself. She talks with them several times a week. She consults with them on life matters from parenting to just her own things. They are a very important influence on her life."

Very often, finding time in a marriage for one's spouse and time for one's parents requires sensitivity to both and the ability to weave the threads of independence and connection into a family tapestry. Lana describes Betty's connection to her parents and also her independence from them:

> I think Betty does a great job in terms of balancing her relationship with them and balancing her relationship with me. While she has a great relationship with her parents, I am also relieved that she doesn't always agree with them. There are times that she may consult or they may offer uninvited opinions, but she has a mind of her own and, ultimately, she and I will make the decision.

Since Lana and Betty come from family backgrounds that have different levels of emotional expressiveness, when situations arise they (and their parents) do not always react in similar ways:

> My in-laws are incredibly kind people, perhaps almost to a fault. They are really liberal. I grew up in a more reserved family. My in-laws are kind of out there—not

in a hippie way—just in a "we're going to talk about everything" way. My son had a little accident and he has a hairline fracture in his wrist. Betty was wrestling with him and she reached down to help him up off the bed and felt a pop. I come from a family that might not share something like this as it is minimal and my family doesn't talk as much as my wife's. Typically, when anything happens, Betty will call her parents. This time her parents overreacted: "He's only three and half. He is really little. You are just too rough with him!" Minimal, but they took it to the nth degree, so Betty talked to them about it. It was the kind of thing where it was already stressful and you don't want your child to be injured and they end up escalating the situation instead of helping to calm us. She has to check them in terms of their reaction, and she tells me about it and we have to be able to work it out and be okay with where we are and what we are doing despite her parents' reaction. That has happened a couple of times, and it is hard to say who knows what that is really about. It could be just their personalities; it could be the distance. They live so far away and, not being here to see it for what it is, they tend to make it worse. The good thing is, it gets resolved. She is able to talk with them about it and she and I are able to work it out.

Betty's brother is married to a woman. Lana, in a situation reminiscent of Michelle's where Lilly's sister is less favored, thinks that Lana is the favored daughter-in-law, which has brought her closer to her in-laws: "I hear a lot of negativity about my fellow daughter-in-law. To be honest, it is great to be the favorite. Who doesn't want to be the favorite? But at the same time, when I have not been the golden child, I can empathize with what it must be like to be my brother-in-law's wife and be really disliked by her in-laws."

Part of Lana's challenge is to build an appropriate boundary with her mother-in-law. Lana's in-laws stay with Lana and Betty when they visit, and there are times when Lana feels her mother-in-law does not give her enough time to herself:

> I need to be able to come home and be in my space. One of the things that Betty's mother will do is, I don't think she has many friends, so when she is here she will follow me around and talk at me everywhere. I am an introverted personality, so that is very difficult for me. Betty is aware and runs interference for me. I told her, "I love your parents but I need to come home, have a few minutes, a glass of wine, and not feel like I am on all the time." Despite all of this, we have grown closer over the years. In the beginning of every relationship you don't show your faults, and over the years the faults have emerged, both mine and theirs. I think it has just helped us grow closer. We have a better understanding of each other and our humanity.

Lana learned a lot about in-laws from her own family:

My mother was very close with her mother-in-law. My grandmother was like a third parent, while my grandfather was nonexistent. He was physically absent and the memory of him was not good. I didn't grow up knowing either of my grandfathers. My grandmother lived next door and died suddenly of a heart attack right before I got out of high school. I was very close to her and she and my mom were best friends. I admired their relationship, so I probably recognized the importance of that relationship and, while I wanted to emulate that, I don't want to have as close a relationship with my mother-in-law as my mother had with hers. I think if my mother-in-law was the same personality as my grandmother, I would want to connect with her, but she is not the same person.

Lana's family was more of a hurdle initially for their relationship as lesbians than Betty's:

The marriage was an issue. Right before Betty and I married, my father said, "I prefer you not use the term 'wedding.' I am an old-fashioned guy." The coming-out process for both of us always had an impact on our relationships with our parents. The marriage piece brought up stuff that we thought had been resolved. It was okay for us to be together and my family could tolerate that, but then the marriage piece came up and that changed the game. After we were married, that became okay. Then we started talking about children. That changed the game again. My father asked, "Why don't you just adopt?" and I said, "Dad, if I was married to a man, would you ask me that question?" There aren't exceptions necessarily because we are from the same gender. We want to have the house and the yard and the cars and the kids and everything that suburban America is about, with a social conscience. I think the fact that we are two women together changes in-law perspectives. Maybe there is a perception that I should be more traditionally motherly and nurturing to my son, whereas I see my relationship with my son just as being something unique between me and my personality and him and his personality and gender to the extent that we respect his need to be around men. We see he enjoys being around men, so gender roles tend to get into the mix of the marriage dynamics and would not even arise in this way in a heterosexual marriage. And there is the challenge of role assumptions, that the female is traditionally in the nurturing role. Well, with two women, how does that work? Or if there were two men? Does that mean the child is being neglected?

Both of Lana's parents came to the wedding and her father, Lana reports, even gave a speech where he said, "'I came here and did not know what to expect and I am amazed.' He demonstrated his ability to evolve when just a few weeks before he said we should not use the term 'wedding.' It helped him broaden his perspective on what marriage really means. My parents have come a long way."

Lana's interactions with her in-laws do not seem that different from what a heterosexual in-law relationship might look like. But echoing earlier themes raised in other case examples, in the broader context of both families, it took some time for family members to accept the idea of "marriage" between two women. Then it took some time to accept the idea of two women having children. Other issues also are raised when looking at the development of a lesbian family, specifically around role modeling when two women raise a son. Once those hurdles were jumped, family members were able to pull together.

Micky: "Our biological fathers are men's men but they both accepted our homosexual relationship."

Married only 18 months after dating for three-and-a-half years, Micky, age 33 and White, works as a waiter. His husband, Jeff, age 37 works in real estate. Micky takes a matter-of-fact approach to his relationship with his father-in-law, Bill, whom he rarely sees. His attitude toward his in-laws is similar to others in this chapter and reflects a realization of the importance parents play in a marriage:

> He's my husband's father. I have to like him (laughs). But seriously, I do like him. I want us to get along because I love my husband and his father is important to him, so I want him to be important to me as well. As far as my mother-in-law, it's very important because it's my husband's mother. She's with me for the rest of my life now, so I would like to have a good relationship with her. My in-laws are both really cool. They are divorced and have both remarried. My father-in-law has a lot of health problems. I probably get along more with my stepfather.

As we show in this chapter, some parents have trouble accepting their son's or daughter's sexuality, but not in this case:

> Bill is accepting of our relationship and he has always been a part of Jeff's life, even though his parents divorced when Jeff was five and Jeff was primarily raised with his mother and stepfather. Jeff would like to be closer with his father, but Bill is a very independent man. We all like to have a few beers, relax, have fun, but Bill's health is poor so he can't get around as well. Jeff is frustrated

because I met his dad two weeks before the wedding and we have barely seen him since. And again it is not because of Bill or Jeff; it's just that we are very busy. When we get together it's great. I just really think it's because men do not talk on the phone every day. We got along great on the weekend we met. We went to the dinner, came back, crashed, went to breakfast and to a few bars. The wedding was a blast. But as of right now Bill is confined to a wheelchair, so it's just really hard for him, and he is a very proud man. I really enjoy Bill's company and he actually told me that he enjoyed mine, so that was a good moment for me. Jeff and Bill love each other, but they can go five months without calling each other, but when they do speak it's right where they left off. I am lucky, especially with Bill being such a man's man. Both of our biological fathers are men's men, but they both accepted our homosexual relationship with open arms, and many heterosexual couples do not have that.

Micky has a good relationship with Jeff's mother, whom he met for the first time at her high school reunion party:

Not to make my mother-in-law sound like a lush or anything, but when I got there she had been drinking and accepted me with open arms. We walked around dancing, drinking, having an absolute ball. Everyone kept asking, "Is this an escort?" and she was like, "No, this is my future son-in-law." I was so happy because I had not yet even proposed and it was so welcoming. I remember thinking, "I want to be a part of this family."

Micky and Bill's relationship seems more driven by stereotypical gender roles of men not speaking on the phone and by Bill's reaction to being incapacitated than by Micky and Jeff being gay. One of Micky's fondest moments with Bill was during a conversation about the nature of Micky and Jeff's relationship:

I think the best interaction was when Bill said that he was so proud of Jeff. We were having one of those, "So, you are going to marry my kid?" talks, and it was really cool. He said that if we ever needed anything money, bail money (laughter), he was joking, but then he went on to seriously say if there was ever anything that we needed that he would be right there. Bill said that Jeff has always been a smart kid and a good judge of character. Bill said that Jeff sized me up as the one, so that was good enough for him. That was probably the most special moment that I had with anyone in his family.

Micky knows he has a good thing with his in-laws after seeing his parents' struggles with Micky's paternal grandmother:

My dad gets along well with my mom's parents, but my dad's mother is horrible. My parents have been married for a long time and had to go to marriage counseling over her interference because it was causing such big problems in their marriage. My mom said their therapist coached them to not respond to her and I shouldn't either because it was hurting dad. She is a mean, bitter old lady.

With this relationship, Micky and Jeff have run into no roadblocks in their in-law relationships because they are gay. In addition, Micky has relationships with Bill as well as Jeff's mother that are not mediated by Jeff. The next two men have more complicated relationships with their father-in-law.

Sam: "I wonder if I weigh all the not-so-great things he did, or do I just take how he is now?"

Sam is White, 27, and a social worker married to a 43-year-old Latino, Diego, from Colombia. Given their age difference, there is a greater age gap than usual between Sam and his father-in-law, Miguel. There is also greater geographic distance. When asked how important his relationship was with his father-in-law, it was not surprising to hear from Sam that the relationship is not that important and has little impact on Sam's day-to-day existence. While Sam and Miguel get along well enough, Sam feels some ambivalence. It is a feeling that many people have for their parents-in-law when they learn more and more about how their spouse was treated growing up:

> He's great and has a good relationship with Diego now, but when Diego was a kid he did not. He was a pretty horrible dad and husband, so I feel conflicted about all the horrible things he did in the past, though he's been nothing but nice to me now. He's never been anything but supportive and welcoming, so I wonder if I weigh all the not-so-great things he did, or do I just take how he is now?

As a result of his past behavior, Sam walks on eggshells around Miguel when he sees him:

> I'm definitely more guarded and a little cynical about him and our relationship. I feel like maybe I don't want to get super-close because you never know how much people really change. While Miguel and Diego have a relationship, it's largely surface-level, as is my relationship with my own father. I guess it's just not super-profound.

Sam and Diego used to live in Cartagena and, since moving to the United States two years ago, have not seen Miguel and Diego's stepmother. Even when living in the same country, it was a three-hour drive and they did not see each other often. Sam also has a surface-level relationship with his stepmother-in-law (Diego's mother died): "It's not a deep bond or connection. I get along fine with her. She has a sharp side to her, but she's never shown that to me."

Miguel threw a big barbecue for them when they became engaged, though Sam still wonders about Miguel's level of acceptance of him as a gay man:

> Being gay definitely impacted the relationship Diego has had with his dad. Prior to me, Diego was in a relationship with someone for 13 years. He was living with his boyfriend and his boyfriend's mom for seven years. That was just after his mom passed away, so he really thought of his boyfriend's mom as his own mom. Definitely Diego being gay shaped how Miguel treated him. There isn't anything outright, but he has lived in a small town in a rural area his whole life except for two years in the military. He just has provincial views of the world. He's gotten to the point where he's okay with it, but it's always on the back of my mind: What is he not saying? Is there anything he still isn't approving of? He didn't go to our wedding. But he said it was because he wouldn't know anyone and that would make him feel uncomfortable. He sent us a wedding gift, so I don't think he objected to it. Afterwards, his dad's wife was all, "I wanted to go, but he said no. I wanted to be there, but he wouldn't let us."

Sam does not often have direct conversations with Miguel and, if there is an issue, Diego will be the go-between:

> Like, when we were moving or the wedding, Diego went and talked to him by himself. So I said, "Okay, it's your dad, so if you want to deal with it, I'm okay with that." As I've spent time with them, I feel I've gotten closer. Of course, the periods when I'm not living in the same country as them, we are more distant. In some ways, I think of him more like my grandparent as opposed to my father-in-law or my parent. I have an amazing relationship with my grandparents and they're a very integral part of my life. I always felt my dad had good relationships with his in-laws, my grandparents, so I had very positive experiences of in-law relationships. For my mother's side, I would say not nearly as good or seamless as my dad's relationships with my mom's parents. I think that was distance: My mom lived 400 miles from her in-laws. There's only so much of a close relationship that you can create when you're so far apart.

To some extent, the distance between Sam and Miguel replicates the distance and distancing Sam saw in his own family. Sam feels ambivalence toward Miguel, which matches his receiving mixed messages. While Miguel's outward behavior has been supportive (sponsoring a dinner in their honor), Sam suspects Miguel's feelings, based on his past behavior and living in a small community, are less accepting.

Roger: "They still don't actually know we're married."

While many of these relationships are ones where there is communication and attempts to work through differences, Roger's is characterized by clear rejection. A 33-year-old, White, electrical engineer, Roger and Ron, 32, married two years ago after a year of dating. Roger's relationship with his father- and mother-in-law in the role of son-in-law is nonexistent: "We mostly avoid them. They weren't happy when Ron came out to them, and they still don't actually know we're married. It is so complicated. Ron did not tell them because it was the only thing that made sense. Ron was worried they would stop talking to him completely."

Prior to Roger and Ron getting together, there had been periods when, because of family strife, Ron's parents did not talk to Ron. Having achieved a rapprochement, Ron feared his being married to a man would cause a permanent rift. Roger reported:

> I met them a few times. They didn't know we were dating the first time, so they were friendly. After they started talking to Ron again I would see them occasionally. They generally keep their distance and so do I. They live in Wyoming and we almost never see them. We all prefer it that way. My parents have not met my in-laws because my in-laws don't know we're married.

When asked how he envisioned his in-law relationship, Roger said that he was already not in a "traditional" marriage so he had no expectations: "The first time we met, Ron's father was nice enough because he thought I was Ron's friend. Since then he has been cold and we just avoid each other."

Roger does not see that changing in the future unless his father-in-law has a "perspective shift":

> Ron's father became more hostile. Most of my experiences are indirect. I hear about them through Ron. He just kind of ignores me, so I'd say it has basically been distant from the beginning. Occasionally he looks in my direction and says

hi. But basically, in every interaction, he has refused to acknowledge me. My mother-in-law is not as blatant in her rejection but is basically the same.

While we have talked about the ambivalence in some relationships, here there is none—Roger only feels resentment: "I don't understand why they have such a hard time accepting Ron and me. I've given up on that changing."

Themes

These three women and three men provide a preliminary perspective on the range of experiences that lesbians and gays may encounter with their in-laws. Their experiences are not unique. Other research has found that increased support for same-sex couples from parents-in-law usually comes with marriage and over time.[12] Michelle and Lana, both of whom have grown closer with their in-laws, epitomize greater acceptance over time. Gina, Michelle's mother-in-law, demonstrated her acceptance by placing a picture of Michelle and Lilly on her desk at work. Lana's father finally embraced the notion of a wedding, but only after attending the wedding.

Time can also have a different effect on the relationship. Rachel has moved away from accommodating to Karun and does not feel as close to Karun as she sees how controlling she is. Rachel feels that, as she matures, she does not have to give up so much of herself to please her mother-in-law, that she can be her own person. Miguel held a barbecue to celebrate Sam's marriage to Diego, though we see ambivalence on Sam's part as to the extent to which Miguel has accepted him as a son-in-law and accepted Diego as being gay. Roger has seen no change with time.

Receiving greater acceptance with marriage and time needs to be understood within the context of acceptance in general. Many gays and lesbians have a justified fear of acceptance by society.[13] Many sons-in-law and daughters-in-law, regardless of sexual orientation, worry about being accepted by their new family, daughters-in-law in particular.[14] Put together, fears around acceptance may become amplified. Further complicating the question of acceptance, as is seen in other research, is that adult children sometimes struggle with acceptance by their own parents.[15] In short, acceptance can be difficult for family members; it can become more difficult in relation to in-laws; it can become even more difficult for gays and lesbians.

To add one more complicating factor with the families described here, and not different from opposite-sex couples, acceptance may be forthcoming from one parent-in-law but not another or from one set of parents and not from another set of parents. Michelle wonders if her father-in-law has rejected her relationship with Lilly, while she feels accepted by Gina. Lana and Betty were embraced by Betty's family but initially rejected by Lana's.

A third theme that emerged in these case studies is also not unique to gays and lesbians—sibling rivalry or feeling accepted in relation to another daughter-in-law or daughter. In a previous book on adult sibling relationships, we describe how whether one is the more or less favored child can have a significant effect on how one travels through life. While being favored may feel good, it also can raise feelings of guilt, while not being favored often feels like rejection. Michelle felt increasingly accepted after Gina's relationship with her own daughter soured. Lana also felt more accepted than the other daughter-in-law in the family, while feeling bad for that other daughter-in-law. As Lana, somewhat guiltily, admitted, "To be honest, it is great to be the favorite."

A fourth theme we see is the importance of the social network in helping parents-in-law become more accepting of their own child and, by extension, their son- or daughter-in-law. Michelle's description of some of Gina's friends being supportive is instructive in understanding her change of feelings. The support she received from some friends helped her to feel more comfortable letting go of other friends who were "incredibly religious and incredibly conservative." Micky recounts going dancing with his mother-in-law at her high school reunion and her former classmates joining in the revelry. Lana's father was quite affected at her wedding when he observed how others were embracing the event.

Ambivalence is a useful concept to apply in understanding how some of these relationships function. Rachel feels ambivalent about Karun, loving her for her kindness on the one hand but hating her for her being high maintenance and unsupportive on the other. Sam feels ambivalent toward Miguel. Lana describes mixed feelings toward her in-laws—great admiration for some of their characteristics but also some hesitancy in having too much unwanted contact with them. Michelle says she is close but not very close with Gina and accepts Gina and the overpowering personality she possesses. Michelle appears to have resolved her feelings, so that ambivalence may have been an appropriate characterization earlier in their relationship. Ambivalence can lead to ambiguous communications as family members may be unclear themselves about how they feel and send conflicting messages depending on the time and circumstance. As with all these complex in-law relationships, acceptance and patience are good starting points.

CONCLUSION

The takeaway message from these in-law interviews with both generations is that their experiences can be broadly placed into three different groups:

1. Families where acceptance of the son-in-law or daughter-in-law was never an issue;
2. Families where acceptance was initially withheld and then a shift occurred toward ambivalence or acceptance by at least some of the family members; and
3. Families where acceptance of the younger generation never occurred.

For some families, sexual orientation is not an issue. The parents are accepting of their child's sexual orientation and go into creating a relationship with a new child-in-law open to getting to know that child-in-law. Other in-law issues might come into play but, when they do, they are related to what we typically see in all families regardless of sexual orientation.

For the second group, one or both parents may have been uncomfortable with their child coming out and may have struggled again when the marriage become a public event. Change occurred in many of these families when some members of the broader social network were accepting and when a number of years passed. One way of thinking about this for parents is that the coming out was a form of loss of what the parent had wished for in a child. Then the marriage sends the message that this is real and it is not going away. The parent, as reported from the parent's perspective and from the child's perspective, may have been subjected to the opprobrium of other family members and friends who were not accepting of a gay or lesbian marriage. In some cases, those friends and family members came around and, in other cases, the relationship frayed or broke. Just as these disruptions affect the parent–child relationship, they also affect the in-law relationship and add a layer of stress to what is a developmental stage for a family: adding a new family member through marriage. This is also where we see ambivalence coupled with acceptance. A son-in-law or daughter-in-law may feel accepted but also withhold a part of themselves based on interactions with or past knowledge of a parent-in-law.

In the third group are families where people are still closeted or where significant people in the family network are not on board. Not all accept their child, much less their child-in-law.

Having a gay or a lesbian marriage may be one more hurdle for families to jump in integrating a new member into the family. While the parents-in-law described here were usually comfortable or grew more comfortable over time, often someone else in the family or in the social network was disapproving. While there has been a significant increase in acceptance in U.S. society for gays and lesbians and same sex marriage over the last decade, resistance still exists. Such resistance can affect in-law dynamics in demonstrable ways.

CHAPTER 8

Are All In-Laws Alike?

What We Learned About Differences Between In-Law Groups

No surprise to anyone, the relationships that daughters-in-law and mothers in-law have can be quite different from the relationships between sons-in-law and fathers-in-law. That is the big-picture pattern emerging from our research, but we offer this with the caveat that trying to paint a monolithic portrait of such complex relationships is difficult to impossible. These relationships are dynamic, are embedded in culture, gender roles, and gender definitions, and often change from one generation to the next as societal norms and expectations shift. Just as in music, where no single composition represents classical, rap, jazz, rock, blues, folk, be-bop, or world music, no sample of in-laws portrays every major and minor, dominant and tonic chord of family life.

Is there any benefit in making comparisons then? The roles of the mother and mother-in-law, daughter and daughter-in-law, are wrapped up with being a woman, wife, and mother just as the roles of the father and father-in-law, son and son-in-law, are wrapped up with being a man, husband, and father (we apologize here and elsewhere for the gender binaries we are describing, and recognize that our understanding of those too are changing across generations). Thus, significant differences may appear within and across families depending on how the family members view women's roles, men's roles, and parenting roles. And, of course, significant differences about these roles may exist not only within a family but between two families when joined by marriage. Such differences often vary by culture and by the idiosyncratic nature of each family in that, even within the same culture, wide variations exist. The benefit of making comparisons is that family members and mental health practitioners can use these comparisons as a basis for self-understanding, and as a beginning point in assessing in-law relationships in families, and intervening when in-law issues arise.[1] History is informative but not determinative—unless we look at where family patterns and beliefs have been, and put them in a context, we will not know where we are and where we may be going.

Each family is unique and may be the exception to a significant trend that we found among the close to 1,500 in-laws who participated in our surveys and research interviews. We find as we give lectures on our findings that someone will invariably raise a hand and say, "That does not apply to me. I do not walk on eggshells with my daughter-in-law" or "You just said a majority of sons-in-law feel close to their father-in-law. My wife wants nothing to do with her father and I support her in that." As we present the broad trends we found, we caution that these are only trends and that we are interpreting them through our lenses. In other words, we do not agree with Leo Tolstoy, who wrote in *Anna Karenina* that all happy families are alike and all unhappy ones are different. We suggest all families are unique in their own ways and our research simply identifies patterns that apply to many, but by no means all, families. Still, examining the trends in the ways families are alike is informative in understanding in-law relationships. To be clear, we are not presenting what we wished relationships would look that—we are presenting what we found them to look like among those in our research. We begin with the perspectives of daughters-in-law and sons-in-law.

COMPARING DAUGHTERS-IN-LAW AND SONS-IN-LAW

First of all, when we look at this dyad, the daughters-in-law's relationship with their mother-in-law is viewed less positively than the sons-in-law's relationship with their father-in-law. Daughters-in-law are less likely to report they admire their mother-in-law, ask her for advice, feel close to her, enjoy spending time with her, trust her, or share similar interests (our relationship quality questions). In addition, daughters-in-law are more likely to avoid their mother-in-law, walk on eggshells when around her, maintain emotional distance, have conflicts with her, or report feeling anxiety when with her.

In essence, this relationship is more of a struggle for daughters-in-law than for sons-in-law. Why might this be so? We return to the belief that women are more central to the family's day-to-day functioning and, as the primary caregivers of children,[2] are more relationship oriented. It is reasonable to anticipate mothers-in-law would have more interest and be more invested in their relationships with daughters-in-law. Because of their centrality and investment and the inherent complexity of families, when roles between the women are ambiguous, discomfort may arise. As family is so important to women, a lack of clarity would affect them more than men. We are not saying that a lack of role clarity does not affect men and that family is not important to men; we are saying a lack of role clarity around the in-law role may not affect men *as much* as it affects women. We suggest part of these differences reflect a different set of expectations for the relationships. In short, men may not put as much energy into the relationship. A father-in-law, because of his socialization as a man, may make fewer interpersonal requests of the son-in-law, and the son-in-law expects less and offers less. In some relationships, the men may consciously or unconsciously agree to not engage with each other on the same level as the women, so the men are less reactive. As the American Psychological Association (APA)'s report on boys and men asserts, men experience gender role conflict related to different domains of the male gender role, including power and competition. This can be related to "restrictive affectionate behavior between men (discomfort expressing care and affectionate touching of other men)."[3] While focusing on competition and power struggles, it could be that men, according to the APA, are less engaged with their own emotions, and thus their highs and lows would be more modulated when they are asked to respond to statements related to their feelings.

Second, despite the greater struggles of daughters-in-law, when asked about closeness to mothers, fathers, mothers-in-law, and fathers-in-law in separate questions, both daughters-in-law and sons-in-law reported feeling closer to their mothers than to their fathers and closer to their mothers-in-law than to their fathers-in-law. Further, although sons and daughters reported similar closeness to their mothers and mothers-in-law, sons-in-law reported feeling closer to both their fathers-in-law and their mothers-in-law than daughters-in-law do. Finally, we asked if they were closer to their same-gender or opposite-gender in-law, with daughters-in-law reporting feeling closer to their same-gender in-law and sons-in-law reporting feeling closer to their opposite-gender in-law, reinforcing the differences found in the separate questions and a question asking for a direct comparison.

Our findings indicate that both daughters-in-law and sons-in-law state they feel a little closer to their mother-in-law than their father-in-law. The sons-in-law and daughters-in-law also feel closer to their own mother than to their own father. Specifically, 77% of the sons-in-law strongly agreed or agreed that they felt close to their father and 83% strongly agreed or agreed they felt close to their mother; 72% of the daughters-in-law strongly agreed or agreed they felt close to their father and 79% strongly agreed or agreed they felt close to their mother. Gender role expectations for mothers and fathers may account for some of these differences. When asked to compare closeness across their in-laws, 50% of daughters-in-law reported being closer to their mother-in-law than father-in-law, with 27% neutral, while only 26% of sons-in-law reported being closer to their father-in-law, with 32% neutral. Thus, both sets of children-in-law are more likely to be emotionally connected to their mother-in-law (and mother). This may mean the older generation of women plays a more significant role, which, because of this greater connection, makes them more likely to generate reactions from children-in-law, like feelings of interference, when asserting themselves into, for example, parenting or holiday meal planning, which a slightly more distant father might not generate. While the differences we highlight here may be small, they help explain some of what traditionally have been points of contention for some families around the reception given to mothers-in-law by children-in-law.[4] In short, caring and closeness sometimes generate concerns and conflict.

These responses also speak to the universal trope that sons-in-law have difficulties with their mothers-in-law. In our data, most do not and, in fact, report feeling closer to their mother-in-law than to their father-in-law. We think the responses are a clear indication that the son-in-law and mother-in-law relationship is not the universal *bête noir* that it is reputed to be. While we do not want to put comics out of business, it may be time to retire the mother-in-law jokes or to expand the repertoire to include father-in-law jokes.

Third, the birth of the first child is more likely to bring the son-in-law and father-in-law closer than it is to bring the daughter-in-law and mother-in-law closer. In fact, in what may seem counterintuitive but makes sense the more you think about it, the daughters-in-law with children feel less close to their mother-in-law than daughters-in-law without children.

While one-quarter of the daughters-in-law believed their relationship with their mother-in-law improved with the birth, over one-third of the sons-in-law thought their relationship with their father-in-law improved. One in 10 of the daughters-in-law thought the relationship got worse, whereas only one in 50 of the sons-in-law thought it got worse. When comparing daughters-in-law with children with those without, our data showed that daughters-in-law with at least one child felt less close to their mother-in-law, admired her less, were less likely to ask her for advice, were less likely to enjoy spending time with her, and experienced more conflicts with her. In addition, those daughters-in-law reported their husband was less happy with the relationship the daughter-in-law had with his mother. To understand this, the role the daughter-in-law plays postnatally, as a mother of the child, must be appreciated. In most families, the mother carries out the bulk of childcare and is more likely to facilitate access to the child. The mother-in-law may want greater access to her new grandchild at the same time that the daughter-in-law is trying to learn how to be a parent. The daughter-in-law may be trying to establish boundaries, leaving the mother-in-law unsure as to where she fits into the picture with her son, her daughter-in-law, and the new grandchild. Before a child is born, the daughter-in-law may not feel as much of a need to establish such a boundary.

As for sons-in-law, few items on the survey differentiated those with children from those without children. With the birth, the father-in-law, along with his wife who, like him, may be helping out their daughter, will likely have more contact with the son-in-law, and that contact is around the grandchild. Both son-in-law and father-in-law may find they have much in common as they spend time together along with the women in child-related interactions. Sons-in-law with children generally have better relations with their father-in-law than daughters-in-law with children. They feel less anxiety when around him and have a higher degree of trust toward him than daughters-in-law feel toward their mother-in-law. As one son-in-law, a 35-year-old French tennis instructor married to a Brazilian, told us, when he became a father, his father-in-law started paying much more attention to him. The tennis instructor was not just another guy; he was now the father of his grandson. Their contact increased and the son-in-law felt he was being given more respect.

The fourth point is that daughters-in-law have a harder time balancing time with both sets of parents than sons-in-law. Sons-in-law perceive their own parents as interfering more in their marriage than daughters-in-law perceive about their own parents. Daughters-in-law are more likely to feel their mother-in-law interferes in their marriage than sons-in-law feel about interference from their fathers-in-law.

Perhaps unsurprisingly, daughters-in-law are more likely to feel great pressure to split time with both families than are sons-in-law.[5] We also learned that sons-in-law believe that their parents, their wife's in-laws, are more interfering, essentially agreeing with daughters-in-law about their mother's interference. Daughters-in-law also feel their mothers-in-law, their husband's mother, hinder their marriage. This perception of greater interference may be related to the mother-in-law (the son-in-law's mother) attempting to have a more active role in the family or the daughter-in-law feeling a greater need to put a boundary around her family system than sons-in-law feel about their father-in-law. As we have explained in earlier chapters, the son-in-law's mother often feels she has to walk on eggshells around the mother of her grandchildren. If she is unclear about her role, she may be perceived by her son, as well as by her son's wife, as interfering, which has the effect of hindering her marriage.

Fifth, daughters-in-law experience their mother-in-law as more jealous than sons-in-law experience in relation to their father-in-law. Specifically, daughters-in-law answered that their mother-in-law was more likely to be jealous of the daughter-in-law's relationship with her own parents as well as being more likely to be jealous of the relationship her husband has with her parents.

Two examples may best explain these three-way in-law relationships. In the first example, let's assume that Tameka, married to Michael, has two children and goes to her mother for assistance. Tameka's mother-in-law, Betty, wishes she could be part of such a close mother–child relationship and is envious of it—something she communicates to Tameka in a manner that makes Tameka sense jealousy on Betty's part. In the second example, Tameka and her husband Michael get together with both Tameka's and Michael's parents every so often, a group of six. Michael's mother, Betty, observes how well Michael gets along with Tameka's parents—they work in the same profession and enjoy the same activities. Tameka senses that Betty is also jealous of Michael's relationship with her parents.

It may be that mothers-in-law are more likely to feel jealousy and communicate it, but it may also be that daughters-in-law have greater sensitivity to feelings of jealousy on the part of parents-in-law than sons-in-law and so are more likely to report it. For daughters-in-law, having that perception would make balancing both sides of the family more difficult for them as they will have greater concerns about not hurting feelings. In fact, in a similar finding that reinforces the role that daughters-in-law play in relationship building, sons-in-law were more likely to say their wife wanted them to work on their parent-in-law relationship than daughters-in-law reported about their husband. Men are not as likely to encourage their wife to improve relationships to the extent that women are to encourage their husband, which may, again, speak to the different levels of sensitivity or attention given to family relationships.

Finally, it is not always about differences; certain similarities appear. For example, sons-in-law and daughters-in-law spent similar amounts of time with their parent-in-law, with slightly more than one-third of each group spending, on average, one hour or less a month communicating in some form with their same gender parent-in-law. They also had similar levels of agreement as to whether they felt caught between their spouse and their parent-in-law, which, if it occurred, would be a sign of triangulation.

We assumed that daughters-in-law would be spending more time with their mothers-in-law. Not so. It may be that with more women in the workforce of both generations, the time is not available that previous generations had. It also may be that the nature of the time, which is not captured by our surveys, was where the differences, if there were any, could be found. For example, a fishing trip once a month, while one "contact," may amount to as much time as a number of phone calls and hour-long lunches across the same month. One of the biggest struggles for couples is balancing the competing demands of time with friends, with family, at work, and pursuing personal interests, such as exercising, reading, or hobbies. It may be that daughters-in-law are less willing to have their lives dictated by their husband's parents or that sons-in-law are more willing to spend time with their in-laws, thus equaling out what once may have been disparities. (Of course, time spent with in-laws is often affected by the in-laws' child as well as other children of the in-laws.) We do note, though, that while daughters-in-law may not spend more time with their mother-in-law, they do still experience, in some cases, greater difficulty balancing both sides of the family.

When issues do arise, the men and women are equally capable of dealing directly with their parent-in-law about those issues without including their spouse. More than a third of both daughters-in-law and sons-in-law said they can talk directly to their in-law without first talking with their spouse about important matters. This could be a reflection of healthy, non-triangulating behavior on their part and could be due to their spouse encouraging direct communication. In other words, if a son-in-law has an issue with his father-in-law, his wife may encourage him not to involve her, or he may decide not to involve her on his own.

COMPARING MOTHERS-IN-LAW AND FATHERS-IN-LAW

Our first point is that mothers-in-law struggle more with their relationship with their daughter-in-law than fathers-in-law struggle with their son-in-law. In our data mothers-in-law were more likely to say they walk on eggshells, avoid their child-in-law, feel anxious, feel left out by their child and child-in-law, have a different parenting philosophy than their child-in-law, and have problematic conflicts with their child-in-law. This pattern seems driven by struggles that emerge from having grandchildren.

Consistent with what we, and others, have found, women invest a great deal in their families and experience more struggles and boundary ambiguity in relation to each other than do men. This is clearly amplified when there are grandchildren to care for and raise, which may exacerbate role ambiguity in the arena of parenting. How do we conclude this? When we run these analyses on the parents-in-law with grandchildren, the pattern of differences remain. When we compare mothers-in-law and fathers-in-law who do not have grandchildren from the child/child-in-law couple, differences are not found—mothers-in-law and fathers-in-law look very similar.

While it is harder for mothers-in-law than fathers-in-law in the areas cited, it is important to emphasize that it is a minority of women who experience these troubling feelings, as we show in Chapter 3. We could also consider why it is easier for men than women: Are men more outwardly focused and less invested in family relationships, especially parenting grandchildren? Are they less emotionally affected by the normal ups and downs in families? Or is it that their counterpart, the son-in-law, is also less emotionally invested in family relationships and more outwardly focused? Both father-in-law and son-in-law may be "colluding," in part, because of how they are socialized, to be less reactive to each other and to push aside disagreements, including around parenting, if disagreements arise in the family. Men are less willing to go to couple's therapy.[6] They are more likely to subscribe to and be inhibited by traditional masculine stereotypes that may blunt their emotional availability and their willingness to be vulnerable.[7] This may shift the emotional work of the family to the women who are more engaged in feelings. It may also be that, because of women's greater involvement in the emotional life of the family, the men take a more reserved position as a counterweight. Conflicts then are less likely to arise between the men because they are less likely to have them or are less willing to allow themselves to feel them.

Second, we found that across multiple survey questions, mothers-in-law are more likely to experience highs or lows, or both, in the relationship, as demonstrated by their greater likelihood than fathers-in-law to strongly agree or to strongly disagree on key relationship items. These include: I am close with my child-in-law; I feel I have to walk on eggshells with my child-in-law; my child-in-law is or will be a good parent; I maintain emotional distance from my child-in-law; my relationship with my child is hindered by my child-in-law; some aspects of my child's marital relationship make me uncomfortable; I sometimes feel caught between my child and my child-in-law; I can talk directly with my child-in-law about important matters; and I enjoy spending time with my child-in-law. Fathers-in-law's responses group more in the middle.

Not only are women more emotionally expressive than men, as we have stated, they may experience stronger emotional reactions both to the good and bad that occur in in-law interactions than men because of their often more central position and greater investment in family interactions.[8] Men's greater emotional constriction, such as discomfort expressing vulnerable emotions, as detailed by the APA's report, may make it difficult for them to experience and express a wide range of emotions. As a caveat to this, and given the limited racial and ethnic diversity in our sample, a more culturally diverse sample may show other degrees of difference in the way that emotions are shared and roles performed in the family. Men are socialized by their family as well as by their peer group, cultural background, and society. Thus the lens we bring to understanding our findings is specific to the current sample.

Third, mothers-in-law are more concerned about the relationship between their daughter-in-law and their son and more likely to be affected by those concerns than fathers-in-law in relation to their son-in-law and daughter. Specifically, mothers-in-law were more likely to be concerned about their son's choice of a wife, to be disturbed by some aspects of the marital relationship between their son and daughter-in-law, and to believe their daughter-in-law hinders their relationship with their son. In addition, they are more likely to feel left out by their son and daughter-in-law. Mothers-in-law are also more likely to believe that their daughter-in-law holds the power in the relationship and that their daughter-in-law gets angry at them. Fathers-in-law believe there is a greater balance of power in their relationship with their son-in-law.

The mothers-in-law's greater concerns at the outset about the marriage they see their son getting into set the tone in some relationships later on as such doubts seem connected to poorer relationship quality with their daughter-in-law. As watchful as fathers are reputed to be of their daughters, these mothers may be more watchful of their sons both at the outset of a relationship that results in marriage and as the marriage progresses. While a larger minority of the mothers-in-law endorse negative feelings related to their daughter-in-law and son (e.g., 20% felt their daughter-in-law hindered their relationship with their son, while only 6% of fathers-in-law felt their son-in-law hindered their relationship with their daughter), our findings still reflect an interesting trend in families that helps us understand the potential levels of reactivity of fathers and mothers about their children's marriage.

Finally, as for similarities between the parents-in-law, we found that after the birth of the first child, close to half of both groups reported a positive impact on the parent-in-law and child-in-law relationship. Both fathers-in-law and mothers-in-law have similar (and high) levels of agreement that they admire their child-in-law. Further, both sets report high levels of agreement that their child-in-law is, or will be, a good parent.

Parents are also usually thrilled to have a grandchild, especially if the birth results in sufficient contact with that grandchild. Both fathers- and mothers-in-law whom we interviewed enjoyed and greatly anticipated the grandparent role. While we have called attention to the struggles, the high level of enjoyment spending time together and the belief that the son-in-law and daughter-in-law will be or is a good parent bode well for the long-term success of the relationship.

HOW DO THE GENERATIONS DIFFER?

Mothers-in-Law and Daughters-in-Law

Our first point is that although both sets report positive relationships, in almost every way, mothers-in-law report a sunnier relationship with daughters-in-law than daughters-in-law report with their mother-in-law. Specifically, in our data, mothers-in-law report feeling closer to their daughter-in-law, are more likely to say they admire their daughter-in-law, that they trust her, that they share similar interests, and that they enjoy spending time with her. Similarly, mothers-in-law are less likely to report they maintain emotional distance from their daughter-in-law, walk on eggshells around her, feel anxiety when together, report problematic conflicts, or avoid her.

Why, across the board, would mothers-in-law hold a sunnier view of the relationship? Wishful thinking? A greater interest in being part of the daughter-in-law's life than the daughter-in-law has in having the mother-in-law a part of her life? Or just different perspectives on life and relationships? It may be that there is greater societal pressure on mothers-in-law to say they are close to their daughter-in-law than there is on daughters-in-law say they are close to their mother-in-law. When mothers-in-law compare notes with other mothers-in-law, the topic of daughters-in-law may come up frequently and it is more socially acceptable to describe a close relationship than one that is emotionally distant. At the same time, many mothers-in-law we have talked to anecdotally say they walk on eggshells around their daughter-in-law because they want access to their son and their grandchildren. One mother-in-law told us she feels like her daughter-in-law keeps up a protective shield around herself that the mother-in-law cannot penetrate.

Yet daughters-in-law, it should be noted, are even more likely to walk on eggshells around their mother-in-law, to feel anxiety when around her, and to avoid her. Many are clearly keeping their distance. They may feel they have to protect the relationship they have with their husband and their own autonomy by keeping a boundary around their newly formed family as they further strive for balance in their own life. They are more in the process of becoming who they are and are finding their way. As a result, they may have to try and clarify boundaries for themselves.

Second, daughters-in-law are more likely to believe their parenting philosophy is different from their mother-in-law's philosophy. Mothers-in-law are more likely to believe they and their daughter-in-law are on the same page. We wonder if the differences in parenting philosophy have any relationship to what the daughter-in-law's husband, the mother-in-law's son, has told his wife about the way he was raised (or the daughter-in-law's unhappiness with the way he was raised). Such a history could affect the daughter-in-law's view of her mother-in-law's parenting and how comfortable she is with her mother-in-law parenting her children. Thus, there are more historical data from which to scrutinize both the mother-in-law's past and present parenting performance. The mother-in-law may feel she should be on the same page as her daughter-in-law in order to maintain contact with her grandchildren and so may gloss over any differences that appear.

Third, daughters-in-law are less likely to say they can ask for advice from their mother-in-law. This finding surprised us, as we assumed the younger women would feel they could seek out wisdom from the older women about a range of matters, from balancing work to raising children. We also thought that older women, the mothers-in-law, would need advice less. What we may not have considered is the mother-in-law may be giving unsolicited advice, reducing the likelihood that advice would be sought. So it should be noted we do not actually know how much advice is going in each direction, nor what all that advice may be about, as we only asked if they asked for advice. It also may be, and similar to other responses about feeling less close to their mother-in-law than mothers-in-law feel to their daughter-in-law, that the daughters-in-law do not want advice because that might be seen as inviting their mother-in-law into their lives more than they want them involved in their lives. The mothers-in-law may feel that asking for advice is a good way to engage their daughter-in-law.

Fourth, a higher percentage of daughters-in-law reported that their mother-in-law was needy with them than the mothers-in-law reported about their daughter-in-law. While only 15% of the daughters-in-law said their mother-in-law was needy with them, an even smaller percentage of the mothers-in-law (9%) saw their daughter-in-law as needy. It may be important for daughters-in-law who are seeking to establish a boundary around their relationship with their husband to not appear needy if they wish to keep some distance from the mother-in-law.

Fathers-in-Law and Sons-in-Law

First of all, although both sets of men report good relationships with each other, in almost every way and much like mothers-in-law, fathers-in-law report a sunnier relationship with their son-in-law than sons-in-law report with their father-in-law. Specifically, fathers-in-law report feeling closer to their son-in-law, that they admire him more, that they trust him more, that they are more likely to share similar interests, and that they enjoy spending time with him. Fathers-in-law are less likely to maintain emotional distance, walk on eggshells, feel anxiety when together, or report problematic conflicts.

Similar to the mothers-in-law, fathers-in-law report easier relations with their son-in-law than the sons-in-law report with their father-in-law. Many of the same reasons may be at the heart of these differences. For some sons-in-law, given the way men are socialized to be self-sufficient, there may be a great push away from too much closeness so they can prove to themselves, their wife, and their in-laws that they are able to stand on their own feet. The son-in-law may also look to his wife as a measure of how close she wants him to be with her father. Fathers-in-law may characterize the relationship as close to fit their own narrative around family closeness, feeling that, by wishing it, maybe it is more likely to happen.

Second, sons-in-law are more likely to believe that their parenting philosophy is different from their father-in-law's philosophy. Fathers-in-law are more likely to believe they and their son-in-law are on the same page. Here again, the men have the same pattern as the women. With the evolving nature of gender roles, older men who subscribe to traditional values about discipline and childrearing are likely to hold different philosophies than the younger generation of men. Because fathers-in-law believe they are closer to their son-in-law than the reverse, they may be more likely to believe their parenting philosophies are aligned. In addition, in the event that sons-in-law heard negative things from their wives about the father's parenting history, the sons-in-law may feel reluctant to say they subscribe to the same parenting approach.

COMPARING WOMEN'S AND MEN'S RELATIONSHIPS

The differences between the daughters-in-law and sons-in-law and the fathers-in-law and mothers-in-law come with one clear message: Women, regardless of whether they are daughters-in-law or mothers-in-law, struggle more with their relationships with each other. They are also more likely to believe they have made mistakes in their in-law relationships. When asked if they thought they had ever made a mistake in their relationship with their child-in-law, almost one in three of the mothers-in-law said "yes," while only a little more than one in eight of the fathers-in-law thought they had made a mistake. More than one in four of the daughters-in-law thought they had made mistakes with their mother-in-law, while only one in seven of the sons-in-law thought they had made mistakes with their father-in-law. (This finding is generally consistent with another sizable study of relations of daughters- and sons-in-law's in the Midwest that found more ambivalence among women in their in-law relationships than among men.[9])

One other interesting difference appeared in relation to mothers-in-law: They felt less encouragement from their husband in dealing with their daughter-in-law than fathers-in-law felt from their wives in dealing with their son-in-law. In other words, the men were more likely to receive support when trying to relate to their son-in-law than the mothers-in-law felt when interacting with their daughter-in-law. Maybe the men needed less support. But maybe this is consistent with the emotional caretaking or kinkeeping role that women are more likely than men to fulfill in the family.[10] Repeatedly, we saw reconfirmation in our findings about men's and women's distinct roles in the family. What we do not know for certain, as we have only surveyed for the last few years, is whether these differences would have been greater 10 or 20 years ago. We believe, and as is supported by others' research, that differences in gender-related family behavior are narrowing and that gender roles and responsibilities throughout society are slowly moving toward more equitable dynamics.

Finally, fathers-in-law in particular continue to be the less *invested* member of the family when it comes to the issues we explored. They are not as close as mothers-in-law with their children or their children-in-law (which reflects our findings that the children report being closer to mothers and mothers-in-law). They avoid triangulation to a greater degree than mothers-in-law which can be seen as a good thing but also may be the result of less engagement. It is not that fathers-in-law are absent. They are seen as being supportive by their wives; 39% of mothers-in-law view their spouse/partner as having a somewhat or very positive influence on their relationship with their daughter-in-law (while 59% of fathers-in-law view their spouse/partner as having a somewhat or very positive influence on their relationship with their son-in-law.) Mothers- in- law also report their partners encourage them to work on their relationship with their daughter- in- law. It is that fathers-in-law are just not perceived as being *as involved* as mothers-in-law in the family or as encouraging as much closeness. It is a matter of degree.

As we view the family as a system, we see the complementarity of partners' (in this analysis, fathers' and mothers') roles. Both cannot always be engaged equally, and the significant engagement of one, the mother-in-law, may leave other roles for the father-in-law to pursue. And, as we saw from the interviews, fathers-in-law may be playing the role of financial advisor and home repair expert, roles that are, of course, also played by mothers-in-law, though typically not as frequently.

CONCLUSION

It is a tale of two cities. In almost every way we look at the data, in-law roles are more of a struggle for women than men as children-in-law work harder to create boundaries and space for their marital relationship. Generational changes are afoot that will have a profound effect on the family in the future. In the final chapter, we discuss possible ways of improving relationships.

CHAPTER 9

How to Improve In-Law Relationships

As we have detailed, most of these in-law relationships are close and many are functional and cordial. A few, as we have also explained, are problematic. In this chapter we focus on what we have learned from our research that can help guide family members to improve their relationships and can help practitioners working with families who are struggling. First, by reading others' stories, readers can place their own story in a broader context. Second, by learning what trends were found in in-law relationships, readers can understand the broader familial and societal forces at play. It will be helpful to consider that these are both horizontal and vertical family relationships. By this we mean that family members are dealing not only with people in their own generation but potentially with both younger and older generations as well. For instance, a daughter-in-law is dealing horizontally with her spouse, while at the same time she is dealing vertically with her own parents and her spouse's parents. And if she has children, she is also dealing with her parents and her parents-in-law's interactions vis-à-vis those grandchildren across three generations. While this three generation dynamic portrays a typical family position to be in, it is not always easy, given the number of family members involved.

To apply what we have learned, we first offer four family focused approaches (which we have found useful in our past research with siblings[1]) to help families and clinicians make sense of these complex dynamics. These lenses can guide how one approaches in-law relationships. Briefly, they include knowing one's family history, communicating clearly with family members, understanding where boundaries should be drawn in the family, and understanding how societal beliefs about family roles may combine with family narratives about someone to narrowly define them. For those new to these theories, this may be a bit of a deep dive so stick with us. We also suggest potential directions that may aid individuals seeking to improve these underattended-to family relationships.

FAMILY THERAPY MODELS

Murray Bowen and Family Systems

To understand the present, one must understand past patterns of behavior in one's family. Murray Bowen, a psychiatrist and pioneering family therapist,[2] has written about the importance of how family patterns are passed down from one generation to the next. He uses the term differentiation as referring to the ability to operate with a balance of thinking and feeling independently from one's parents. Being able to act independently—such as emotionally and financially—while staying connected is the goal. A lack of differentiation from one's family of origin is termed "fusion" and refers to, in adulthood, relying too much on support and approval from one's parents. For example, a daughter who is fused to her parents may select a partner to please them who also might be fused with his or her parents. If there is little differentiation and a greater reliance on parents, newlyweds will be less able to act independently to balance their individual and couple needs with the time and attention needs of each set of parents.

On the opposite end of the continuum from fused, but also problematic, are family relationships that are cutoff. A daughter who has an ambivalent or strained relationship with her parents and feels uncomfortable being in the room with them may choose a partner who is also uncomfortable with his or her family and can potentially side with her to keep her parents at bay. The couple might then construct a life of avoiding both sets of in-laws and thus deprive themselves, and their children, of possible sources of support.

A son- or daughter-in-law can play a part in starting the cutoff, in supporting it if his or her spouse is already cut off and wants no contact with his or her parents, or in helping the spouse become closer to his or her parents by helping with reconciliation.

Bowen also formulated a theory about relationship triangles in the family. Triangles form when a couple is anxious or in conflict and unable to resolve their own issues. Couples who are struggling may pull in a parent/in-law consciously or unconsciously as a way to redirect their conflict. Similarly, a parent/in-law may insert herself or himself into the couple's relationship or may want to get involved for her or his own needs as triangulating behavior can originate from either generation. Some triangles may have an historical genesis when they get passed down to the younger generation and are recreated.

Bowen's theory offers fertile ground for thinking about how in-law relationships are manifested based on whose shoulders the family members stand on. Typical questions for practitioners and those struggling with their in-laws to consider would be:

1. What has been the family's experience with in-laws in prior generations?
2. What has been the family's experience with in-laws in this generation—that is, have siblings or cousins already married and brought in a new in-law?
3. Are new family members welcome or is there the sense that the family is a tightly knit group of "us versus them"?
4. Every new in-law will bring beliefs and routines around childrearing, vacations, work hours, closeness, privacy, and so on. Is being different a challenge to the family or is it accepted, and even welcome?

Bowen is known for his use of genograms, or family trees, to illustrate intergenerational patterns. Genograms usually include a brief description of family members and depict the nature of their relationships across and within other generations. Drawing and discussing family genograms can provide insight into how relationships in previous generations may be driving current in-law interactions.

Virginia Satir and Communications Theory

Another clinical lens for guiding practice with families—communications theory—was developed by Virginia Satir, a social worker and early family therapy practitioner and theorist. Satir wants family members to communicate clearly and directly with each other. She postulated that family members with low self-esteem have difficulty communicating their feelings to others in a coherent manner. When verbal and physical communications are not aligned, the receivers of the communication are confused about what is being conveyed. Self-awareness is the first step in learning to communicate more effectively. To communicate effectively, one's body posture, tone, and other nonverbal communications need to match what is said. Satir also believes that everything can be talked about, that avoidance is maladaptive, and that when issues are brought into the open, they can be worked through.[3]

From the research on in-law relationships, we learn that disclosure and openness about family history and feelings may help new in-laws to feel more included. We also know too much disclosure too soon or disclosure of the wrong sort may cause an in-law to back off,[4] particularly if that in-law comes from a family where self-disclosure or open discussion of difficult issues is infrequent.

For Satir, the ideal model for healthy communication is the person who can directly say what she feels and accept feedback. If there is fallout from that direct communication, Satir would say that fallout is important to know about and work through. Satir's approach may be helpful in families in which communication is indirect or contradictory.

Using Satir's approach, typical questions to consider might include:

1. Do family members communicate directly and honestly and are the non-verbal and verbal components of the communication consistent with each other?
2. How does communication and information flow between the generations? Do parents-in-law and children-in-law feel comfortable communicating directly or is the child/spouse the conduit?
3. Are the styles of communicating the same in both spouses' families or is there a great deal of shifting back and forth between communication styles when going from one family to the next?

Facets of both Satir's and Bowen's theories could be combined to explore what is unfolding with any one family by looking at family history and how they talk about it.

Salvador Minuchin and Structural Family Therapy

Now let's look at another way of thinking about families. Structural family therapy, developed by Salvador Minuchin, an Argentine psychiatrist, and others, offers an action-oriented approach to help families when communication and insight-focused therapy fall short. This theory is particularly useful when considering in-law relationships because it views healthy families as being able to adapt to changes and as having a parental executive system in place with a boundary around it. The boundary, if healthy, prevents children from inappropriately intruding into their parents' lives, and parents from inappropriately drawing children into struggles or conflicts between the parents. A boundary should also exist around the children's sub-system, growing clearer as children mature into adults, so that parents do not interfere in their lives while still maintaining a nurturing relationship.

If the boundaries between family members are ambiguous, parents and children can become enmeshed on one extreme or disengaged on the other. Enmeshment (consider Bowen's term "fused") refers to an unhealthy closeness where families feel they have few options for independent thoughts, feelings, or action; disengagement (consider Bowen's discussion of cutoff) can feel like a lack of nurturance. Minuchin and Bowen viewed triangulation similarly—a third party is roped into a two person relationship to mitigate the tension within the dyad.

The relevance for in-law relationships is to consider where the newlyweds draw the boundary between their own identity as a couple and their membership in each of their families of origin. With every new marriage, the spouses' obligation to each other is to be the primary source of emotional support and intimacy as they form a new family. To do this, they must figure out where their boundaries are with their own families. As previously noted, cultural imperatives and family history may also have an effect on the level of closeness desired between the generations. Additionally, when conducting the qualitative interviews for this book, the notion of boundaries was brought up spontaneously many times by those we interviewed, which makes it a useful and easily accessible concept for helping people to understand who is included and excluded when delving into these complex family relationships.[5] To create a visual depiction of family boundaries, and similar to Bowen's use of genograms, structural family therapists use figurative representations, called mapping, to understand the current relationships and the boundaries between members.

When thinking in terms of structural family therapy, questions to consider would be:

1. Are the boundaries clear in the family?
2. Are those boundaries rigid, missing, or flexible?
3. Are people being triangulated (e.g., the children-in-law and one of the parents in-laws) to displace or avoid conflict?
4. Is there a sense that the family can adapt to the inevitable changes that occur in families by re-evaluating their roles as new members join and current members need support or care?

Narrative Therapy

Narrative therapy is another model that can be used to help families who wish to change how they consider their family. Developed by Michael White and David Epston, clinical social workers from Australia and New Zealand, the therapy is based on the idea that people's lives are socially constructed both by family history and by society. Narrative therapy holds that stories get written about family members that may be unproductive and need to be rewritten. Those stories can be difficult to rewrite as they are affected by societal beliefs, for example, that mothers-in-law interfere. The theory asserts that the events and history of a family, or an individual, can be woven together with new narratives. Learning more about an in-law can help a family understand that he or she is more than just an interference.

The goal is to "thicken" the story rather than rely on a thin description of someone. By carefully asking more questions of the person, a broader definition can be found. Gloria Horsley, in writing about therapy with in-laws, describes a case where a mother-in-law was seen as fragile and nervous, a description that developed after she had an automobile accident when she first was learning how to drive. She never drove again. The family viewed her as weak and dependent, a description that spilled over to other women in the family. It was not until Horsley asked the family to focus on the mother-in-law's strengths—such as navigating the transit system independently and being an active community volunteer despite not driving—that the narrative around her behavior, and the behavior of other women in the family, began to change to a more strengths-based one.[6]

For in-laws, and mothers-in-law in particular, popular culture and the media create impressions and commonly held beliefs. The way they are framed can have a powerful impact such that whatever a mother-in-law does, her behavior may be seen as conforming to the popular notions about mothers-in-law. Asking about the external descriptions can open the door to exploring other, more accurate descriptions, based on who *this* person is, not on what an unhealthy stereotyped narrative suggests. For example, mothers-in-law as "meddlesome" or "intrusive" can be reframed as mothers-in-law as "very helpful" or "care deeply."

Typical questions to consider in the mindset of narrative therapy would be:

1. What stories or narratives have been created about in-laws in the family or in the wider culture?
2. Are those stories reinforced by current attitudes or actions in the family?

3. To what extent are those narratives originating from or reinforced by society's depictions of in-laws?
4. If the narratives are negative, is the family open to finding positive stories about the in-law?

Summary

We can use many lenses to understand these complicated relationships, which are often tinged with ambivalence and ambiguity.[7]

As we enter the complicated lives of families where much may remain unknown, a caution for clinicians when working with family members: Levels of closeness in a family vary across generations and from one culture to the next. Some cultures encourage (even require) more family togetherness, while other cultures value independence of thought and action. What is adaptive for a particular family needs to be viewed within the history and the cultural dimensions of that particular family.

Finally, it is too facile to contend that *all* families are governed by their history or communications patterns, that boundaries are the best way to look at a family, or that the stories the family has told about itself are the ones that get reified in the present and future. These theories or lenses are offered as ways for families and practitioners to get a foothold on what is happening. The art remains in finding the best key to unlock the unique mystery that is any one particular family.

OUR RESEARCH AND BUILDING GOOD IN-LAW RELATIONSHIPS

Drawing on our survey data, we are able to see what characteristics of in-law relationships are most highly related to a good in-law relationship. We see commonalities across the samples and some characteristics that are uniquely related. These, to various extents, are action-oriented characteristics that parents-in-law can engage in to build better relations.

What Parents-in-Law Say Works

1. Having similar interests;
2. Believing the child-in-law is or will be a good parent;
3. Being close with one's own child and having that child be happy with the relationship with the child-in-law;
4. Not maintaining emotional distance from the child-in-law.

While these were the most consistent predictors of a good relationship for both sets of parents-in-law, a few other characteristics were significant and worth noting. These include, for the mothers-in-law: approving of the marriage; having a good impression of the quality of the marriage; and not feeling they have to walk on eggshells around the daughter-in-law. For the fathers-in-law, these include: having a history of being close with their own in-laws and being able to talk directly with their son-in-law without involving their daughter. These four main findings point to specific things that people can do to reconsider and work on their in-law relationship. Some of these are more workable and some may not be realistic or effective in improving irreparably damaged relationships.

Building Similar Interests

Finding commonality with a son- or daughter-in-law is one way to build a relationship if it is not there or maintain a relationship if it is. We heard from parents-in-law who cooked, fished, drank beer, and enjoyed camping with their child-in-law. Others watched sports together, liked to travel, and discussed politics. We heard from those who felt they shared few interests (and disagreed about politics). Making an attempt to become interested in a son- or daughter-in-law and their avocations can be one way to connect with them.

Believing the Child-in-Law Will Be a Good Parent

When a mother- or father-in-law admires their child and child-in-law's parenting approaches, they rest more easily, knowing their grandchildren will be well raised. Yet many parents with good relationships disagreed with their child and his or her spouse about parenting but were able to let those disagreements go. They acknowledged that they had a different parenting philosophy and that, maybe, their approach was outdated. Serious concerns about parenting approaches can be understandably upsetting to parents-in-law. For a few parents there were what we, as social workers, would consider justifiable concerns. Those are not easily addressed here. For the bulk of parents, one approach is praising what is liked about the parenting approach (assuming something can be found), which may help to shape the parenting behavior and be more welcome than criticizing. Other strategies can draw on the theories we offer: Parents can seek to understand the family background, culture, and the history of the son- or daughter-in-law and how that drives parenting approaches. At the same time, the parent-in-law can look at his own background and see what part his child is playing in the parenting approach. A parent-in-law can also consider the narrative that is developing around the parenting differences. Most parents want to raise their children well. It may be that by being open and curious about how the next generation is thinking about parenting, the impression of the parenting will become more fleshed out and thickened. There will be a more formed view and not just a surface impression.

Being Close with One's Own Child and Having One's Child Be Happy with the Relationship with the Child-in-Law

These are obvious signs that the relationship with the child-in-law is working. While this is not new information, it reconfirms the interconnectedness of family relationships. These characteristics reiterate the point that it is difficult though not impossible (as we have shown in previous chapters) to be close with a child-in-law without being close to one's child. The child-in-law usually takes cues from his or her spouse. For in-laws interested in building a closer relationship with their own child, one avenue, out of many, is through building a stronger relationship with the child-in-law.

Reducing Emotional Distance from a Child-in-Law

For some, this finding may be a call to take a risk and to be more self-disclosing. Others' research has found that appropriate self-disclosure can bring in-laws closer.[8] How that plays out with any particular dyad is hard to predict, but it does open up the possibility that sharing more, while not sharing inappropriately or interfering, may help to build a closer relationship with a son-in-law or daughter-in-law.

The findings that were predictive for one or the other set of parents-in-law merit mention also. Mothers-in-law who approved of the marriage and think the marriage is going well have better relationships with their daughter-in-law. Their son's selection of an appropriate spouse and his happiness in the marriage are important to the mother. For the fathers-in-law, a personal history of closeness with his own in-laws paves the way for a good future with his son-in-law, as does the ability to communicate directly with the son-in-law. This last characteristic is in the control of the father-in-law, who can work on communication with his son-in-law, whereas the other characteristics are in the past so out of the control of the parents-in-law.

What Children-in-Law Say Works

1. Having similar interests;
2. Having similar parenting philosophies;
3. Having parents who are not jealous of the relationship the son-in-law or daughter-in-law has with the in-laws;
4. Having a spouse who is happy with the relationship with the son- or daughter-in-law's parents.

While these were the most consistent predictors of a good relationship for both daughters- and sons-in-law, a few other characteristics were significant and worth noting. These include, for the daughters-in-law, having a mother-in-law who was not seen as interfering and having a mother-in-law who is close with her son, the daughter-in-law's husband. For the sons-in-law, these include being close with their own father and being able to talk directly to their father-in-law without involving their wife (similar to what fathers-in-law said was important for a good relationship).

What do these four findings mean for daughters-in-law and sons-in-law? They can point to specific areas to work on to improve their relationship with their in-laws.

Building Similar Interests

As with the parents-in-law, sharing common interests is a sign of good relations and is something that in-laws can work toward to improve their relationship. When people are asked about their interests, it opens up a venue for understanding them. We are not suggesting that avid bicyclists become chess players like their father- or mother-in-law, but having some awareness of what the Chess World Cup is (okay—we admit we Googled this one!), and maybe even learning the game, might help to show an interest in and build a better relationship with the intended person.

Having Similar Parenting Philosophies

Daughters- and sons-in-law should certainly have a strong impression of what their spouse's parents' parenting philosophy might be—it would have shown up in their spouse and in the way the parents treat their spouse. How much independence is given? How "hands-on" were or are they? How important is spirituality or excelling in sports or academics? How is punishment handled? When parents are providing childcare, having similar parenting approaches becomes particularly important. Here, an understanding of the context that the parents-in-law came from coupled with the ability to have an open conversation about parenting philosophy, as Virginia Satir suggests, can go a long way toward getting on the same page. Finally, and as Minuchin suggests, a boundary may have to be drawn, with adult children explaining to parents and parents-in-law what their parenting approach is. If both parents and parents-in-law can then support that intentional parenting, healthy interactions across three generations are likely to ensue.

Dealing with Jealousy from One's Own Parents

When a son- or daughter-in-law has a good relationship with the parents-in-law, his or her own parents may be jealous, and this can affect how the family system functions. It is difficult to balance multiple relationships including both sets of parents and to make them seem equal. Sometimes adult children are not close with their parents, have ambivalent feelings toward them, or experience ambivalent feelings from them.[9] Processing such feelings can open up the possibilities for close and possibly unfettered relationships with in-laws. Jealousy from parents may be openly discussed or may be suspected when, for example, parents complain about not having as much time with grandchildren as the other grandparents. Attending to it by reassuring and including parents as much as is comfortable, if even only with more frequent telephone contact, may help to reassure parents about their role in the couple's life.

Having a Spouse Who Is Happy with the In-Law Relationship

Here we reiterate the importance of the interconnectedness of family matters. If a daughter has a good relationship with her parents, she should want her partner to have one, too, and that happiness is a sign of a good in-law relationship. To build a better relationship with a parent-in-law, then, a son- or daughter-in-law should use his or her spouse as a guide and find out what may be needed to help improve the relationship.

IMPROVING IN-LAW RELATIONS: OTHER ISSUES TO CONSIDER FROM RESEARCH AND PRACTICE

Our research points us in the direction of other observations that may be helpful with our clinical lenses in undertstanding how to improve in-law relationships.

One son-in-law told us: "Now they are older, our roles are almost switched. We take care of them instead of them kind of taking care of us. So that's why it's switched."

Relationships can change significantly over the course of a lifetime. When the children-in-law first enter the family, they may be in their 20s and starting a career, a significant relationship, and possibly a family of their own. They may be tethered to their parents and friends, may be trying to balance competing demands on their time, and may have limited financial resources. Parents-in-law are usually healthy and independent when they first meet. However, within 25 years or so, aging and illness can catch up with them. Whereas parents may have helped with childcare and financial resources early on, later in life they may need physical and financial assistance. These lifespan changes shift the nature of the relationships.

In addition, some families' culture may expect greater contact and sharing of lives while others' culture may value greater intergenerational separation and independence that would lead to emotional distancing. Some may move geographically closer or farther apart. Grandchildren may bring families emotionally closer or cause greater distance, if in-laws feel excluded. Significant challenges can arise and impact these relationships, such as substance abuse, mental health struggles, dementia, and other health issues. Generations may have moved closer to each other, if care is needed, or farther away if parents have retired to warmer climes or children have moved for work or to be closer to the other parent set. Hence, the amount of time together may change dramatically one way or the other.

Also with time, people know each other better, often come to appreciate and understand each other better, and grow more tolerant with each other. Family members are likely to be more mature and less reactive. Things that may bug a mother-in-law about the daughter-in-law when she first enters the family may be seen in a larger context of other positive attributes, as in this example from Angela, who struggled at first with her daughter-in-law: "She was very controlling in every aspect of her life . . . we had a disagreement about my ex-husband and it just escalated. Then my youngest son died and she was beyond helpful. That's where the controlling stuff came into play. She took care of every detail that we had to do for my son's death. It really healed our relationship."

From our research, three key points emerged around time.

First, when we looked across all our samples of in-laws as well as within each sample, neither the age of the in-law nor the amount of time the child-in-law was in the family was related to the quality of the relationship. In other words, older parents-in-law and older children-in-law who have been in the family for years do not report better relationships when compared with younger in-laws and those who have only been in the family a few years. This could be because of the complicated nature of life. There are ebbs and flows of caretaking and being taken care of that cause distancing or closeness between family members. It may be that many relationships get established early on for better or for worse, and do not change.[10]

Second, while the quality of the relationship across ages is not different, individual relationships can shift markedly. In our one-year follow-up surveys of the in-laws, approximately one in 10 reported marked changes for the better and one in 10 reported marked changes for the worse in their relationship.[11] Angela provides one example of how things can improve. Leon provides another as he describes the shifts that occurred in relation to his son-in-law: "I played more of a fatherly role early in their marriage. Now that we are older, I would say more a trusted friend and similar to my own children in that I can ease up on the parenting and enjoy the friendship. It was gradual. I really respect his hard work and don't feel the need to give advice because I trust his process."

Another father-in-law, Miles, whose son-in-law married into the family 10 years ago, described him as fulfilling classically male family roles: "He has proven to be an ambitious, dedicated spouse, father, family man, willing to contribute to his side of the family as well as ours."

Brandon chalked up the improvement in his 15-year-long relationship with his 80-year-old father-in-law to becoming a new father: "It evolved as we started a family, and we've become closer. I can talk to him about parenting now and things that I wouldn't have before. I love and admire my wife and that makes me admire the values that my father-in-law instilled."

Carrie also credits her becoming a parent with improvements: "The amount of time we speak and the frequency we communicate with each other is the same, but it's definitely become a more positive interaction over time . . . Why? The kids. My mother-in-law says I'm a good mom, and that's important to her."

We also have stories detailing how relationships have worsened over the years. When relationships got worse over the course of the year, it could be because of, or leading up to, marital separation or divorce. In a handful of cases, drug addiction and mental health struggles are blamed. Other times, the daughter- or the son-in-law being a bad parent or spouse is blamed. Harry, quoted in Chapter 5, lost respect for his son-in-law the better he got to know him: "He changed! I saw that other side of him that I wasn't seeing when I wasn't around him. I would see stuff that she was kind of complaining about him to do. He's not stepping up being the man he's supposed to be to support my daughter."

Having children can cause rifts also, as in this next example from Alba: "My mother-in-law and I got along in the beginning, but after I started to have children, our relationship became strained. I think she just likes conflict. I know how to deal with her because I confront her. Her behavior does not affect me, but I will not let her disrespect my daughter."

It is important to note that divorce does not always end in-law relationships. Some maintain a good relationship because they still care about each other, because the parent-in-law is still a valued grandparent, or because a parent-in-law feels their own child's behavior was reprehensible. Kathleen encapsulates all three reasons. After 35 years of marriage, she and her husband divorced. Kathleen and her mother-in-law were always close and her mother-in-law came to believe that her son's behavior caused the breakup. Kathleen has two daughters who have an on-again, off-again relationship with their father but are very close with their paternal grandparents. Kathleen remains close with her former mother-in-law and they exchange emails and holiday cards.

Third, a significant minority of in-laws do not spend a lot of time together in face-to-face contact or in electronic contact. When asked how many hours they spent interacting in a typical month (in person, on the phone, online, emailing, and texting), between 27% and 35% said they spent one hour or less with each other. Between 4% and 11% reported they spend 20 hours or more a month together. Mothers-in-law reported more time together with daughters-in-law than fathers-in-law reported with sons-in-law; daughters- and sons-in-law reported similar amounts of time with parents-in-law. In addition, we did not find that daughters-in-law were doing significantly more of the caretaking of both sets of parents than sons-in-law were.[12] Generally, and it is cyclical, when more time is spent together, the quality of the relationship is better—and if the relationship is better, people will spend more time together.

To improve in-law relationships, it is vital to have a sense of the typical ebbs and flows that can occur across the lifespan as well as within a short period of time. Specific acts of kindness between the generations can go a long way toward changing family relationships.

The Family Developmental Stage of These Horizontal and Vertical Relationships

How we conceptualize these relationships can help us to live with in-laws more productively. With marriage, both newlyweds have to negotiate some form of attachment that carries the definition of child (*son*-in-law or *daughter*-in-law) to one or more new "parents." The newlyweds also have to help their spouse attach to a new set of parents and possibly help their own parents negotiate with another set of parents.[13] The parents, who have separated in a developmentally appropriate way from their own child, now have to attach to a new "child." These "attachments" can cause challenges. Some parents-in-law were very clear that they did not consider themselves a parent to their child-in-law, even when they sometimes felt pulled into that role by their daughter- or son-in-law. Others were thrilled to play that parenting role.

The in-law relationship requires an understanding of not only the developmental stage of the relationship but also the vertical and horizontal nature of it. As a daughter-in-law solidifies her relationship with her spouse, a horizontal relationship, she is potentially shifting the vertical relationship with her own parents (she may not be as available to them as she was; she may begin to keep things from them). As she builds a relationship with her in-laws, she is also potentially shifting the relationship with her own parents just as her becoming closer to her spouse also shifts her relationship with her in-laws. Understanding the shifting dynamics can help to make the struggles that arise across a lifespan more manageable. It is not that "things" are just happening; they are occurring in a family context whose dynamics change with births, deaths, divorces, major life events, and the additions of new in-laws. Families should anticipate these changes and prepare for them by talking about them.

Ambivalence and Ambiguity

Having mixed feelings about someone and being unclear about some of their expressions and behaviors are part and parcel with life's vagaries. Holding simultaneously positive and negative feelings toward an in-law needs to be viewed as a typical part of adult relationships. Just as parents often hold such feelings toward their own adult children, it would be expected they would hold them toward their children's spouses. Likewise, adult children often hold ambivalent feelings toward their own parents. Most readers can easily relate to having loving feelings toward parents while also remembering hurtful experiences with them. These feelings form over many years and become more complicated when one is married to someone who is also interacting with the parents in their role as parents-in-law. They are reflective of the complicated nature of in-law relationships and are not a sign that a relationship is in trouble. A mature understanding and acceptance of the nature of ambivalence, in many facets of one's life, can help one travel through life's ups and downs more easily.

Ambiguity arises when people are unclear about another person's actions and about how one should act. Ambiguity is typical when families join together through marriage or when family members are assuming new roles as family dynamics shift. We heard it so often from both children-in-law and parents-in-law when they were unclear about caregiving, childrearing, or other family responsibilities. Family members should anticipate and talk about it when expectations are unclear.

Interference

When we ask mothers- and fathers-in-law for advice about how to improve relations with their in-laws, "Bite your tongue," "Stay out of it," "Keep your mouth shut," and "Don't give advice" are often heard. We heard these suggestions from both fathers-in-law and mothers-in-law, though mothers-in-law, perhaps as a result of all the mother-in-law jokes, seemed more concerned about being seen as interfering than fathers-in-law. When daughters- and sons-in-law offered advice, it rarely centered on interfering except in the context of not interfering in the relationship between their spouse and their spouse's parents. In a world where there can be a thin line between giving advice and interfering, with the two people involved seeing the opposite in the same interaction, the better the relationship, the easier it is to give advice without it being perceived as interference. To that end, parents-in-law also advised keeping communication open, being nice, and staying out of the middle of the children's relationship. Usually, advice is given to one's child and that can be interpreted by the child's spouse as interference. Other times, communication goes directly to the in-law, which also can be viewed as interference. Asking permission to give input or even saying, "Let me know if you ever want feedback; otherwise I will keep my mouth shut" is one way a mother- or father-in-law can approach a daughter- or son-in-law. This is best said at a time when there is no feedback to give.

Setting Boundaries

In most cultures, and as we discussed, one of the key developmental tasks of life entails separating from one's family of origin and establishing an independent identity while also staying connected to them in an adult way. Advice from the younger generation is a reflection of this developmental task. We heard one should "Accept parents-in-law as they are," "Don't confront them," "Keep your opinions to yourself," "Don't interfere in your in-law's relationship with your spouse," "Take the time to make it work by spending time with them," and "Set boundaries as a couple."

One son-in-law, Cooper, advised keeping negative feelings to oneself:

> Find that niche and go with it. Bond with them over things that they enjoy no matter what that is because you are doing it for them, your spouse, and for yourself, and possibly your kids. They are your spouse's parents and if you still cannot get along with your in-laws, bite your tongue because by making negative comments in front of your spouse about your in-laws you are not changing the in-law. But you are hurting your spouse because somewhere deep inside your spouse is that little kid and that is their mom and dad.

Another son-in-law, Patrick, cautioned about understanding the differences between his role and his spouse's role:

> Have mutual respect and know where boundaries are. For me, recognizing that my in-laws' relationship with Mary will be different from their relationship with me. Their relationship has developed over 42 years. It is what it is and I respect that, but I am a different person. It is going to have different boundaries and they are going to have a different role with her than with me.

This daughter-in-law, Shauna, talked about the importance of reaching out, staying in contact, and being open—but within reason: "I would say initiating contact with my mother-in-law, her Skyping with our son, and my being open to hearing their opinions and advice while respectfully letting them know where the boundaries are."

Another daughter-in-law, Tracy, who described her mother-in-law as playing a central role in communicating with extended family, told us that she, too, has learned the importance of communication:

> I think something I learned that was really helpful in our relationship is that I be upfront and open about how things were going when they were difficult. I think that has helped whenever we have disagreements, which are few and far between at this point. But when they happen, I bring up my concern and talk with her straightforward about it. I think that is always the best, instead of feeling frustrated and not saying anything.

The importance of setting boundaries cannot be overstated. Without them, the couple will have a hard time establishing an identity, which will likely result in a strained marital relationship. In-law interference has been cited as one of the reasons for divorce.[14] At the same time, a strained marriage will also affect in-law relationships, particularly the more the parents/parents-in-law are aware of the strain. They may be consciously or unconsciously brought into what is happening between the couple and have a reaction that, as we heard from people we interviewed, further exacerbates the relationship difficulties.

Boundary setting can be accomplished by understanding how past family relations may be affecting the present ones. Such insight can lead to communicating openly about where boundaries should be drawn and taking clear steps to establish them that are supportive and loving, yet firm.

Relations Between Two Sets of Parents-in-Law

When the two sets of parents knew each other before the marriage because they lived in the same area, they usually get along better. Their children may have grown up together and they may have friends in common. But in an increasingly mobile society, this is less likely to be the case. We have cited stories from highly inclusive families where everyone feels comfortable together at significant family events as well as those families where the in-laws do not know each other well and only saw each other at the wedding. When the two sets of in-laws do not get along, it is often a reflection of underlying issues between the generations—for example, a daughter-in-law does not get along well with her mother- or father-in-law so her parents do not get along with that in-law, either.

The children have to be careful when considering to what extent they want to get in the middle of the two sets of parents. Some children feel it is their responsibility to make the relationship work, while others work hard to arrange as little contact as possible to ease tensions. Children openly talking about this with each other can help them operate as a team. Part of what this entails is paying attention to the narratives around each set of parents and seeing if different narratives may be written which can result in a new outcome. Seeing a set of parents as needy can be rewritten as seeing them as loving and wanting more contact with their children.

Triangulation and Supporting the Spouse

Setting boundaries is one way of avoiding triangulation. Triangulation occurs when a third party has to mediate between two others because the two are unable to resolve their differences. With in-laws, triangulation might look like (1) a mother-in-law telling her son to tell his wife, the daughter-in-law, that the mother-in-law should be included in more family events; (2) a son-in-law feeling caught between his father-in-law and his wife when the father-in-law complains to him about her; (3) a son-in-law complaining to a father-in-law about his daughter, the son-in-law's wife. In all three examples, a family member could feel inappropriately pulled into a conflict and caught between a parent and a spouse. Being on the same page with the spouse, even anticipating how to respond to attempts at triangulation, would be important in the first two examples. Specifically, the son or son-in-law could say he feels caught when the mother or father-in-law makes such a request or complains about his wife. In the third example, similar language could be used, with the father-in-law saying he feels uncomfortable hearing complaints about his daughter. These steps would help to set a boundary also.

Another way to support the spouse is suggested by Karen Fingerman and colleagues, who found that getting together alone with one's in-law after the wedding was linked to more positive feelings about the relationship.[15] Such contact could send a message to the spouse that she or he does not have to play a mediating role.

Frozen Conflicts

Borrowing from international law, the term "frozen conflicts" is used to describe "territorial disputes in locations that have neither a peaceful resolution nor armed hostilities."[16] Thomas Grant, a senior research fellow at the University of Cambridge, offers characteristics of frozen conflicts that could apply metaphorically to highly conflictual in-law relationships:. These include that hostile activities have occurred, that there is now stability between the parties, and that " . . . a settlement process involving outside parties has been sporadic and inconclusive."[17]

The term is used to describe an entrenched, hostile stalemate between a government and separatist forces.

Some of the stories we heard from in-laws sound to us like frozen conflicts. Two "armed" camps of family members, while not openly warring anymore, are deeply entrenched in their positions and even with outside intervention are unable to reconcile. Sometimes these conflicts pervade other relationships as siblings and relatives become involved. There are usually highly complicated backstories, with those on each side feeling justified in their actions. Settlement processes when a country is mired in a frozen conflict may occur if there is a significant shift in the context accompanied by a push for reconciliation and peace. In families, members should be attuned to opportunities for change that might naturally occur in a family (a death, a wedding, a birth) and be willing to consider attempts to *thaw* the conflict that are amenable to all. We saw with our follow-up research that frozen conflicts can change from one year to the next. We also saw that seemingly good relationships can take a significant turn for the worse. Sometimes when relationships seem frozen, there may be a sliver of good that is occurring. An attempt should be made to focus on the sliver for the betterment of the family.

The Long View

This is a "sit back and wait" approach, which we heard from both the children-in-law and the parents-in-law. Essentially, they espouse the belief that to get along with an in-law, they had to not focus on a momentary hiccup in the relationship but to think instead about the relationship as unfolding over many years. As one daughter-in-law told us, if the marriage is viewed as a lifelong commitment, then the relationship with the in-law is also a lifelong commitment. Keeping the relationship alive by not letting it get derailed is the operative philosophy while accepting the in-law and avoiding conflicts. Mikucki-Enyart found that in-laws may specifically avoid talking about certain topics to maintain the relationship.[18] This can be a useful strategy particularly when family members hold differing political views.

Mental Health and Substance Abuse Struggles in an In-Law

We asked on our surveys about the presence of mental health or substance abuse struggles in the respondent and family members.[19] Daughters-in-law reported much higher incidences of mental health and substance abuse issues in all family members (themselves, their parents, their spouse, and their in-laws) than did sons-in-law. Mothers-in-law reported higher incidences in themselves, their child-in-law, their own child, and their spouse than did fathers-in-law. It is hard to believe that the difference between the two samples (an average of 17.5% reported by the daughters-in-law for all family members and an average of 11% for the sons-in-law; an average of 13.5% reported by the mothers-in-law for all family members and 6% reported by the fathers-in-law) is that great.

It may be that men purposely or unconsciously under-report such issues—that they exercise a kind of denial, do not consider the same types of struggles to be significant, or are simply not as aware of them. Thus, family members should anticipate that they might not always be on the same page about the presence of these issues or how to approach them.

We do know that the presence of such struggles can strain in-law relationships, particularly the more generations that are involved. Such issues are best approached when seen as a disease and not as a character flaw or choice. This may require the narratives around these issues to be rewritten. We also know that when mental health or substance issues are overcome, such a victory can bring family members together and a narrative of strength can be celebrated.

Useful Web Advice

Sometimes Googling "in-laws" and reading web advice can be helpful for some quick tips. One site[20] suggests, when starting out the relationship with in-laws, knowing your own limits about being in groups, being polite, complimenting family members, controlling alcohol consumption, asking questions about family history, spending time with people individually to build the relationship, and facilitating contact between the two sets of in-laws. We can add to this one quick tip—keep your sense of humor!

Calling Parents-in-Law "Mom" and "Dad"

Cultures and families vary greatly about when they consider someone an equal member of the family and what they wish to be called. We found great variation here. Some parents-in-law ask to be called mom or dad; some ask to be called by their first name. In one situation, a father-in-law wanted to be called Dr. Fred. Some children-in-law decline to call their in-law mom or dad, saying they have their own parents already. Names can be a matter of some tension and need to be considered with the input of the son- or daughter-in-law's spouse.

In one touching story, Nolan, who had lost his father at a young age and then his grandfather, told his new father-in-law that he did not feel comfortable calling him dad because he had suffered so much loss. Twenty years later, when he was in his 40s, both Nolan and his father-in-law survived health crises at the same time. When Nolan, at that point the healthier of the two, picked up his father-in-law at the hospital, his father-in-law told Nolan how much he loved him. Nolan began calling him dad from that point forward.

With names, we encourage both generations to be open to the other generation. Asking what names to use is a good place to start while remembering that names, such as son or mom and dad, have meaning that is often connected to prior generations.

Gender Differences When Thinking About Improving In-Law Relationships

As we discuss in Chapter 8, differences appear between how male in-laws and female in-laws manage these relationships.

What to do about gender? We return to the theories that begin this chapter. On a family level, people make choices based on their history and the context in which they are living in their relationships. Those choices are also shaped by broader cultural and societal expectations for women and men, for sons and daughters, and for in-laws. Drawing a genogram that includes role expectations around gender can help people understand how they have come to the beliefs they have about their role in the family. It can also be the beginning of a conversation about what they are interested in doing in the future. Talking about issues in an open, non-defensive way can be hard to go about at first but, with practice, can help to clear away family driftwood when people are open to deeper conversations—and we realize that some family members may not be. But it can be incumbent on the family member who is most interested in change around gender expectations to start the conversation even if the response is not what was hoped for. Boundaries, boundaries, boundaries. People who seek change, whether a daughter-in-law or a father-in-law, will need support from their partner. Having a boundary around that relationship can be the crucible within which couples can talk about their expectations for each other and, in turn, for their in-law interactions. Finally, and using the tenets of narrative therapy, family roles are shaped by societal expectations. A discussion about what the expectations are for the in-law roles can help to change the narrative around them.

We can recommend working broadly to re-envision the roles that men and women fulfill in the family as spouses and as parents. In what has been a complementary handshake, women are more central to the maintenance of the socio-emotional workings of the family while men have been more central to the financial workings, although those roles are becoming less distinct. Men are more on the periphery of the family as compared to women; we found in our research that both sons and daughters, as well as sons-in-law and daughters-in-law, feel closer to their mother and their mother-in-law than their father and father-in-law. Parenting is very important to the men and women we surveyed. The image of men not caring about parenting and leaving it to their wife would be wholly inaccurate, according to our findings. Yet men do not take, and perhaps are not asked to take, as active a role. We would love to see, as we saw in our research with younger siblings where brothers and sisters were equally communicative with each other, a continued and encouraging increased sharing of roles by men and women in the family.

CONCLUSIONS

Despite the struggles expressed by some in our research, our book is a testament to the triumph of relationships, the flexibility of two families with multiple generations, to come together, form a new family, and be a model for future generations. We found in our research that a majority of the in-law relationships are generally positive and working, with some working extremely well and providing a great deal of support and love. Also within that majority are in-law relationships that are functioning at a comfortable or satisfactory level where both generations have adapted to and are contented with each other. In-laws may labor from time to time to watch what they say and may feel the need to walk on eggshells, but they are making it work for the benefit of all. A minority of the in-law relationships, between 10% and 15%, are quite strained. Some of these, in this minority, may not be salvageable, while others can improve to a point where interactions become more satisfying. The need for improvement is not just limited to those that are strained. Those in the majority can also improve, and it is our belief that good family relationships can become great family relationships.

ACKNOWLEDGMENTS

We first would like to thank our in-laws, living and dead, for their love and support—the three Dans and Millie (GG) and Madeline and Eugene (MW).

We greatly appreciate all those in-laws who so graciously gave us their time by participating in this research. You have provided the bulwark for our understanding of this complex topic. Without you, this book would not have been written.

Micah Saviet, MSW, and Jessica Gelfarb, MSW, two marvelous research assistants, helped get the survey data into the Excel files, edited manuscripts from the research, and coded many, many qualitative interviews. Thank you! Thanks to Rabbi Andy Busch who assisted with biblical interpretations.

We were fortunate to receive financial support from the University of Maryland School of Social Work under the deanship of Rick Barth and thank him for his leadership in and support of social work research in general and this research in particular.

Finally, thank you to the social work students who conducted qualitative interviews for this research:

2015—Tiara Anderson, Benjamin Barer, Tia DeLoach, Jayme Engel, Brett FreedenBerg, Morgan Garber, Lauren Haines, Michelle Hammack, Monet Hinton, Lori LaGrossa, Dorian Lanni, Kristan Miller, Tiffany Mosely, Katherine Petzold, Rachel Sherman, Lillian Soloweszyk, and Sumayyah Taufique.

2016—Nancy Basner, Alexa Cavaseno, Carrie Cleveland, Melissa Cussins, Kareen Hill, Cynthia Moyer, Chidiogo Nkume, Kelsey Pellarin, Colleen Russo, Linnea Shore, Lacy Weinblatt, Laura Whitney, Allison Yankey, Amena Zaman, and Colleen Zorn.

2017—Christiana Bockari, Alexa Bruck, Allison Cavanaugh, Katherine Fleming, Julia Franger, Maxie Franklin, Sydney Gross,

Alexandra Kasoff, Camilla Pearson, Gina Servelle, Daria Silas, Colleen Sippel, and Dominique Thompson.

2018—Jenna Adler, Danielle Boucree, Nicolle Castro Caroca, Cynthia Chung, Briana Cragwell, Sierra Deleon, Lucy Donofrio, Shira Galay, Monique McIntyre, Jessica Piper, Jessica Reedy, Nina Rosenberg, Jasmine Savoy, Hannah Seen, Elizabeth Stafford, Michelle Steele, Joshua Sullivan, Austin Tucker, Ali Warhaftig, Laura Weimer, and Brittany White.

2019—Ariella Bernstein, Margaux Blau, Clare Bubniak, Taylor Buckley, Melissa Erickson, Katie Golden, Justice Harris, Ava Hawkinson, Laura Knox, Katie Lewis, Rachel Lilly-Pawlowski, Brenda Nettey, Jennifer Pinder, Laina Russell, Shannon Sammis, Morgan Strehl, and Liana Ventimiglia.

Research Methods

We gathered the qualitative and quantitative data analyzed for this book in three ways: (1) surveys administered through Qualtrics; (2) surveys and interviews conducted by MSW students as part of an advanced research course; and (3) surveys and interviews conducted by the authors.

QUALTRICS DATA

The Qualtrics data analyzed for this study were collected with a 115-item quantitative survey (the first five questions were the screening questions) developed by the authors, piloted in live interviews by the authors and master's students enrolled in an advanced-level research course, and then formatted in the Qualtrics platform by the authors. Qualtrics is an online survey platform in which researchers may design, format, and administer their own surveys via email. Qualtrics has an infrastructure to administer surveys for social science researchers to a sample of respondents who meet screening criteria for inclusion in a study. The authors, supported by a grant from the University of Maryland School of Social Work, hired Qualtrics to administer this survey in 2017. Respondents were blind to the nature of the survey or study, and so initial screening questions ensured that respondents met the study's family relationship criteria for inclusion. Those screening questions included, for daughters-in-law, for example: 1) being female; 2) being married to a male; 3) having a living mother-in-law; and 4) having or had interpersonal interactions with that mother-in-law. Respondents also had to agree to thoughtfully provide their best answers to each question in this survey. In order to be eligible, respondents needed to answer "Yes" to all five screening questions, after which they were presented the entire survey.

Respondents were part of the Qualtrics Panel and are compensated, sometimes with gift certificates, for their participation in surveys. Qualtrics made the survey available to potential respondents with the goal to survey 250 respondents across each of the four in-law types. The samples were emailed again one year later and asked to complete a similar, though shorter, survey that also included new questions not asked originally. For the Qualtrics study, we focused on heterosexual marriages. Other research we conducted explored gay and lesbian couples' in-law relationships as well as parents of gay and lesbian married children (discussed in Chapter 7).

QUALTRICS SAMPLE DESCRIPTIONS

Here, we detail the response to that survey strategy and the resulting four samples of in-law respondents who completed the surveys and provided the data analyzed for the research reported here.

Mothers-in-Law

Qualtrics made the survey available on July 20, 2017, and over the next 11 days 1,086 potential mother-in-law respondents initiated the screening questions in the survey, resulting in a sample of 267 who met the screening criteria and completed the full survey by July 31, 2017, at which time the survey was closed. That mother-in-law sample of 267 respondents had a mean age of 63 and ranged in age from 37 to 88. About half ($n = 137$; 51%) were married to the father of the son who was married to the daughter-in-law, while 130 (49%) were not; 78 (29%) reported having been divorced from the son's father. The mean length of time in years the daughter-in-law had been married into the mother-in-law's family was 11. Of those 267 mothers-in-law, 203 (76%) reported being European American or White, 19 (7%) Black or African American, 15 (6%) Latina or Hispanic American, five (2%) Asian American, four (2%) belonging to multiple races or ethnicities, one (<1%) Native Hawaiian or other Pacific Islander, and 19 (7%) another race or ethnicity. In terms of religious affiliation or spirituality, 99 (37%) reported being Protestant, 67 (25%) Catholic, 23 (9%) not affiliated with a religion (agnostic, atheist, secular humanist), 21 (8%) Jewish, 11 (6%) spiritual, three (1%) Buddhist, two (1%) Islam, and 36 (14%) endorsed another religion or spirituality. Mother-in-law respondents had an average of 14 years of education (two years beyond a high school degree) with a range of four to 24 years. In terms of combined household income, 87 (33%) endorsed $40,000 or less, 87 (33%) between $40,001 and $80,000, 49 (18%) $80,001 to $120,000, 28 (11%) $120,001 to $160,000, and 16 (6%) above $160,000.

Daughters-in-Law

Qualtrics made the survey available to respondents on July 20, 2017. Over the next 12 days, 1,112 potential daughter-in-law respondents initiated the five screening questions in the survey, resulting in a final sample of 351 meeting study criteria and completing a full survey by August 1, 2017, at which time the survey was closed. That sample of 351 daughters-in-law had a mean age of 40 and an age range from 18 to 69. Their mothers-in-law had a mean age was 67 and their ages ranged from 43 to 94. The mean length of time these daughters-in-law had been married into the mother-in-law's family was 12.7 years. Of the 351 daughters-in-law, 250 (71%) reported being European American or White, 35 (10%) reported being Asian, 23 (6%) Latina or Hispanic, 14 (4%) Black or African American, three (1%) American Indian or Alaska Native, one (<1%) Native Hawaiian or Pacific Islander, three (1%) multiple races/ethnicities, and 22 (7%) reported being another race or ethnicity. In terms of religious affiliation or spirituality, 81 (23%) reported being Protestant, 87 (25%) Catholic, 65 (19%) not affiliated with a religion (agnostic, atheist, secular humanist), 15 (4%) Jewish, 13 (4%) spiritual, six (2%) Buddhist, four (1%) Muslim, and 78 (22%) endorsed another religion or spirituality. Respondents had an average of 15 years of education (three years beyond a high school degree) with a range from 7 to 22 years. In terms of combined household income, 54 (15%) endorsed $40,000 or below, 103 (29%) between $41,000 and $80,000, 104 (30%) $81,000 to $120,000, 49 (14%) $121,000 to $160,000, and 41 (12%) above $160,000. For 287 (82%), this was her first marriage and for 288 (82%) it was the first marriage for her husband. Two hundred nineteen (62%) of these daughters-in-law reported having children from this marriage, while 52 (15%) brought stepchildren into the marriage, and 47 (13%) of the husbands brought stepchildren into the marriage.

Fathers-in-Law

Qualtrics made the survey available on July 20, 2017, and over the next 12 days 1,023 potential father-in-law respondents initiated the screening questions in the survey, resulting in a sample of 294 who met the screening criteria and completed the full survey by August 1, 2017, at which time the survey closed. That father-in-law sample of 294 respondents had an average age of 66 and ranged from 34 to 95. About three-quarters (218 [74%]) were married to the mother of the daughter who was married to the son-in-law, while 76 (26%) were not; 58 (20%) reported having been divorced from the daughter's mother. The mean length of time in years the son-in-law had been married into the father-in-law's family was 12. Of those 294 fathers-in-law, 254 (86%) reported being European American or White, 12 (4%) Black or African American, six (2%) Latino or Hispanic American, four (1%) Asian American, two (<1%) belonging to multiple races or ethnicities, one (<1%) Native Hawaiian or other Pacific Islander, and 13 (6%) another race or ethnicity. In terms of religious affiliation or spirituality, 116 (39%) reported being Protestant, 99 (34%) Catholic, 26 (9%) not affiliated with a religion (agnostic, atheist, secular humanist), 16 (5%) Jewish, three (1%) spiritual, two (<1%) Buddhist, two (<1%) Islam, one (<1%) Universalist Unitarian, one (<1%) Hindu, and 31 (11%) endorsed another religion or spirituality. Father-in-law respondents had an average of 16 years of education (four years beyond a high school degree) with a range of one to 24 years. In terms of combined household income, 36 (12%) endorsed $40,000 or less, 88 (30%) between $40,001 and $80,000, 81 (28%) $80,001 to $120,000, 42 (14%) $120,001 to $160,000, and 47 (16%) above $160,000.

Sons-in-Law

Qualtrics made the survey available to respondents on July 20, 2017. Over the next 11 days, 831 potential son-in-law respondents initiated the five screening questions in the survey, resulting in a final sample of 263 meeting study criteria and completing a full survey by July 31, 2017, at which time the survey was closed. That sample of 263 sons-in-law had a mean age of 53 and an age range from 20 to 71. Their fathers-in-law had a mean age was 79 and their ages ranged from 43 to 98. The mean length of time these sons-in-law had been married into the father-in-law's family was 17 years. Of the 263 sons-in-law, 198 (75%) reported being European American or White, 26 (10%) Asian, 23 (9%) Latino or Hispanic, 21 (8%)

Black or African American, two (<1%) American Indian or Alaska Native, one (<1%) Native Hawaiian or Pacific Islander, one (<1%) multiple races/ethnicities, and 12 (5%) reported being another race or ethnicity. In terms of religious affiliation or spirituality, 93 (23%) reported being Protestant, 81 (25%) Catholic, 35 (19%) not affiliated with a religion (agnostic, atheist, secular humanist), 11 (4%) Hindu, six (2%) Jewish, three (1%) spiritual, two (<1%) Buddhist, one (<1%) Islam, and 34 (13%) endorsed another religion or spirituality. Respondents had an average of 16 years of education (four years beyond a high school degree) with a range of zero to 26 years. In terms of combined household income, 17 (7%) endorsed $40,000 or below, 54 (33%) between $41,000 and $80,000, 83 (32%) $81,000 to $120,000, 55 (21%) $121,000 to $160,000, and 52 (20%) above $160,000. For 220 (84%) this was his first marriage and for 226 (86%) it was the first marriage for his wife. One hundred ninety (72%) of these sons-in-law reported having children from this marriage, while 28 (11%) brought stepchildren into the marriage, and 29 (11%) of the wives brought stepchildren into the marriage.

The follow-up surveys one year later of all four samples did not look significantly different from a demographic perspective. Their scores on the relationship scale that we constructed also did not look significantly different.

ANALYTIC STRATEGY

The central goal of the research was to explore the nature of four in-law relationships: mothers-in-law with their daughter-in-law, daughters-in-law with their mother-in-law, fathers-in-law with their son-in-law, and sons-in-law with their father-in-law. Three types of analyses were reported and interpreted in this book. The first included frequencies and descriptive statistics of survey responses. The second type of analyses were bivariate correlations, a statistical estimation of how two variables, such as survey question response patterns, covary or, put simply, tend to show a systematic pattern. Those correlations are reported when we report that those who responded to one question in a certain way tended to respond to another question in a certain way. For example, when we state that mothers-in-law who reported not knowing their daughter-in-law well before the marriage were less close to that daughter-in-law, it is based on a correlation between the response patterns across those questions. The third type of analyses were multivariate linear regressions in which an outcome was predicted by a set of predictors. The outcome variable used in all these analyses was a seven-survey-item scale that was a measure of the overall quality of the relationship.

The outcome variable, which was an overall measure of the quality of the in-law relationship, was the mean of a set of seven survey items. All seven survey items had the same 5-point response option set: *Strongly Agree* (coded 4), *Agree* (3), *Neutral* (2), *Disagree* (1), or *Strongly Disagree* (0). Those seven items included five that were positive indicators of relationship quality and two that assessed negative relationship characteristics: 1) *My mother-in-law and I have a close relationship*, 2) *Overall, I admire my mother-in-law*, 3) *I can ask my mother-in-law for advice*, 4) *I enjoy spending time with my mother-in-law*, 5) *I trust my mother-in-law*, 6) *I avoid my mother-in-law*, and 7) *I have problematic conflicts with my mother-in-law*. Before estimating the mean of this scale for each sample, the two negatively worded questions were reverse-coded. This scale had strong internal consistency reliability across the four samples (Cronbach's α ranged from .88 to .93).

The predictor or independent variables for the regression analyses across the four samples were determined by a series of analyses to identify the survey items most predictive of relationship quality.

SURVEYS WITH INTERVIEWS

In addition to the Qualtrics-generated data, MSW students administered surveys and conducted interviews, as did the authors. The students were enrolled in an advanced research class and were asked to interview people over the age of 21 who had a living in-law of the same gender. Only one member from a family was surveyed or interviewed.[1] Students interviewed people they knew, though not their own family members, people they learned about through acquaintances using snowball sampling, and people they met in public spaces. Prior to conducting the surveys and interviews, the students completed Institutional Review Board coursework, including HIPAA and CITI training, and were trained in administering a survey and conducting a qualitative interview. The students operated as a research team and discussed issues that arose during the administration of the survey and the interview.[2] This helped to sensitize the research team to the population.

In-laws were first asked to complete a survey and then to describe their relationship with their in-law as a way to acclimate them to the topic. They were then asked more specific questions from a structured interview protocol. The interviews were transcribed and any audiotapes of the interviews were then erased. Some interviews lasted more than an hour while some were only 30 minutes, when the in-law did not have much to say or gave brief answers.

For research articles generated from this process as well as for this book, the qualitative interviews were read separately by two members of the research team and, depending on what was being explored, were thematically coded. To develop an initial sense of the relationships, all the interviews were read to see what the range of responses were. This process is part of the immersion in the data that other researchers recommend.[3] The team members, depending on the issue being explored, coded for specific answers as well as more broadly for positive, negative, and mixed relationships from the general accounts. They then would meet to resolve any coding differences.[4] Relationships that were identified from the interviews as being positive and negative, for example, were cross-checked with the survey responses to assess the level of qualitative and quantitative data pattern agreement.

In each new wave of data collection with the MSW students, open-ended interview questions were added, informed by our analyses of interviews and data collected up to that point, including what we learned from the samples from Qualtrics. This increased sensitization to the topic resulted in adding questions focused on getting respondents' descriptions of changes in the in-law relationships across transitions and the trajectory of these relationships over time.

As the authors, we did not know the identities of those whom the MSW students interviewed as consent forms were separated from transcripts and surveys when we received them. We have further changed all identifying information about the interviewees to hide their identities. Occasionally, a composite identity appears to better illustrate a point from the analysis of the data and to further disguise the interviewees who so graciously gave of their time.

We have included examples of interview guides, one for the father-in-law and one for the son-in-law. The women's are similar with the wording adjusted. The surveys have similar questions to the Qualtrics surveys, which are included for the women.

INTERVIEW SAMPLE DESCRIPTIONS

Here, we detail the characteristics of four samples of in-law respondents who completed the surveys and the interviews.

Mothers-in-Law

The sample included 79 mother-in-law participants who had a mean age of 62 years and a range from 37 to 83. The majority (80%) were married to the father of their son who was married to their daughter-in-law, while 10% were divorced; and of the remaining eight, 4% reported not being married and 6% indicated they were widowed. The mean length of time since the daughter-in-law had entered the family was eight years. Sixty-six percent of the mothers-in-law indicated that they had grandchildren from the marriage between their son and daughter-in-law, while 34% did not. Of the 79 mothers-in-law, 80% endorsed being White; 15% Black or African American; 2% Asian; and 2% indicated mixed races/ethnicities or other race or ethnicity not listed. In terms of religious affiliation or spirituality, among 78 of the mother-in-law respondents, the following religious identities were reported: 24% Jewish; 14% Catholic; 14% Protestant; 8% no religious affiliation; 5% Christian; 5% Mormon (Church of Jesus Christ of Latter-day Saints); 1% Sikh; and 22% another religion or spirituality. Respondents had an average of 16 years of education (four years beyond a high school degree) with a range from 10 to 22 years. Participants were also asked how they self-identified by class, as measured by their household income. Four percent endorsed being lower-middle class; 38% endorsed middle; 45% endorsed upper-middle; and 13% endorsed upper.

Fathers-in-Law

The sample included 85 father-in-law participants who had a mean age of 66 years and a range from 51 to 87. The majority (87%) were married to the mother of their daughter who was married to their son-in-law, while 8% were divorced; and of the remaining four, 2% reported not being married and 2% indicated they were widowed. The mean length of time since the son-in-law had entered the family was eight years. Sixty-three percent of the fathers-in-law indicated that they had grandchildren from the marriage between their daughter and son-in-law, while 36% did not. Of this sample of 85, 78% endorsed being White; 18% Black or African American; and, of the remaining four, 1% endorsed being Latino or Hispanic, 1% identified as Asian, and 2% indicated mixed race or ethnicities or other race or ethnicity not listed. In terms of religious affiliation or spirituality, the following religious identities were reported: 37% Jewish; 15% Protestant; 15% Catholic; 10% no religious affiliation; 7% Christian; 2% Muslim; 2% atheist/agnostic; 2% spiritual; 1% Mormon (Church of Jesus Christ of Latter-day Saints); and 16% another religion or spirituality. Respondents had an average of 16 years of education (four years beyond a high school degree) with a range from 12 to 25 years. Participants were also asked how they self-identified by class, as measured by their household income. Eight percent endorsed lower-middle class; 40% endorsed middle; 43% endorsed upper-middle; and 8% endorsed upper.

Daughters-in-Law

The sample included 93 daughter-in-law participants who had a mean age of 36 years and a range from 23 to 61. Of this sample, 85% indicated that this was their first marriage, while 8% indicated that it was not their first marriage, and 2% indicated that it was not the first marriage for their spouse. Three percent indicated that it was not the first marriage for either themselves or their spouse. The average amount of time that these daughters-in-law had been married to their current spouse was nine years. Fifty-four percent of the daughters-in-law indicated that they had children from their current marriage, while 43% did not. The majority (68%) of the daughters-in-law identified as being White; 19% identified as Black or African American; 4% as Latina or Hispanic; 3% as Asian; and 5% reported mixed race or ethnicities or other race or ethnicity not listed. In terms of religious affiliation or spirituality, the following religious identities were reported: 21% Protestant; 20% Catholic; 15% no religious affiliation; 10% Jewish; 9% atheist/agnostic; 5% Christian; 3% Muslim; 1% spiritual; and 13% another religion or spirituality. Respondents had an average of 16 years of education (four years beyond a high school degree) with a range from 12 to 24 years. Respondents indicated how they self-identified by class, as measured by their household income: 4% endorsed lower class; 19% endorsed lower-middle; 42% endorsed middle; 33% endorsed upper-middle; and 2% endorsed upper.

Sons-in-Law

The sample included 89 son-in-law participants who had a mean age of 37 years and a range from 21 to 71. Of this sample, 90% indicated that this was their first marriage, while 9% indicated that it was not their first marriage. One respondent indicated that it was not the first marriage for either himself or his spouse. The average amount of time that these sons-in-law had been married to their current spouse was nine years. Sixty-one percent of the sons-in-law indicated that they had children from the current marriage, while 39% did not. The majority (66%) in this sample identified as being White; 18% as Black or African American; 8% as Latino or Hispanic; 4% as Asian; and 3% as mixed race or ethnicities or other race or ethnicity not listed. In terms of religious affiliation or spirituality, 25% were Protestant; 15% no religious affiliation; 12% Jewish; 12% Catholic; 9% Christian; 3% Muslim; 3% spiritual; 3% atheist/agnostic; and 17% another religion or spirituality. Participants had an average of 16.5 years of education with a range from 12 to 24 years. The respondents were asked how they self-identified by class as measured by their household income: 2% endorsed lower class; 13% endorsed lower-middle; 49% endorsed middle; 29% endorsed upper-middle; and 6% endorsed upper.

LIMITATIONS

Qualtrics Survey

The current findings need to be interpreted in light of the limitations of this research. The first limitation is that all data were self-reports from the respondents and therefore subject to the limitations of individual perceptions and interpretations of social relationships. The second limitation is similar in that data were collected from one family member who reported about her or his thoughts and feelings, as well as the perceived feelings of other members of that family who did not provide corroborating data or any of their own data. Third, although the sample size was sufficient for the analyses reported and the effect sizes found were substantial, this is a survey sample frame established by Qualtrics for its online survey platform. People who sign up to complete surveys through Qualtrics, while coming from multiple states across the United States, are not representative of in-law relationships throughout the United States. Our sample is largely White and does not reflect the racial and ethnic diversity in the United States. Because of these characteristics, caution should be taken in generalizing our findings.

Even with these limitations, we believe our findings are consistent with other scholarly conclusions in this area of limited research and that these findings lend additional aspects of particular relevance to clinicians and can inform the direction of future research.

Survey and Interview Sample

Limitations of the research conducted by the MSW students and by us include that it is a non-representative, cross-sectional convenience sample gained by social work students and social workers. Those interviewed may have provided a socially desirable picture of their in-law relationships. In addition, social workers tend to be politically progressive and their contacts may be more likely to be acceptant of and ascribe to nontraditional roles. The fathers-in-law, for example, with positive relationships seemed comfortable with their sons-in-law sharing housekeeping and childcare. A different sample may offer a more traditional view of how the daughter (or son) and son-in-law relationship should function and how masculinity is defined. In addition, and like the Qualtrics surveys, the sample only includes the perspective of one person in the relationship and in the family. Multiple interviewers conducted the interviews. Despite training, this could result in different presentations and interpretations of the questions that were asked and in the depth and quality of the qualitative interview process in general. Another limitation is that this sample is predominantly White (72%) and 18% African American and does not reflect the diversity of the U.S. population, though we have attempted to highlight the accounts of people from other races and ethnicities. Finally, those interviewed by the students tended to be from the east coast, where most of the students were from. Many of those interviewed, though, had in-laws with whom they were relating who lived in other states, with one-third of the parents-in-law and children-in-law living more than 240 miles from each other.

FUTURE RESEARCH

Many questions remain for future research. For example, how do men's and women's socialization in different regions of the country and across different generations affect the way they interact with each other? Are there racial differences in the relationships that we were not able to unpack, and are interracial in-law relationships different? With interracial and interethnic marriage on the rise, gaining an understanding of these family relationships can help sustain healthy marriages. How does divorce in either set of parents affect the relationship?[5] We did not learn about the timing of a reported divorce nor the quality of the continuing relationship between the divorced parents. We wonder if divorce early in a son- or daughter-in-law's background or in the background of their parents-in-law might affect their in-law relationships differently than if the divorce occurred in their adulthood.

Future research can also explore in greater depth how relationships develop over time, which would require a years-long longitudinal study. We only looked at our sample one year later. With people living longer, under-standing lifespan development and its impact across two or three genera-tions is crucial. This would entail looking at intergenerational childcare as well as care of aging parents and in-laws. Future research should also explore the nature and dynamics of the key relationship triangles connected to these relationships. For example, to what extent are women mediating the rela-tionship between the father-in-law and son-in-law? Exploring this would be consistent with women's roles as social managers in many families.[6]

Given the rapidly changing acceptance of gay and lesbian marriages, from the married couple's perspective and from their parents' perspective, this is an area that continues to be ripe for research, with larger sample sizes available post-*Obergefell*. Finally, concurrently collecting data from multiple members of a family about these understudied family relationships may provide insights not available when analyzing data from one respondent in a family.

SURVEYS AND INTERVIEW GUIDES

For readers interested in the questions that we used on the Qualtrics survey, we have included without the initial demographic questions a ver-sion of the key questions for the mothers-in-law and daughters-in-law from the Qualtrics survey (the wording was changed for the men's surveys). For those interested in the qualitative interview and the key guiding statements that the MSW students and we used, we have included after the survey items those asked of the fathers-in-law and sons-in-law (the wording was changed for the women's interviews).

Qualtrics Survey: Mother-in-Law

How much do you agree with the following statements about your family?

Strongly agree=SA, Agree=A, Neutral=N,
Disagree=D, Strongly disagree=SD,
Does not apply/Don't know=DNA/DK

1. I am/was close with my mother.
2. I am/was close with my father.
3. I am close with my son.
4. I have/had a close relationship with my own parents-in-law.
5. My mother had a good relationship with her mother-in-law.
6. My father had a good relationship with his father-in-law.

7. My daughter-in-law and I have a very close relationship.
8. Overall, I admire my daughter-in-law.
9. I can ask my daughter-in-law for advice.
10. I sometimes feel caught between my son and my daughter-in-law.
11. My son is happy with the relationship I have with this daughter-in-law.
12. My daughter-in-law is close with her mother.
13. My daughter-in-law is close with her father.
14. I did not approve of my son's marriage to this daughter-in-law.
15. I maintain some emotional distance from my daughter-in-law.
    Only present the next two questions if the son/daughter-in-law have children
16. I provide significant childcare (babysitting) to my son/daughter-in-law.
17. My spouse provides significant childcare to my son/daughter-in-law.
18. I provide significant financial support to my son or daughter-in-law.
19. My spouse provides significant financial support to my son or daughter-in-law.
20. I feel I have to walk on eggshells with my daughter-in-law.
21. My son does not know my true feelings about this daughter-in-law.
22. My daughter-in-law and I have different parenting philosophies.
23. My daughter-in-law and I have similar interests.
24. Some aspects of my son's marital relationship make me uncomfortable.
25. My son has a better relationship with his parents-in-law than with me.
26. I sometimes feel left out by my son and daughter-in-law.
27. My spouse would like me to work harder on my relationship with my daughter-in-law.
28. Our son is usually more loyal to us than to my daughter-in-law.
29. I believe my daughter-in-law is (or will be) a good parent.
30. In relation to a job/career, I wish my daughter-in-law would work harder.
31. I am happy with my marital relationship.
32. I knew my daughter-in-law well before the marriage.
33. I have not struggled with mental health or substance abuse issues.
34. My daughter-in-law has not struggled with mental health or substance abuse issues.
35. My son has not struggled with mental health or substance abuse issues.
36. I avoid my daughter-in-law.
37. I have problematic conflicts with my daughter-in-law.
38. My daughter-in-law is domineering with me.
39. My daughter-in-law is interfering towards me.
40. My daughter-in-law is trustworthy to me.
41. My daughter-in-law is kind to me.

42. My daughter-in-law is withholding from me.
43. My daughter-in-law is helpful to me.
44. My daughter-in-law gets angry with me.
45. My daughter-in-law is condescending towards me.
46. My daughter-in-law is warm to me.
47. My daughter-in-law is stubborn with me.
48. My daughter-in-law is available to me.
49. My daughter-in-law is attentive to me.
50. My daughter-in-law is manipulative towards me.
51. My daughter-in-law is needy with me.
52. I usually speak with my daughter-in-law directly about important matters between us rather than going through my son.
53. My daughter-in-law is receptive to my offering advice about: Parenting; Appearance; Job or career; Her marital relationship
54. Have you received financial support from your daughter-in-law or son? If yes, how significant was the financial support provided? Are you receiving any other type of significant care/help from your son or daughter-in-law? Who provided the bulk of that care/help? If yes, how significant was the care/help provided?
55. Within the first year or so of your son and daughter-in-law's wedding, did you experience a change for the better, the worse, or no change in your relationship with your daughter-in-law?
56. If applicable, since your son and daughter-in-law had their first child, did you experience a change for the better, for the worse, or no change in your relationship with your daughter-in-law?
57. If applicable, since you started receiving financial support or care/help from your son and daughter-in-law have you experienced a change for the better, for the worse, or no change in your relationship with your daughter-in-law?

Qualtrics Questionnaire: Daughter-in-Law

How much do you agree with the following statements about your family?

Strongly agree=SA, Agree=A, Neutral=N,
Disagree=D, Strongly disagree=SD,
Does not apply/Don't know=DNA/DK

1. I am/was close with my mother.
2. I am/was close with my father.
3. My mother had a good relationship with her mother-in-law.

4. My father had a good relationship with his father-in-law.
5. My mother-in-law and I have a very close relationship.
6. Overall, I admire my mother-in-law.
7. I can ask my mother-in-law for advice.
8. I enjoy spending time with my mother-in-law.
9. I sometimes feel caught between my husband and my mother-in-law.
10. My husband is happy with the relationship I have with this mother-in-law.
11. My husband is close with his mother.
12. My husband is close with his father.
13. My mother-in-law did not approve of this marriage.
14. My mother-in-law is closer to another child-in-law than to me.
15. I maintain some emotional distance from my mother-in-law.
    Only present this and the next question to those who responded they have children
16. We receive significant help with childcare from my mother-in-law.
17. We receive significant help with childcare from my father-in-law.
18. We receive financial support from my mother-in-law.
19. We receive financial support from my father-in-law.
20. I feel I have to walk on eggshells with my mother-in-law.
21. My husband does not know my true feelings about my mother-in-law.
22. My marriage feels hindered sometimes by my mother-in-law.
23. My mother-in-law and I have different parenting philosophies.
24. My mother-in-law and I have similar interests.
25. Some aspects of my husband's relationship with my mother-in-law make me uncomfortable.
26. My mother-in-law is jealous of the relationship I have with my parents.
27. My mother-in-law is jealous of the relationship my husband has with my parents.
28. My husband and I have a hard time balancing time with both sides of the family.
29. My parent(s) interfere in our marriage.
30. My husband would like me to work harder on my relationship with my in-laws.
31. I feel closer to my mother-in-law than to my father-in-law.
32. My husband is usually more loyal to me than to his parents.
33. I am happy with my marital relationship.
34. I knew my mother-in-law well before the marriage.
35. I have not struggled with mental health or substance abuse issues.
36. Neither of my parents has struggled with mental health or substance abuse issues.

37. My husband has not struggled with mental health or substance abuse issues.
38. My mother-in-law has not struggled with mental health or substance abuse issues.
39. My parent(s) are jealous of the relationship I have with my mother-in-law.
40. I avoid my mother-in-law.
41. I have problematic conflicts with my mother-in-law.
42. My mother-in-law is domineering with me.
43. My mother-in-law is interfering towards me.
44. My mother-in-law is trustworthy to me.
45. My mother-in-law is kind to me.
46. My mother-in-law is withholding from me.
47. My mother-in-law is helpful to me.
48. My mother-in-law gets angry with me.
49. My mother-in-law is condescending towards me.
50. My mother-in-law is warm to me.
51. My mother-in-law is stubborn with me.
52. My mother-in-law is available to me.
53. My mother-in-law is attentive to me.
54. My mother-in-law is manipulative towards me.
55. My mother-in-law is needy with me.
56. I usually speak with my mother-in-law directly about important matters between us rather than going through my husband.
57. My mother-in-law gives me advice in relation to my:
    Parenting; Appearance; Job/Career; Relationship(s) with my parent(s); Marriage.
58. My mother-in-law is supportive of me in relation to my:
    Parenting; Appearance; Job/Career; Relationship(s) with my parent(s).
59. Have you or your husband provided your parents-in-law with physical care/help? If yes, how significant was the physical care/help provided? Who provided the bulk of that care/help?
60. Have you or your husband provided your parents-in-law with financial support? If yes, how significant was the financial support provided?
61. After you were first married, did you experience a change for the better, for the worse, or no change in your relationship with your mother-in-law?
62. If applicable, did you experience a change for the better, for the worse, or no change in your relationship with your mother-in-law after you and your husband had your first child?
63. If applicable, since you and your husband provided physical care/help or financial support, have you experienced a change for the better, for the worse, or no change in your relationship with your mother-in-law?

Father-in-Law Qualitative Question Guide 2019

1. Describe in broad terms what the relationship is like with your son-in-law.
2. How has the in-law relationship turned out to be different or similar to what you thought it would be?
3. Describe your relationship with your son-in-law's parents.
4. Tell me how well you knew your son-in-law before the marriage and what the transition to getting to know him has been like.
5. How has the relationship changed within the first year of marriage and then in subsequent years? Please describe what that has been like. Is there an event that has made you closer or more distant?
6. (If applicable) You shared on the survey that your daughter/son and son-in-law have a child. Since the birth, did you experience a change for the better, for the worse, or no change in your relationship with your son-in-law after he and your child had their first child? Please describe what that has been like.
7. (If applicable) You shared on the survey that you provided child care support to your daughter/son and son-in-law. Since you began providing that care, did you experience a change for the better, for the worse, or no change in your relationship with your son-in-law? Can you describe what that has been like and give an example of an event or situation that exemplifies that change?
8. (If applicable) You shared on the survey that you provided financial support to your daughter/son and son-in-law. Because of providing that support, did you experience a change for the better, for the worse, or no change in your relationship with your son-in-law? Please describe what that has been like.
9. (If applicable) You shared on the survey that there were financial differences in your daughter/son and son-in-law's upbringing. How do you see the impact of those differences in your relationship with your son-in-law?
10. (If applicable) You shared on the survey that your daughter/son and son-in-law are different races/ethnicities/religions. How do you see the impact of those differences in your relationship with him?
11. (If applicable) You shared on the survey that your son-in-law has struggled with a substance abuse/mental health issue. Please describe a situation when that struggle has affected your relationship.
12. On a scale of 1 to 10, where 1 is the worst and 10 is the best you can imagine your relationship with your son-in-law, what rating would you give for the best your relationship has been since they were married?

Please describe an event or situation that would help us understand your experience of when it was the best the relationship has been.

13. On a scale of 1 to 10, where 1 is the worst and 10 is the best you can imagine your relationship with your son-in-law, what rating would you give for the worst your relationship has been since they were married? Please describe an event or situation that would help us understand your experience of when it was the worst the relationship has been.

14. On a scale of 1 to 10, where 1 is the worst and 10 is the best you can imagine your relationship with your son-in-law, what would you rate your relationship today and why?

15. Many people have conflicting feelings in a relationship with an in-law. Please describe the range of feelings you have towards your son-in-law.

16. Do you ever feel you do not understand some of the things your son-in-law does? Please describe if this is the case.

17. Do you have any advice for how to strengthen/improve son-in-law or other in-law relationships?

Son-in-Law Qualitative Question Guide 2019

1. Describe in broad terms what the relationship is like with each of your parents-in-law.

2. How important is your relationship with your father-in-law? Describe your father-in-law's relationship with your father.

3. How has the in-law relationship turned out to be different or similar to what you thought it would be?

4. Tell me how well you knew your father-in-law before the marriage and what the transition to getting to know him has been like.

5. How has the relationship with your father-in-law changed within the first year of marriage and then in subsequent years? Please describe what that has been like. Is there an event that has made you closer or more distant?

6. (If applicable) You shared on the survey that you have a child. Since the birth, did you experience a change for the better, for the worse, or no change in your relationship with your father-in-law? Please describe what that has been like.

7. (If applicable) You shared on the survey that your father-in-law provided child care support to you and your spouse. Since he began providing that care, did you experience a change for the better, for the worse, or no change in your relationship with your father-in-law? Can you describe what that has been like and give an example of an event or situation that exemplifies that change?

8. (If applicable) You shared on the survey that your father-in-law provided financial support to you and your spouse. Because of providing that support, did you experience a change for the better, for the worse, or no change in your relationship with your father-in-law? Please describe what that has been like.

9. (If applicable) You shared on the survey that there were socio-economic differences between you and your spouse growing up. How do you see the impact of those differences in your relationship with your father-in-law?

10. (If applicable) You shared on the survey that there are differences in races/ethnicity/religion with your spouse. How do you see the impact of those differences in your relationship with your father-in-law?

11. (If applicable) You shared on the survey that your father-in-law has struggled with a substance abuse/mental health issue. Please describe a situation when that struggle has affected your relationship.

12. On a scale of 1 to 10, where 1 is the worst and 10 is the best you can imagine your relationship with your father-in-law, what rating would you give for the best your relationship has been since you were married? Please describe an event or situation that would help us understand your experience of when it was the best the relationship has been.

13. On a scale of 1 to 10, where 1 is the worst and 10 is the best you can imagine your relationship with your father-in-law, what rating would you give for the worst your relationship has been since you were married? Please describe an event or situation that would help us understand your experience of when it was the worst the relationship has been.

14. On a scale of 1 to 10, where 1 is the worst and 10 is the best you can imagine your relationship with your father-in-law, what would you rate your relationship today and why?

15. Many people have conflicting feelings in a relationship with an in-law. Please describe the range of feelings you have towards your father-in-law.

16. Do you ever feel you do not understand some of the things your father-in-law does? Please describe if this is the case.

17. Do you have any advice for how to strengthen/improve father-in-law or other in-law relationships?

NOTES

PREFACE
1. A few participants at workshops we gave related to a book on sibling relationships were also invited to participate by completing the survey and interview.
2. See Greif & Woolley (2018), Greif, Leitch, & Woolley (2019), Greif & Woolley (2019a), Greif & Woolley (2019b), Woolley & Greif (2019).
3. The phrase appears in Hungerford's 1878 novel *Molly Bawn*. Shakespeare, in *Love's Labour's Lost* (Act 2, Scene 1), wrote, "Beauty is bought by judgment of the eye."

CHAPTER 1
1. Hawkins et al. (2012).
2. Willson, Shuey, & Elder (2003).
3. Mikucki-Enyart (2011), p. 245. See also Greif & Woolley (2016) and Merrill (2007) for a discussion of ambiguity and ambivalence.
4. Carroll, Olson, & Buckmiller (2007), pp. 210–211.
5. See Fingerman et al. (2008); Willson et al. (2003).
6. Coontz (2006), p. 27.
7. Middleton (1962). On rare occasions, fathers and daughters would marry, according to Middleton. He also notes shifts in commoner marital practices between the Pharaonic period and the Ptolemaic period such that sibling marriage was less likely.
8. Coontz (2006), pp. 24–26.
9. Abbott (2010) writes that polyandry may occur in societies where the land cannot support a growing population. Men can then share rather than forgo fatherhood (p. 23). Some societies, like the Cheyenne and the Bemba tribe in Zambia, had restrictions on son-in-law and mother-in-law interactions. For the Cheyenne, the son-in-law worked for his parents-in-law and communication with his mother-in-law went through his wife. For the Bemba, if the son-in-law and mother-in-law run into each other by chance, the son-in-law has to look at the ground as he backs away. Reasons for this avoidance are hypothesized to be to prevent any semblance of sexual contact between the two and to show respect for the mother-in-law (Pans, 1998).
10. Stockard (2002).
11. UNICEF (2019).
12. UNICEF (2014).

13. Abbott (2010), p. 27.
14. The sense of connectedness spawned in the African American community is still upheld today. Goodwin (2003), in comparing interactions with in-laws, found that in-laws were a greater source of support to recently married African American women than to recently married European American women.
15. Massie (2011), p. 469.
16. Ehmer (2002), p. 313.
17. Ehmer (2002), p. 315.
18. Ehmer (2002), p. 316.
19. Kertzer (2002), p. 62.
20. Ehmer (2002), p. 297.
21. The findings from one interesting small study of parents of college students (*n* = 76 households) suggest that, hypothetically, mothers and fathers would be more upset to learn that their daughter-in-law had committed sexual infidelity than emotional infidelity and would be more upset to learn that their son-in-law had committed emotional infidelity than sexual infidelity (Fenigstein & Peltz, 2002). This is consistent with chastity being seen as more important in a daughter-in-law than a son-in-law.
22. Apostolou (2010).
23. Livingston & Caumont (2017).
24. Apostolou (2011). For more on evolutionary selection and preferences expressed by parents, see Apostolou (2013) and van den Berg et al (2013).
25. Silverstein (1990). See also Turner, Young, & Black (2006), who make the same point about attraction to another being related to gaps in one's own family.
26. See also Turner et al. (2006).
27. Merrill (2007).
28. Marotz-Baden & Cowan (1987). Note the year of this in relation to current interactions in families. For those interested in sisters- and brothers-in-law, which is beyond the focus of this book, see Yoshimura (2014).
29. Duvall (1954), p. 187. See also Stryker (1954) for a 60-plus-year-old view of men's and women's relationships with in-laws. Stryker found that women are more dependent on their mothers than men, that marital adjustment is more related to the wife's relationship with her parents, and that a husband's relationship with his mother-in-law is negatively related to how close his wife is to her mother and his relationship with his father-in-law is positively related to how close his wife is to her father. Stryker and Serovich & Price (1994) were two of only a handful of researchers who dug into the role of father- or son-in-law.
30. Duvall (1954), p. 35.
31. Duvall (1954), pp. 22–23.
32. Serovich & Price (1994).
33. Lee & Szinovacz (2016), p. 663.
34. Poushter, Fetterolf, & Tamir (2019). This was based on a poll of 30,133 in 27 countries.
35. DeSilver (2014). In this Pew Research Center paper, the rising cost of childcare is driving more mothers with young children to decide to stay home and raise their children full-time.
36. Cohn, Livingston, & Wang (2012).
37. Tatlow (2017), p. A5. For more on in-law relationships in China, see, e.g., Shih & Pyke (2010).
38. Greif & Woolley (2016).

39. Greif & Deal (2012).
40. Petronio (2002).
41. U.S. Census Bureau (2016).
42. Prentice (2008).
43. Lee & Szinovacz (2016).
44. Bialik (2017).
45. Murphy (2015).

CHAPTER 2

1. For examples of recent in-law research in other countries, see Cao, Fine, Fang, & Zhou (2018) for China; Cofie et al. (2018) for Ghana; Danielsbacka, Tanskanen, & Rotkirch (2018) for Finland; Cheraghi, Mezaheri, Motabi, Panaghi, & Sadeghi (2019) for Iran; Choi, Nam, Kim, & Park (2019) for Korea; and Kung (2019) for Taiwan. Stryker (1954) is male and conducted research on in-laws before the 1960s.

2. Mikucki-Enyart's (2011) article is based on two studies. The first study focused on mothers-in-law and includes five fathers-in-law reporting on their relationship with their daughter-in-law and five fathers-in-law reporting on their relationship with their son-in-law. The second is also largely focused on mothers-in-law and includes six fathers-in-law reporting on their relationship with their daughter-in-law and seven fathers-in-law reporting on their relationship with their son-in-law. For more on Mikucki-Enyart's research see her 2018 and 2019 publications. Willson et al. (2003), using a rural Iowa population in a panel study, looked at ambivalence between adult children and their parents and parents-in-law. For their comparisons, they used a sample of 181 sons-in-law talking about their fathers-in-law, 256 mothers-in-law talking about their daughters-in-law, 248 mothers-in-law talking about their sons-in-law, and 143 daughters-in-law talking about their fathers-in-law. Serovich & Price (1994), in an older study and as noted in the text, looked at 309 daughters-in-law and sons-in-law who were part of the National Survey of Families and Households. Fingerman (2004) used a convenience sample to explore grandparents' relationships with their grandchildren and the parents of their grandchildren. Sixty-six grandmothers and 66 grandfathers were interviewed, 35 of which included grandfathers talking about their sons-in-law. For both groups of grandparents, as would be expected, ties to daughters were the strongest and ties to sons were the next strongest. Specifically for fathers-in-law, ties to sons-in-law were stronger than ties to daughters-in-law.

3. Peters-Davis, Moss, & Pruchno (1999).
4. Apter (2009).
5. Fry (2019).
6. Polenick et al. (2017).
7. Globerman (1996).
8. Globerman (1996), p. 43.
9. Henz (2009).
10. Peters-Davis et al. (1999); see also Kleban et al. (1989), who also studied a population at the same geriatric center, and Lee, Spitze, & Logan (2003), who looked at data from the late 1980s.
11. Chesley & Poppie (2009).
12. Globerman (1996).
13. Greif & Woolley (2016).

14. Fischer (1983), p. 191.
15. Merrill (2007), p. 88.
16. Mickuki-Enyart (2011).
17. Wiik & Bernhardt (2017).
18. Rittenour & Soliz (2009).
19. Prentice (2008), p. 82.
20. Morr Serewicz (2008).
21. Morr Serewicz & Canary (2008). See also, Morr Serewicz, Hosmer, Ballard, & Griffin (2008). Morr Serewicz also describes the importance of the adult child in her Linchpin Theory. If things are going well between parent and child and child and spouse, they are likely to go well between the child-in-law and parent-in-law.
22. Rittenour & Soliz (2009), p. 69. Rittenour (2012) subsequently analyzed a sample of 624 daughters-in-law gained from listserv groups, chatrooms, and websites, and explored communication patterns. Findings were similar to her study with Soliz but also provided information on the extent to which a daughter-in-law is expected to be able to accommodate to a mother-in-law. One interpretation from her findings is that a daughter-in-law who never expects her mother-in-law to be "real" family will have a harder time building a positive relationship with her.
23. Prentice (2008), p. 82.
24. Apostolou (2015), p. 384.
25. Minuchin, Rosman, & Baker (1978), p. 10.
26. Morr Serewicz (2014).
27. Bengston, Giarrusso, Mabry, & Silverstein (2002).
28. Connidis & McMullin (2002); see also Merrill (2007) for the application of ambivalence to understanding in-law relationships.
29. Pillemer & Suitor (2002) discuss this in relation to parents feeling a child may not be capable of taking care of them. The selection of a child-in-law carries the expectation that one's child and his or her spouse will facilitate such care.
30. Luscher (2002).
31. Willson et al. (2003).
32. Willson et al. (2003).
33. Santos & Levitt (2007), p. 828.
34. Mikucki-Enyart (2011; 2019).
35. Lee & Szinovacz (2016); Willson et al. (2003).
36. Willson et al. (2003).
37. Turner et al. (2006).
38. Silverstein (1990), pp. 401–402.
39. Fingerman et al. (2012), p. 121.
40. Serovich & Price (1994).
41. Fowler & Rittenour (2017) found, among students at a university in California and people the students recruited, that the age of children-in-law and the age of parents-in-law were not related to the children-in-law's perception of positive or negative behavior from their parent-in-law. Over three-quarters of the 179 participants were women and most reported on their mother-in-law.
42. Willson et al. (2003).
43. Marotz-Baden & Cowan (1987).
44. By example, Jackson & Berg-Cross (1988), in studying African American daughters-in-law in Washington, DC, found that they used a tactful assertiveness strategy and a compliant strategy more often than an avoidant or a defensive

strategy when struggling with both their mother and their mother-in-law. This study presents the question whether other races would use different strategies.

CHAPTER 3

1. Yaffe (2017), pp. 142–143.
2. To determine what variables or individual and family characteristics are most highly predictive of high-quality in-law relationships, we used a similar strategy for all four in-law groups. We use here the mother-in-law relationship with the daughter-in-law as an example. To determine what practitioners could learn from the data in designing interventions for mothers-in-law, we created blocks of variables that were survey questions about various individual, relationship, and family factors that were hypothesized to predict in-law relationship quality. These blocks looked at (1) demographics; (2) the mother-in-law's history before the daughter-in-law entered the family; (3) the daughter-in-law's family background; (4) the mother-in-law and daughter-in-law relationship; and (5) a family triangle block of survey item variables that captured the dynamics of three-way relationships that included the in-law relationship of interest, such as the son and husband/partner in the case of the mother-in-law. The outcome variable used in these regression analyses was the mean of seven survey questions, five assessing positive relationship and two assessing negative relationship characteristics (a similar analytic strategy was used in Woolley & Greif, 2019). The items that proved significant as predictors in analyses of each of those individual blocks of variables were then placed in a final regression analysis including variables across all five blocks. Those four analyses revealed substantial R-squared coefficients suggesting a large proportion of the variance in in-law relationship quality was captured by those analyses (R-square coefficients ranged from .60 to .71, essentially capturing from 60% to 71% of variance in relationship quality). Such high R-squared coefficients indicate those analyses revealed a set of relationship factors that were highly predictive of relationship quality. We can then suggest interventions related to the factors those analyses revealed. The central limitation to these analyses is the possibility of important relationship quality factors not measured in the current surveys.
3. Daatland (2007) reported on research based in Norway.
4. We did not survey, for any of the four in-law groups, when people moved to the United States. This may account for a level of assimilation/biculturalism/acculturation stress that may affect difference.
5. Murphy (2015).
6. Only those with grandchildren answered this question.
7. Paula Span (2018), writing in the *New York Times*, made a similar point in an op-ed that speaks to the advantage that the maternal grandmother has in contact with the grandchildren.
8. Geographic distance between the mother-in-law and the daughter-in-law was related to the son feeling closer (of course, emotionally closer sons may choose to live closer), though we did not ask how far the other set of in-laws lives from the adult children.
9. See Nancy-Boyd Franklin YouTube interview by Kim Butler, October 15, 2008, for more on this context.
10. Turner et al. (2006) make a similar point about the systemic nature of families.
11. The marital status of the mother-in-law was unrelated to the provision of childcare or the provision of financial assistance.

CHAPTER 4

1. England et al. (2016).
2. "Biracial" was the term used by the respondent. The mother-in-law is Vietnamese and we do not know what the race or ethnicity of the father-in-law is. Versions of these two cases and a son-in-law case in Chapter 6 also appear in Greif & Saviet (2020).
3. See Chapter 2 for more on this.
4. Thirteen percent had children that were the product of a previous relationship.
5. As might be expected, none of those who reported their relationship had worsened after the birth reported having a good relationship with their mother-in-law, while almost all of those who said things changed for the better with the birth felt close to their mother-in-law before the birth.
6. Lee & Szinovacz (2016).
7. The statement read, "I feel/felt closer to my mother-in-law than my father-in-law." As the response options ranged from strongly agree to strongly disagree with neutral as a midpoint, someone who feels equally close to both may have disagreed with the statement.
8. See, e.g., de Guzman & Nishina (2017) for interracial marriages and Abbott (2010) about the belief of some of the importance of praying together as a family.
9. Pew Research Center (2009).

CHAPTER 5

1. See, e.g., Carr (2005).
2. Latshaw (2015).
3. Greif (2009).
4. Morr Serewicz (2008).
5. Kieffer (2008). See also Haaz, Kneavel, & Browning (2014), who found, among a sample of 90 women whose parents had divorced, that those who maintained close bonds with their father experienced increased intimacy in their own marriage.
6. Taken from Ted Gioia's 2018 *Wall Street Journal* book review of *Paul Simon: The Life* (May 5, p. C5).
7. Lee & Szinovacz (2016).
8. See an earlier Chapter 3, note 2, that describes the approach to the analysis.
9. Many of these cases were adapted from Greif & Woolley (2018).
10. About one-third did not know what the relationship was like.
11. A caveat is that we do not know the age of the father-in-law when his parents' divorce occurred. Divorce during the father-in-law's youth would presumably have a greater impact on the father-in-law than parental divorce when the father-in-law was an adult.
12. We use a significance of .05 as the cut-off in our discussion and this had a significance of .052. Hence, it is worth considering in future research as a variable affecting the relationship.
13. Eighty-five percent of these interfaith couples had children.
14. Greif & Woolley (2018).
15. Fischer (1983).
16. One-quarter of the son-in-law's parents were divorced; there was no relationship between his parents being divorced and the father-in-law's relationship with his son-in-law.

17. Twenty-eight percent of the fathers-in-law said they did not help out financially—which might mean they wanted to or their support was needed and it was not given—while 33% reported the daughter and son-in-law did not need financial support.
18. See, e.g., Greif & Deal (2012) where some wives said they tried to help their husbands make friends with other men.

CHAPTER 6

1. Peters-Davis, Moss, & Pruchno (1999).
2. Santos & Levitt (2007).
3. Bryant, Conger, & Meehan (2001).
4. Serovich & Price (1994).
5. Santos & Levitt (2007).
6. Kaplan, Foelsch, Heller, Nye, & Aquino (2015).
7. E.g., Cicirelli, 1989; Gilligan, Suitor, & Nam, 2015; Globerman, 1996; Greif & Woolley, 2016.
8. Medved (2014).
9. An additional analysis of African American sons-in-law in our sample was done by Ericka Lewis, Michelle Sermon, and Michael Woolley and was presented at the January 2020 annual conference of the Society of Social Work and Research in Washington, DC. Here is their abstract from the study:

Our study's sample consisted of Black/African-American sons-in-laws who participated in the qualitative interviews (N=11). Sons-in-law were between the ages of 25 and 60 and married, on average, for 8.6 years (SD=5.3). Fifty-five percent of sons-in-law (n = 5) reported having at least one biological or stepchild. Three themes emerged, as sons-in-law identified interactions and situational factors that impacted their relationship with their fathers-in-law. First, sons-in-law believed having similar interests or participating in activities helped to shape their relationship with fathers-in-law. Next, sons-in-law consistently reported how explicit and intentional communication with fathers-in-law, following a significant life event, strengthened the in-law relationship. For example, sons-in-law considered marriages and children's births as events where fathers-in-law communicated their expectations of sons-in-laws in their new role as a husband or father. As a result, in-laws were able to discuss culturally masculine values and establish a mutual respect for one another as providers and protectors for their family. Finally, sons-in-law described instances of social fathering, where fathers-in-law served as role models, as contributors to building the in-law relationship. Sons-in-law seemed to appreciate receiving advice from fathers-in-law on issues related to employment and child rearing. Sons-in-law found these opportunities to be helpful in building a relationship with their father-in-law, particularly for sons-in-laws who did not have a close relationship with their biological fathers. These findings suggest that quality interactions, explicit communication, and opportunities for social fathering can aid in the relationship-building process for male in-laws in Black families. These exchanges allow for discussion and consensus-building around values specific to men of color supporting and protecting the family unit. Additionally, understanding the role of Black fathers-in-law in strengthening sons-in-law's parenting skills may also lead to evidence-based interventions that include multi-generational approaches to healthy child development. (Lewis, Sherman, & Woolley, 2020)

10. A version of these cases appears in Greif & Woolley (2019a).
11. According to Polenick et al. (2017), if the wife is too dedicated to her parents, the marriage will suffer.
12. Carroll et al. (2007); Merrill (2007).
13. We suspect having a divorce in the family could be related to less closeness between family members but are hesitant to discuss this relationship as we did not ask at what age the son-in-law's parents separated or divorced. A separation or divorce when the son-in-law was a child would have a different impact than if the separation occurred when the son-in-law was an adult.
14. Livingston (2017).
15. Eleven percent of both the sons-in-law and their wives brought stepchildren into the marriage; within this group, a little more than half of the stepchildren were brought in by both spouses.
16. When we looked at the response to this question and our seven-question measure of relationship quality, the pattern shows the sons-in-law with the very highest-quality relationships with their fathers-in-law tended to cluster among those who reported the relationship got better after the birth of a child or did not change. Another cluster, just below the highest-quality scores of sons-in-law, reported it was mixed—in some ways it got better and in some ways worse. Finally, although only a handful reported the relationship got worse, half of them were among the few sons-in-law with the lowest-quality relationships with their fathers-in-law.
17. Sons-in-law who indicated their father-in-law struggled with mental health or substance abuse issues reported a poorer-quality relationship with them.
18. Gay (1988).
19. Please note that this was significant at the .051 level whereas all the other correlations were significant at the <.05 level.

CHAPTER 7
1. Widiss (2016).
2. People also self-identify, for example and not exclusively, as bisexual, pansexual, asexual, questioning, queer, intersex, or transsexual. For information on trans* families, see, e.g., McGuire et al. (2016). An earlier analysis and interpretation of some of these cases appear in Greif, Leitch, & Woolley (2019).
3. Alonzo & Buttitta (2019).
4. Brown (2017).
5. Alonzo & Buttitta (2019); Cao et al. (2016).
6. Oswald (2002).
7. Department of Justice (n.d.).
8. Reczek (2016). See also LaSala (2001) who talks about ambivalence in relationships and changes over time in levels of acceptance.
9. Biblarz & Stacey (2010).
10. A version of this case appears in Greif & Woolley (2018).
11. Ocobock (2018). Ocobock cautions that racial and class minorities are less advantaged by marriage. Ocobock also focuses on bisexual and queer communities, communities that are beyond what we are able to cover in this chapter, but we believe much of what we found could apply.

12. Ramos et al. (2009); Ocobock (2013).
13. Merril (2016).
14. Morr Serewicz (2014)
15. Fingerman et al. (2008).

CHAPTER 8

1. A number of other researchers make comparisons, too, including, but not limited to, Bryant et al. (2001), Chesley & Poppie (2009), Fingerman et al. (2012), Serovich & Price (1994), and Willson et al. (2003).
2. American Psychological Association (2018). We wish to reiterate that parents and parents-in-law may not specifically identify as male or female, though we grouped them as such for this research.
3. American Psychological Association (2018), p. 3.
4. Serovich & Price (1994) had slightly different findings. In their study, sons-in-law had a better relationship with both in-laws than daughters-in-law and sons-in-law felt closer with fathers-in-law than mothers-in-law.
5. Whereas other tests of significance focused on mean responses, here we found differences in variance. This means, as we have indicated elsewhere, that women's responses tend to have a larger range and distribution of values than men's but that their mean responses may not be significantly different. Similarly, Willson et al. (2003) found that reactions to mothers and to mothers-in-law had both a higher positive and a higher negative aspect to them, implying that these mothers and mothers-in-law may draw a greater reaction than fathers and fathers-in-law. Men also reported more positive relations toward parents and parents-in-law.
6. Williamson, Karney, & Bradbury (2019).
7. Beel et al. (2018).
8. These differences appear in the variance though they may not appear in the mean, as explained in note 5 in this chapter.
9. Willson et al. (2003).
10. See Kalmijn & Leopold (2019) in relation to kinkeeping of sisters and mothers.

CHAPTER 9

1. See Greif & Woolley (2016).
2. Bowen (1974); Nichols & Davis (2016).
3. Nichols & Davis (2016).
4. Morr Serewicz & Canary (2008).
5. Sylvia Mikucki-Enyart (2011), whose work we cite in Chapter 2, surveyed 149 parents-in-law to explore how they incorporated their children-in-law into their family's privacy boundaries. Mikucki-Enyart was interested in where the boundaries were drawn around the family and who was included within those boundaries. What she found is that if parents are uncertain as to how to maintain a sense of boundaries, they avoid certain topics of discussion altogether (note Satir's clear caution about this). What makes parents uncertain can stem from concerns about the character of the child-in-law, including financial solvency and responsibility, and the child-in-law's commitment both to the marriage and to being a member of the family. The parents' read on their child-in-law's desire for contact with them also feeds their uncertainty. As a result, some parents felt less satisfaction with their in-law relationships and "shut down" as a response, thereby making it harder for the children-in-law to feel included. See also Petroni (2002).

6. Horsley (1996). Horsley includes other therapeutic theories in her very comprehensive book.
7. Santos & Levitt (2007) describe in-law relationships as inherently ambiguous—they originate involuntarily through marriage and can end through divorce. They exist in a society where marriage supersedes family, thus leaving in-laws with no clear roles (p. 828).
8. Rittenour & Soliz (2009).
9. Silverstein (1990); Turner et al. (2006).
10. Responses to another item on the survey indicate, across the samples, that about one-third of the in-laws said relationships got better with time. The rest said relationships ebbed and flowed or got worse. It could be that with a large sample of in-laws, some improve, some worsen, and some do not change so differences get washed out in an analysis.
11. Using our relationship quality multi-item variable, there were no differences between those who participated again in the survey and those who did not.
12. Globerman (1996) and Henz (2009), for example, had different findings, as discussed in Chapter 2.
13. Attachment theorists focus on the quality of early attachment between parent and child as predicting attachments formed in adulthood (Duck, 2011).
14. Hawkins et al. (2012); this was reconfirmed through a personal communication with divorce lawyer Richard Jacobs, June 12, 2019.
15. Fingerman et al. (2012), p. 121.
16. Harrington (2014).
17. Grant (2017), p. 390.
18. Mikucki-Enyart (2018).
19. For sons- and daughters-in-law, we asked about their own mental health and substance abuse history, the history of their parents, their spouse, and their same-sex parent-in-law. For mothers- and fathers-in-law, we asked about their own substance abuse and mental health history as well of that of their child, and their child-in-law.
20. https://www.wikihow.com/Interact-With-Your-New-In-Laws#. Tasha Rube, retrieved August 5, 2019.

APPENDIX
1. Turner et al. (2006) used a similar approach.
2. Padgett (2016) discusses this process.
3. Bradley, Curry, & Devers (2007).
4. Bradley et al. (2007) also recommend this approach.
5. Morr Serewicz (2014).
6. See, e.g., Lee & Szinovacz (2016).

REFERENCES

Abbott, E. (2010). *A history of marriage: From same-sex unions to private vows and common law, the surprising diversity of a tradition.* New York, NY: Seven Stories Press.

Allendorf, K. (2017). Like her own: Ideals and experiences of the mother-in-law/daughter-in-law relationship. *Journal of Family Issues, 38,* 2102–2127.

Alonzo, D. J., & Buttitta, D. J. (2019). Is "coming out" still relevant? Social justice implications for LGB-membered families. *Journal of Family Theory & Review, 11,* 354–366.

American Psychological Association, Boys and Men Guidelines Group. (2018). *APA guidelines for psychological practice with boys and men.* Retrieved from https://www.apa.org/about/policy/boys-men-practice-guidelines.pdf

Apostolou, M. (2010). Parental choice: What parents want in a son-in-law and a daughter-in-law across 67 pre-industrial societies. *British Journal of Psychology, 101*(4), 695–704.

Apostolou, M. (2011). "Oh my child, what an inappropriate spouse for you!" Asymmetrical preferences and parent–offspring conflict over mating. *Social and Personality Psychology Compass, 5*(5), 285–295.

Apostolou, M. (2013). Parent–offspring conflict over marital age and the age of a spouse. *Journal of Evolutionary Psychology, 11*(1), 5–16.

Apostolou, M. (2015). I am right for your child! Tactics for manipulating potential parents-in-law. *Human Nature, 26,* 378–391.

Apter, T. (2009). *What do you want from me? Learning to get along with in-laws.* New York, NY: W.W. Norton.

Beel, N., Jeffries, C., Brownlow, C., Winterbotham, S., & Du Preez, J. (2018). Recommendations for male-friendly individual counseling with men: A qualitative systematic literature review for the period 1995–2016. *Psychology of Men & Masculinity, 19,* 600–611.

Bengston, V., Giarrusso, R., Mabry, J. B., & Silverstein, M. (2002). Solidarity, conflict, and ambivalence: Complementary or competing perspectives on intergenerational relationships? *Journal of Marriage and Family, 64,* 568–576.

Bialik, K. (2017). *Key facts about race and marriage, 50 years after* Loving v. Virginia. Washington, DC: Pew Research Center, June 17.

Biblarz, T. J., & Stacey, J. (2010). How does the gender of parents matter? *Journal of Marriage and Family, 72,* 3–22.

Bowen, M. (1974). Theory in the practice of psychotherapy. In J. Guerin (Ed.), *Family therapy: Theory and practice* (pp. 314–342). New York: Gardner Press.

Bradley, E. H., Curry, L. A., & Devers, K. J. (2007). Qualitative data analysis for health services research: Developing taxonomy, themes, and theory. *Health Services Research*, *42*, 1758–1772.

Brown, A. (2017). *Five key findings about LGBT Americans*. Washington, DC: Pew Research Center, June 13.

Bryant, C. M., Conger, R. D., & Meehan, J. M. (2001). The influence of in-laws on change in marital success. *Journal of Marriage and Family*, *63*, 614–626.

Cao, H., Fine, M., Fang, X., & Zhou, N. (2018). Chinese adult children's perceived parents' satisfaction with adult children's marriage, in-law relationship quality, and adult children's marital satisfaction. *Journal of Social and Personal Relationships*, *35*, 1–25.

Cao, H., Mills-Koonce, W. R., Wood, C., & Fine, M. A. (2016). Identity transformation during the transition to parenthood among same-sex couples: An ecological stress-strategy-adaption perspective. *Journal of Family Theory and Review*, *8*, 30–59.

Carr, D. (2005). The psychological consequences of midlife men's social comparisons with their young adult sons. *Journal of Marriage and Family*, *67*, 240–250.

Carroll, J. S., Olson, C. D., & Buckmiller, N. (2007). Family boundary ambiguity: A 30-year review of theory, research, and measurement. *Family Relations*, *56*, 210–230.

Cheraghi, M., Mazaheri, M. A., Moptabi, F., Panaghi, L., & Sadeghi, M. S. (2019). Beyond the couple: A qualitative analysis of successful in-law relationships in Iran. *Family Process*, *58*, 936–953.

Chesley, N., & Poppie, K. (2009). Assisting parents and in-laws: Gender, type of assistance, and couples' employment. *Journal of Marriage and Family*, *71*, 247–262.

Choi, H., Nam, B., Kim, S., & Park, C. (2019). Contact with parents and parents-in-law, gender, and marital satisfaction. *Journal of Marriage and Family*, *81*, 1192–1205.

Cofie, L. E., Barrington, C., Sodzi-Tettey, S., Ennett, S., Maman, S., & Singh, K. (2018). A qualitative study of women's network social support and facility delivery in rural Ghana. *PLoS ONE*, *13*(11), e0206429. https://doi.org/10.1371/journal.pone.0206429

Cohn, D. V., Livingston, G., & Wang, W. (2012). *After decades of decline, a rise in stay-at-home mothers*. Washington, DC: Pew Research Center, April 8.

Connidis, I. A., & McMullin, J. A. (2002). Sociological ambivalence and family ties: A critical perspective. *Journal of Marriage and Family*, *64*, 558–567.

Coontz, S. (2006). *Marriage, a history—How love conquered marriage*. New York, NY: Penguin Books.

Daatland, S. V. (2007). Marital history and intergenerational solidarity: The impact of divorce and unmarried cohabitation. *Journal of Social Issues*, *63*, 809–825.

Danielsbacka, M., Tanskanen, A. O., & Rotkirch, A. (2018). The "kinship penalty": Parenthood and in-law conflict in contemporary Finland. *Evolutionary Psychological Science*, *4*, 71–82.

Department of Justice (n.d.). *2018 Hate Crime Statisitics*. https://ucr.fbi.gov/hate-crime/2018/topic-pages/victims, retrieved 7/23/2020

De Guzman, N. S., & Nishina, A. (2017). 50 years of *Loving*: Interracial romantic relationships and recommendations for future research. *Journal of Family Theory & Review*, *9*, 557–571.

DeSilver, D. (2014). *Rising cost of child care may help explain recent increase in stay-at-home moms*. Washington, DC: Pew Research Center, April 8.

Duck, S. (2011). *Rethinking relationships*. Thousand Oaks, CA: Sage.

Duvall, E. R. (1954). *In-laws, pro & con: An original study of interpersonal relations*. New York, NY: Association Press/Forgotten Press (republished, 2012).

Ehmer, J. (2002). Marriage. In D. I. Kertzer & M. Barbagli (Eds.), *Family life in the long nineteenth century: 1789–1913* (pp. 282–321). New Haven, CT: Yale University Press.

England, P., Allison, P. D., & Sayer, L. C. (2016). Is your spouse more likely to divorce you if you are the older partner? *Journal of Marriage and Family, 78*, 1184–1194.

Fenigstein, A., & Peltz, R. (2002). Distress over the infidelity of a child's spouse: A crucial test of evolutionary and socialization hypotheses. *Personal Relationships, 9*(3), 301–312.

Fingerman, K. L. (2004). The role of offspring and in-laws in grandparents' ties to the grandchildren. *Journal of Family Issues, 25*, 1026–1049.

Fingerman, K. L., Gilligan, M., VanderDrift, L., & Pitzer, L. (2012). In-law relationships before and after marriage: Husbands, wives, and their mothers-in-law. *Research in Human Development, 9*, 106–125.

Fingerman, K. L., Pitzer, L. M., Lefkowitz, E. S., Birditt, K. S., & Mroczek, D. (2008). Ambivalent relationship qualities between adults and their parents: Implications for the well-being of both parties. *Journals of Gerontology, Series B: Psychological Sciences and Social Sciences, 63*, 362–371.

Fischer, L. R. (1983). Mothers and mothers-in-law. *Journal of Marriage and the Family, 45*, 187–192.

Fowler, C., & Rittenour, C. (2017). A life-span approach of children-in-law's perceptions of parent-in-law communication. *Journal of Family Communication, 17*, 254–272.

Fry, P. (2019). *Baby Boomers are staying in the labor force at rates not seen in generations for people their age*. Washington, DC: Pew Research Center, July 24.

Gay (1988). *Freud: A life for our time*. New York: Anchor Books.

Globerman, J. (1996). Motivations to care: Daughters- and sons-in-law caring for relatives with Alzheimer's disease. *Family Relations: An Interdisciplinary Journal of Applied Family Studies, 45*(1), 37–45.

Goodwin, P. Y. (2003). African American and European American women's marital well-being. *Journal of Marriage and Family, 65*, 550–560.

Grant, T. (2017). Frozen conflicts and international law. *Cornell International Law Journal, 3*, 361–413.

Greif, G. L. (2009). *Buddy system: Understanding male friendships*. New York, NY: Oxford University Press.

Greif, G. L., & Deal, K. (2012). *Two plus two: Couples and their couple friendships*. New York, NY: Routledge.

Greif, G. L., Leitch, J., & Woolley, M. E. (2019). A preliminary look at relationships between married gays and lesbians and their parents-In-law: Five case studies. *Journal of Gay and Lesbian Social Services, 31*, 290–313.

Greif, G. L., & Saviet, M. (2020). In-law relationships among interracial couples: A preliminary view. *Journal of Human Behavior in the Social Environment, 30*, 605–620.

Greif, G. L., & Woolley, M. (2016). *Adult sibling relationships*. New York, NY: Columbia University Press.

Greif, G. L., & Woolley, M. E. (2018). The father-in-law's relationship with his son-in-law: A preliminary understanding. *Smith College Studies in Social Work, 88,* 152–173.

Greif, G. L., & Woolley, M. E. (2019a). Sons-in-law and their fathers-in-law: Gaining a preliminary understanding of an understudied family relationship. *Journal of Family Social Work, 22,* 292–311.

Greif, G. L., & Woolley, M. E. (2019b). Daughters-in-law and their mothers-in-law: Triangles, ambiguity, and relationship quality. *Social Work Research, 43,* 259–268.

Haaz, D. H., Kneavel, M., & Browning, S. W. (2014). The father-daughter relationship and intimacy in the marriages of daughters of divorce. *Journal of Divorce & Remarriage, 55,* 164–177.

Harrington, R. (2014). https://library.law.yale.edu/news/frozen-conflicts, posted January, 17.

Hawkins, A. J., Willoughby, B. J., & Doherty, W. J. (2012). Reasons for divorce and openness to marital reconciliation. *Journal of Divorce & Remarriage, 53,* 453–463.

Henz, U. (2009). Couples' provision of informal care for parents and parents-in-law: Far from sharing equally. *Ageing and Society, 29*(3), 369–395.

Horsley, G. (1996). *In-laws: A guide to extended-family therapy.* New York, NY: John Wiley & Sons.

Jackson, L., & Berg-Cross, L. (1988). Extending the extended family: The mother-in-law and daughter-in-law relationship of black women. *Family Relations, 37,* 293–297.

Kalmijn, M., & Leopold, T. (2019). Changing sibling relationship after parents' death: The role of solidarity and kinkeeping. *Journal of Marriage and Family, 81,* 99–114.

Kaplan, M. A., Foelsch, P., Heller, N., Nye, C., & Aquino, G. (2015). Bopundary ambiguity and borderline personality traits: Implications for treatment for adolescent girls in foster care. *Journal of Family Social Work, 18,* 366–381.

Kertzer, D. I. (2002). Living with kin. In D. I. Kertzer & M. Barbagli (Eds.), *Family life in the long nineteenth century: 1789–1913* (pp. 40–72). New Haven, CT: Yale University Press.

Kieffer, C. C. (2008). From self-objects to mutual recognition: Towards optimal responsiveness in father and daughter relationships. *Psychoanalytic Inquiry, 28,* 76–91.

Kleban, M. H., Brody, E. M., Schoonover, C. B., & Hoffman, C. (1989). Family help to the elderly: Perceptions of sons-in-law regarding parent care. *Journal of Marriage and the Family, 51,* 301–312.

Kung, H.-M. (2019). Persistence and change in the comparative status of mothers-in-law and daughters-in-law in Taiwanese families: 1979 to 2016. *Journal of Family Issues, 40,* 1937–1962.

LaSala, M. C. (2001). The importance of partners to lesbians' intergenerational relationships. *Social Work Research, 25,* 27–35.

Latshaw, B. A. (2015). From mopping to mowing: Masculinity and housework in stay-at-home father households. *Journal of Men's Studies, 23,* 252–270.

Lee, E., Spitze, G., & Logan, J. R. (2003). Social support to parents-in-law: The interplay of gender and kin hierarchies. *Journal of Marriage and Family, 65,* 396–403.

Lee, H. J., & Szinovacz, M. E. (2016). Positive, negative, and ambivalent interactions with family and friends: Associations with well-being. *Journal of Marriage and Family*, *78*, 660–679.

Lewis, E., Sermon, M., & Woolley, M. E. (2020). Understanding African-American sons-in-law and their relationship with their father-in-law. Paper presented at the Society for Social Work Research, Washington, DC, January.

Livingston, G. (2017). *In U.S. metro areas, huge variation in intermarriage rates.* Washington, DC: Pew Research Center. Retrieved from http://pewrsr.ch/2qASxKH

Livingston, G., & Caumont, A. (2017). *5 facts on love and marriage in America.* Washington, DC: Pew Research Center, February 13.

Luscher, K. (2002). Intergenerational ambivalence: Further steps in theory and research. *Journal of Marriage and Family*, *64*, 585–593.

Marotz-Baden, R., & Cowan, D. (1987). Mothers-in-law and daughters-in-law: The effects of proximity on conflict and stress. *Family Relations: An Interdisciplinary Journal of Applied Family Studies*, *36*, 385–390.

Massie, R. K. (2011). *Catherine the Great: Portrait of a woman.* New York, NY: Random House.

McGuire, J. K., Kuvalanka, K. A., Catalpa, J. M., & Toomey, R. B. (2016). Transfamily theory: How the presence of trans* family members informs gender development in families. *Journal of Family Theory and Review*, *8*, 60–73.

Medved, C. E. (2014). Stay-at-home fathers and family communication. In K. Floyd & M.T. Morman (Eds.), *Widening the family circle: New research on family communication* (2nd ed., pp. 115–132). Los Angeles, CA: Sage.

Merrill, D. M. (2007). *Mothers-in-law and daughters-in-law: Understanding the relationship and what makes them friends or foe.* Westport, CT: Praeger.

Merrill, D. M. (2016). *When your gay or lesbian child marries: A guide for parents.* Lanham, MD: Rowman & Littlefield.

Middleton, R. (1962). Brother–sister and father–daughter marriage in ancient Egypt. *American Sociological Review*, *27*, 603–611.

Mikucki-Enyart, S. L. (2011). Parent-in-law privacy management: An examination of the links among relational uncertainty, topic avoidance, in-group status, and in-law satisfaction. *Journal of Family Communication*, *11*, 237–263.

Mikucki-Enyart, S. L. (2018). Parents-in-law's topic avoidance: Understanding the role of interaction goals and relational characteristics. *Personal Relationships*, *25*, 433–457.

Mikucki-Enyart, S. L. (2019). Children-in-laws' message processing: Associations among uncertainty, perceived avoidance, goal inferences, and marital satisfaction. *Journal of Social and Personal Relationships*, *36*, 3908–3933.

Minuchin, S., Rosman, B. L., & Baker, L. (1978). *Psychosomatic families: Anorexia nervosa in context.* Cambridge, MA: Harvard University Press.

Morr Serewicz, M. C. (2008). Toward a triangular theory of the communication and relationships of in-laws: Theoretical proposal and social relations analysis of relational satisfaction and private disclosure in in-law triads. *Journal of Family Communication*, *8*, 264–292.

Morr Serewicz, M. C. (2014). Relationships with parents-in-law. In K. Floyd & M. T. Morman (Eds.), *Widening the family circle: New research on family communication,* (2nd ed., pp. 85–101). Los Angeles, CA: Sage.

Morr Serewicz, M. C., & Canary, D. J. (2008). Assessments of disclosure from the in-laws: Links among disclosure topics, family privacy orientation, and relational quality. *Journal of Social and Personal Relationships, 25,* 333–357.

Morr Serewicz, M. C., Hosmer, R., Ballard, R. L., & Griffin, R. A. (2008) Disclosure from in-laws and the quality of in-law and marital relationships. *Communication Quarterly, 56,* 427–444.

Murphy, C. (2015). *Interfaith marriage is common in U.S., particularly among the recently wed.* Washington, DC: Pew Research Center, June 2.

Nichols, M., & Davis, S. (2016). *Family therapy: Concepts and methods* (11th ed.). Boston, MA: Allyn and Bacon.

Ocobock, A. (2013). The power and limits of marriage: Married gay men's family relationships. *Journal of Marriage and Family, 75,* 191–205.

Ocobock, A. (2018). Status or access? The impact of marriage on lesbian, gay, bisexual, and queer community change. *Journal of Marriage and Family, 80,* 367–382.

Oswald, R. F. (2002). Resilience within the family networks of lesbians and gay men: Intentionalilty and redefinition. *Journal of Marriage and Family, 64,* 374–383.

Padgett, D. K. (2016). *Qualitative research methods* (3rd ed.). Thousand Oaks, CA: Sage.

Pans, A. E. M. J. (1998). The mother-in-law taboo. *Ethnography, 37,* 71–98.

Peters-Davis, N. D., Moss, M. S., & Pruchno, R. A. (1999). Children-in-law in caregiving families. *The Gerontologist, 39*(1), 66–75. doi:10.1093/geront/39.1.66

Petronio, S. (2002). *Boundaries of privacy: Dialectics of disclosure.* Albany, NY: State University of New York Press.

Pew Research Center/ (2009). *Magnet or sticky? A state-by-state typology.* Washington, DC: Pew Research Center, March 11.

Pillemer, K., & Suitor, J. J. (2002). Explaining mothers' ambivalence toward their adult children. *Journal of Marriage and Family, 64,* 602–613.

Polenick, C. A., Zarit, S. H., Birditt, K. S., Bangerter, L. R., Seidel, A. J., & Fingerman, K. L. (2017). Intergenerational support and marital satisfaction: Implications of beliefs about helping aging parents. *Journal of Marriage and Family, 79,* 131–146.

Poushter, J., Fetterolf, J., & Tamir, C. (2019). *A changing world: Global views on diversity, gender equality, family life and the importance of religion.* Washington, DC: Pew Research Center, April 22.

Prentice, C. M. (2008). The assimilation of in-laws: The impact of newcomers on the communication routines of families. *Journal of Applied Communication Research, 36,* 74–97.

Ramos, C., Goldberg, N. G., & Badgett, M. V. L. (2009). *The effects of marriage equality in Massachusetts: A survey of the experiences and impact of marriage on same-sex couples.* Los Angeles, CA: Williams Institute.

Reczek, C. (2016). Ambivalence in gay and lesbian family relationships. *Journal of Marriage and Family, 78,* 644–659.

Rittenour, C. (2012). Daughter-in-law standards for mother-in-law communication: Associations with daughter-in-law perceptions of relational satisfaction and shared family identity. *Journal of Family Communication, 12,* 93–110.

Rittenour, C., & Soliz, J. (2009). Communicative and relational dimensions of shared family identity and relational intentions in mother-in-law/daughter-in-law relationships: Developing a conceptual model for mother-in-law/daughter-in-law research. *Western Journal of Communication, 73*(1), 67–90.

Santos, J. D., & Levitt, M. J. (2007). Intergenerational relations with in-laws in the context of the Social Convoy: Theoretical and practice implications. *Journal of Social Issues, 63,* 827–843.

Serovich, J. M., & Price, S. J. (1994). In-law relationships: A role theory perspective. *International Journal of Sociology of the Family, 24,* 127–144.

Shih, K. Y., & Pyke, K. (2010). Power, resistance, and emotional economics in women's relationships with mothers-in-law in Chinese immigrant families. *Journal of Family Issues, 31,* 333–357.

Silverstein, J. L. (1990). The problem with in-laws. *Journal of Family Therapy, 14,* 399–412.

Span, P. (2018). The maternal grandparent edge. *New York Times,* March 27, A15.

Stockard, J. (2002). *Marriage in culture: Practice and meaning across diverse cultures.* Belmont, CA: Wadsworth.

Stryker, S. (1954). The adjustment of married offspring to their parents. *American Sociological Review, 20,* 149–154.

Tatlow, D. K. (2017). China is preparing for new top leaders, few of them women. *New York Times,* July 17, A5.

Turner, M., Young, C. R., & Black, K. I. (2006). Daughters-in-law and mothers-in-law seeking their place within the family: A qualitative study of differing viewpoints. *Family Relations: An Interdisciplinary Journal of Applied Family Studies, 55*(5), 588–600.

UNICEF. (2014). *Ending child marriage: Progress and prospects.* New York, NY: UNICEF.

UNICEF. (2019, June). *Child marriage.* New York: UNICEF.

U.S. Census Bureau. (2016). *The single life: The gap between married and unmarried Americans age 15 and older has narrowed since 1950.* September 16. Washington, DC: U.S. Department of Commerce.

van den Berg, P., Fawcett, T. W., Buunk, A. P., & Weissing, F. J. (2013). The evolution of parent–offspring conflict over mate choice. *Evolution and Human Behavior, 34*(6), 405–411.

Widiss, D. A. (2016). Legal recognition of same-sex relationships: New possibilities for research on the role of marriage law in household labor allocation. *Journal of Family Theory and Review, 8,* 10–29.

Wiik, K. A., & Bernhardt, E. (2017). Cohabiting and married individuals' relations with their partners' parents. *Journal of Marriage and Family, 79,* 1111–1124.

Williamson, H. C., Karney, B. R., & Bradbury, T. N. (2019). Barriers and facilitators of relationship help-seeking among low-income couples. *Journal of Family Psychology, 33*(2), 234–239.

Willson, A. E., Shuey, K. M., & Elder, G. H. (2003). Ambivalence in the relationship of adult children to aging parents and in-law. *Journal of Marriage and Family, 65,* 1055–1072.

Wood, L. Maren. (2017). *North Carolina Digital History project, Learn NC.* Retrieved June 27, 2018.

Woolley, M. E., & Greif, G. L. (2019). Mother-in-law reports of closeness to daughter-in-law: The determinant triangle with the son/husband. *Social Work, 64,* 73–81.

Yaffe, D. (2017). *Reckless daughter: A portrait of Joni Mitchell.* New York, NY: Sarah Crichton Books.

Yoshimura, C. G. (2014). Siblings-in-law, unwidened. In K. Floyd & M. T. Morman (Eds.), *Widening the family circle* (2nd ed., pp. 103–114). Los Angeles, CA: Sage.

INDEX

For the benefit of digital users, indexed terms that span two pages (e.g., 52–53) may, on occasion, appear on only one of those pages.

birth of children, impact of (*cont.*)
  on mother-in-law's relationship with
      daughter-in-law, 55–57
  on son-in-law's relationship
      with father-in-law, 147,
      159–63, 210–11
boundaries
  avoiding triangulation with, 238–39
  comparing mothers-and daughter-in-
      law relationships, 217
  in daughter-in-law's relationship with
      mother-in-law, 74–75, 77, 79–81
  in gay and lesbian in-law
      relationships, 196
  importance of setting, 236–38
  structural family therapy, 224–25
boundary ambiguity, 4, 155, 214
Bowen, Murray, 222–23
Browning, S. W., 272n5
Buttitta, Deborah, 178

Cahn, Naomi, 108–9
Canary, D. J., 270n21
Carbone, June, 108–9
caretaker role, ceding to
      daughter-in-law, 59
caretaking, in-law, 13, 20–21, 28
Catherine the Great of Russia, 7–8
chastity, 268n22
Chesley, Noelle, 21
Cheyenne tribe, 267n9
childcare
  in daughter-in-law's relationship with
      mother-in-law, 93–94
  in father-in-law's relationship with
      son-in-law, 138
  by grandparents, 14
  role of father in, 13
  role of mother in, 12–14
  in son-in-law's relationship with
      father-in-law, 160
child marriage, 6–7
child phase, 31
children, birth of. *See* birth of children,
      impact of
children-in-law. *See also* daughters-in-
      law; sons-in-law
  determinants of success, 16–17
  differences in treatment of, 173–74
  in family culture, 12–14

improving relationship with
      parents-in-law, 230–31
intergenerational ambivalence, 27–30
patterns of communication, 25–27
in pop culture, 10–12
view of parents-in-law, 2
China
  child marriage in, 6–7
  Na people of, 6
  women's role as in-law caretakers, 13
class differences, impact of
  on daughter-in-law's relationship with
      mother-in-law, 90–92
  on father-in-law's relationship with
      son-in law, 123–25
  on mother-in-law's relationship with
      daughter-in-law, 54–55
  on son-in-law's relationship with
      father-in-law, 156–58
clinical models
  communications theory, 223–24
  family systems theory, 222–23
  narrative therapy, 226–27
  structural family therapy, 224–25
  summary of, 227
closeness in relationships. *See specific*
      relationships
Colonial period, marriage customs
      during, 7, 268n14
communication
  about gender differences, 242
  comparing daughters-in-law and
      sons-in-law, 213
  in daughter-in-law's relationship with
      mother-in-law, 74–75
  in father-in-law's relationship with
      son-in law, 115, 132–34,
      136–37
  in gay and lesbian in-law
      relationships, 201
  in mother-in-law's relationship with
      daughter-in-law, 23
    examples of, 34, 37–38, 40–41, 45
    giving advice, 62–64
    role of son, 66
    role of spouse, 67
  research on patterns of, 25–27
  shared identity and support, 23–25
communications theory, 223–24
comparing in-law relationships, 207–8

son's relationship with, 79–81,
   82, 99–102
mothers-in-law
   approval of children-in-law, 10
   birth of grandchildren, impact on in-
      law relationship, 22
   boundary ambiguity, 4
   comparing fathers-in-law to, 213–16
   daughter-in-law's relationship with,
      70–72, 208–13
      addiction issues, 83–84
      balancing time between
         families, 104–6
      birth of children, impact on, 92–96
      difference within same
         family, 103–4
      family background, effect on, 89
      father-in-law, role of, 102–3
      highly satisfying
         relationships, 73–78
      husband, role of, 99–102
      key items in relationship, 72–73
      mixed bag or neutral
         relationships, 85–89
      parents, impact on, 96–99
      personality differences in,
         79–82, 85–86
      racial, ethnic, religious, or economic
         differences, 90–92
      struggling relationships, 78–84
   in family culture, 12–14
   gay and lesbian in-law relationships
      acceptance in, 180–83
      evolution of, 186–90
      son-in-law's relationship with, 184
   generational differences with
      daughter-in-law, 216
   jokes about, 10–11, 12, 140
   in pop culture, 10–12
   Qualtrics surveys, 248–49, 258–60
   relationship with
      daughters-in-law, 33–35
      birth of grandchildren, impact
         on, 55–57
      culture, role of, 41–42
      difference within same family, 46
      exclusionary behavior, 58–59
      family background, effect
         on, 51–53
      giving advice, 62–64

   highly satisfying
      relationships, 37–41
   key items in relationship, 35–37
   knowing before wedding, 49–51
   mixed bag or neutral
      relationships, 46–49
   only child families, 46–48
   parents of daughter-in law, effect
      on, 60–62
   personality differences, 48–49
   predictive characteristics in, 227–29
   racial, ethnic, religious, or economic
      differences, 53–55
   role of son, 64–67
   spouse/partner, role of, 67–69
   struggling relationships, 42–46
   role in son-in-law's relationship with
      father-in-law, 169–73
   shared identity and support, 23–25
   son-in-law's relationship with, 209–10
   survey and interviews with,
      252–53, 254
movies, in-law relationships in, 10–11
music, in-law relationships in, 11–12

Na of China, 6
narrative therapy, 226–27
neediness of mother-in-law, 218
neutral relationships
   daughter-in-law's relationship with
      mother-in-law, 85–89
   father-in-law's relationship with son-
      in law, 119–20
   mother-in-law's relationship with
      daughter-in-law, 46–49
   son-in-law's relationship with
      father-in-law, 152–56
newlyweds, 3–4
   boundaries, setting, 225
   determinants of success in
      marriage, 16–17
   developmental stage, 234–35
   knowing child-in-law before wedding,
      49–51, 121
   new in-law interactions of,
      14–15, 16–17
   patterns of communication, 25–26

Obergefell v. Hodges, 177–78, 189
Ocobock, Abigail, 191, 274n11

sons-in-law (*cont.*)
  closeness with other
    child-in-law, 173–74
  family background, effect on, 156
  highly satisfying
    relationships, 144–48
  mixed bag or neutral
    relationships, 152–56
  mother-in-law's role in, 169–73
  parents, impact on, 163–66
  predictive characteristics in, 230–31
  racial, ethnic, religious, or economic
    differences, 156–58
  struggling relationships, 148–52
  under-reporting of feelings, 143
  wife's role in, 166–69
  relationship with
    mother-in-law, 209–10
  examples of, 149, 150, 151, 154, 162
  role in relation with
    father-in-law, 169–73
  relationship with parents, 145, 209–10
  relationship with
    stepfather-in-law, 152
  survey and interviews with,
    252–53, 255–56
soul mates, 10
Span, Paula, 271n7
spouse/partner, role of. *See also*
    cooperation in marriage
  in daughter-in-law's relationship with
    mother-in-law, 102–3
  in father-in-law's relationship with
    son-in law, 138–39
  improving in-law-relationships, 231
  in mother-in-law's relationship
    with daughter-in-law, 67–69,
    219–20
  in relations between sets of
    in-laws, 238–39
  in son-in-law's relationship with
    father-in-law, 166–69
stepfathers-in-law, 152
Stockard, Janice, 6–7
structural family therapy, 224–25
struggling relationships
  daughter-in-law's relationship with
    mother-in-law, 78–84
  father-in-law's relationship with son-
    in law, 116–19

son-in-law's relationship with
    father-in-law, 148–52
Stryker, S., 268n30
substance abuse, effect of,
    240–41, 274n17
  on daughter-in-law's relationship with
    mother-in-law, 106
  on father-in-law's relationship with
    son-in law, 115–16
  on gay and lesbian in-law
    relationships, 183–86
Suitor, J. J., 270n29
surveys
  with interviews, 252–53
    limitations, 256–57
    sample descriptions, 253–56
  Qualtrics, 247–48, 258
    analytic strategy, 251–52
    for daughter-in-law, 260–62
    for father-in-law, 263–64
    for mother-in-law, 258–60
    sample descriptions, 248–51
    for son-in-law, 264–65
system model, 27

time, balancing between families. *See*
    balancing time between families
time, changes in relationship over.
    See evolution of relationship
    over time
triadic relationships
  daughter-in-law/father-in-law/
    mother-in-law, 102–3
  daughter-in-law/spouse/
    mother-in-law, 99–102
  father-in-law/daughter/
    son-in-law, 134–37
  mother-in-law/son/
    daughter-in-law, 64–67
  mother-in-law/spouse/
    daughter-in-law, 67–69
  son-in-law/mother-in-law/
    father-in-law, 169–73
  son-in-law/spouse/
    father-in-law, 166–69
triangulation
  examples of, 97–98, 104, 195
  family systems theory, 222–23
  relations between sets of
    in-laws, 238–39